ON BOYINGTON'S WING

The Wartime Journals of
Black Sheep Squadron Fighter Ace
Lt. Col. Robert W. McClurg

With Leon Marketos

EAGLE EDITIONS
2003

EAGLE EDITIONS
AN IMPRINT OF HERITAGE BOOKS, INC.

Books, CDs, and more – Worldwide

For our listing of thousands of titles see our website
at
www.HeritageBooks.com

Cover art, Black Sheep Squadron, courtesy John D. Shaw

Published 2003 by
HERITAGE BOOKS, INC.
Publishing Division
1540 Pointer Ridge Place #E
Bowie, Maryland 20716

ISBN 0-7884-2476-9

9 780788 424762   5 2 2 9 5

International Standard Book Number: **0-7884-2476-9**

Dedication

This book is dedicated to all the remaining Black Sheep those now flying high cover; to Pappy Boyington, t leader a pilot would ever want or need; to Frank Walton, Intelligence Officer. And finally to my wife, Julie and who bring me joy more than they will ever know.

Acknowledgments:

This effort has been written in conjunction with my f "Jerry" Marketos. Jerry's understanding, patience and dedication to a job well done has been endless. A Corsai before I met him, he has enjoyed doing it almost as much

"I will remember you.
Will you remember me?
Don't let your life pass you by.
Weep not for the memory."

Sarah McLachlan

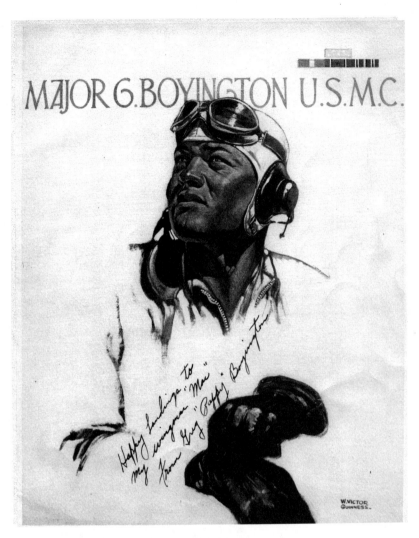

Inscription reads
"Happy Landings to my wingman 'Mac'
from Greg 'Pappy' Boyington"

From publicity tour 1946 (McClurg collection)

Table of Contents:

Foreword

What can be said of the generation of young men who abandoned their dreams and willingly marched off to war? Moreover, how difficult it is, even in retrospect, to fully appreciate the speed and efficiency with which young Americans were transformed from civilians to warriors, and the nation's industrial might underwent a parallel metamorphosis. So it was with young men like Bob McClurg and countless others who left college campuses, career jobs, loved ones and ambitions to serve the nation, armed with weaponry from factories known for automobiles, washing machines and the like.

McClurg wanted to be a fighter pilot though he, like many of those who chose the same path, had never seen an airplane much less flown one. Within a year, however, the survivors of a rigorous, fast paced program departed for combat, pitted, in this case, against the seasoned professionals of Japan's Navy. Fortuitously for McClurg and a few others, they would go into combat flying one of America's newest fighters, and be led in that effort by the quintessential aerial warrior, Lieutenant Colonel Gregory "Pappy" Boyington. Bob McClurg became a member of the now famous "Black Sheep" of Marine Fighter Squadron 214.

These were young men, most of theme naïve in the ways of the world. For many it was the first time away from home. For most, combat was a traumatic passage from adolescence to manhood, with lifetimes of experiences crammed into weeks. Old hands were revered; to many of the veteran pilots, the newcomers attached an almost superstitious trust. When the sense of invincibility that accompanies the young and active was shattered by the loss of friends, new pilots like McClurg were keen to watch, listen to and emulate the best among them. Rank was not as important as reputation. And for all the Black Sheep, their colorful leader was the epitome of the fighter pilot. Flying into combat with Boyington in the lead virtually assured success, and, more importantly, survival. When Boyington was shot down in January 1944, the loss of the plucky leader had an almost devastating effect on the Black Sheep.

Too, the blending of man and machine assumed almost religious fervor. For McClurg and his squadron mates the beautiful Vought F4U "Corsair" commanded close attention, but eventually merited in equal measure a degree of affection that lasted long after flying days were over. To the uninitiated, it may be difficult to understand the love that a pilot may hold for a particular aircraft. Most often that cult-like following is reserved for planes that are either pilots' dreams to fly or thoroughbreds that are high in performance and mercilessly unforgiving of pilot inattention or ineptitude. Among World War II aviators, the argument will rage as to whether the RAF's Spitfire or the USAAF's sleek North American Mustang represents the "dream," but few would disagree that the revolutionary Corsair was a nightmare for many an unwary novice.

Nicknamed variously "U-Bird," "Hose-Nose," or "The Bent-wing Bird," the F4U Corsair ground up unwitting neophytes as readily as it dispatched the enemy in the hands of an expert. Initially deemed unsuitable by the Navy for carrier operations because of its springy landing gear and notoriously poor forward visibility during landing approach, the Corsair was quickly routed to eager Marine squadrons that had been battling the Japanese in the Solomon Islands with the rugged but out-classed Grumman Wildcat. Shortly after, modifications that included a raised pilot seat, bubble canopy and extended tail wheel strut rendered the Corsair much friendlier to the pilot during landing approaches and ground operations. In early 1943, the Corps had its first Corsair ace and the aircraft had established its reputation among Japanese airmen who underscored their respect by naming it "Whistling Death." By 1944 the Corsair was the mount of choice for many of the Corps' top aces. Later, despite its poor rating as a carrier-based aircraft, the F4U was ordered aboard ship, Leatherneck Corsair squadrons fleshing out the Fleet's carrier air groups by the time of the Okinawa campaign.

Claiming the longest production run of any WWII American fighter, Vought and licensed producers Goodyear and Brewster eventually turned out almost 12,000 Corsairs by war's end, and another 649 in the postwar period. In 1950, as North Korean forces raced south across the 38th parallel, the venerable Corsair donned war paint once again and, together with recalled pilots who had thought they'd seen their last war, soldiered ably as a fighter bomber. Today, the aircraft is a fighter pilot's icon.

That is what this book is all about; the matching of a spirited thoroughbred with young, eager and aggressive jockeys. And while the Corsair stands in tribute to the genius of American industry, Bob McClurg and the many young men who went to war are the vestiges of a great generation, without whom the Corsair would have been useless. These were young men who grew up in a time of deprivation; a nickel came from the sweat of the brow, with ambition made keener to gain the security that national economic failure had all but foreclosed. Steeled in the crucible of the Great Depression, that generation was inured to putting off the good things, raising its sights instead to aim for a better future. Little wonder they willingly delayed the good life to answer the Call to Colors. This is a story by one such man, but so typical in that he, like many others, gave his best. It made him an excellent combat pilot - an ace - and forever marks him as an example of the American spirit.

Colonel Denis "Deej" Kiely, USMC (Ret.)
Director of Membership and Public Relations
Naval Aviation Museum Foundation Inc.
Pensacola, Florida

Preface

It seems that simple human nature causes people to have a high degree of interest in conflict and conquest. Some of us are interested in the technical aspects, while significant other attentions are given to the drama involved. As it would happen, the WWII Marine Fighter Squadron I belonged to (VMF-214, known as "The Black Sheep") experienced combat that provided rich food for technical interests. As luck would have it, our colorful leader, Gregory "Pappy" Boyington, was also of high interest to the public all by himself. Add to that the unconventional way our squadron came into existence, and a 1970s television series loosely based on our exploits, and an already high interest entered a whole new dimension.

Many of the original Black Sheep squadron members (including myself) have been in various states of disbelief over the years, as we watched the attention given to our combat history and to our image. A further shock has been to observe how the television show (which never intended to accurately document our experiences) had so much influence in the perception of our combat environment, and our conduct. As the years progress, analysis of our squadron and others continues. The picture has been painted in many different ways by various contributors, and the outcome is a perceived history that may not exactly reflect what we went through. This has resulted in some degree of stress for those of us who know how it really was. Our leader, "Pappy" Boyington wrote his autobiography in the late 1950's. Entitled "Baa Baa Black Sheep," I think it was a best seller.

Later on in the 1970's, our intelligence officer, Frank Walton, (among others) was highly incensed by the television show's portrayal of us as outlaw misfits. For his part, Walton wrote a book "Once They Were Eagles," which aimed to shed light on who the Black Sheep really were.

For many years, I had thought about writing my own memoirs. My purpose would be to provide a firsthand account of how things were, perhaps extending Walton's effort. In December, 1995, I teamed with an acquaintance to begin this work. To accurately reconstruct my past has required countless hours, and through this effort we have come to realize that we owe thanks to many. Some of those are:

- For the use of photos, thanks to Henry Bourgeois, Bob Strickland, Leon Marketos and the USMC.
- Thanks to John Shaw for allowing us to use the image of his painting "Black Sheep Squadron" on the cover of our book.
- Special thanks to Bob Strickland for his support and information regarding Japanese Ace Takeo Tanimizu.
- Thanks to Deane Doolen for allowing us to use portions of his outstanding work in tribute to Robert Alexander.
- To Colonel Denis "Deej" Kiely USMC (Ret), Director of membership and public relations at the Naval Aviation Museum in Pensacola, FL; thanks for writing the foreword for this book, and for entertaining us.
- Thanks also to Bill Vanderhey, who spent many hours copying the entire log of declassified VMF-214 combat reports at the archives in Washington, D.C.

As timing would have it, the 50th anniversary of the end of WWII was preceded slightly by the Persian Gulf War. Interest remains high; since I began the effort on my own writing, at least three other books have been published about the Black Sheep or our leader (none by actual WWII Black Sheep squadron members).

The result of our effort has come together (now), in 2003.

At last, the time has come for me to contribute my part...

xiv

Childhood

Admittedly, the beginning of all this sounds like a bit of a hard luck story, as the Great Depression coincided with my childhood years. Those of us who belong to my "senior" age group probably remember those times; the younger ones will probably remember this stuff as being what the older ones talk about...

I was born in early 1919 in Coshocton, Ohio, the youngest of the brood. Dad was an executive with one of the major rubber companies, and Mom was a busy housewife with a boy, a girl, and a boy. Things changed in 1922, when Dad passed away suddenly and Mother was left to rear the 3 of us. We moved to New Castle, PA, and lived with my mother's sister (Aunt Matilda) for some time, while Mom got our lives organized and entered the teaching profession to support us. As fate would have it, Matilda's husband passed away soon after, so it was Mom and her three kids, with Matilda and her two kids... all in one big house in New Castle.

Matilda wasn't my favorite aunt. I don't think Aunt Matilda was a bad woman, but she was strict and had the unpleasant habit of using castor oil as a disciplinary tool. I wouldn't call myself a problem child, either; I wasn't much for destruction or vandalism. This was the 1920's, when people didn't concern themselves much with such things. But there were times when my desire to take a walk down Highland Avenue would overcome my desire to take a walk to someplace else (like school), and off I'd go. Mom eventually rented a place on Highland Ave., and got us out of Matilda's house, but we knew about our new quarters for a few weeks before we actually got to move in. I had to endure the teasing thought of knowing we would get to live there, but the day didn't come quite fast enough. I loved the idea of being out of Matilda's reach, and would sometimes go to check our new place out. The apartment remained locked until we moved in, but the appeal to a grade school boy was too attractive. Mom was either attending school or working somewhere, and my unplanned absence would leave Aunt Matilda frantic. There were trolley cars which ran the streets in those days; trolley cars make great reconnaissance vehicles... A panicked Matilda would ask the trolley car operator "Did you see a little boy?" Of course, the trolley car operator would say "Why, yes...," and give away my whereabouts. Aunt Matilda would come and get me, and I'd get a dose of castor oil. "All right, Bob, This should make you think twice before doing that again..." Sure, that was, until next time I wanted to... And so I came to hate castor oil even more than most of us.

In grade school, I was a comedian of sorts. But my comedy went to such an extent that Mother began to get calls from the teacher. The whole class was disrupted by my "entertainment," and for years the teachers were concerned that I might not pass to the next grade if I didn't start paying attention. For this, I was rewarded with the red seat in the front row. I think I sat there for most of my grade school career, breaking from my comedic nature only long enough to do the minimum required to pass through. "The ruler" across my knuckles was also something I knew well. By the time I reached junior high, my comedy was turning into aggression. I got into many fights, and became known for that instead. I conjured up many stories to explain torn shirts to my mother; these were shirts she really couldn't afford to replace at the time. Teachers realized that much of my attitude might be resulting from a missing father figure, and they counseled me as well as they could on that subject. My fighting career continued, until one of my previous victims grew more than I did, and cleaned my clock one day. Then the tough guy wasn't so tough any more, and that was about the end of that. I have to think now that the guy did me a favor.

For a calendar reference, this was about the time I entered high school (1933), which was also during the time things had really become financially difficult for this country. For me, high school was a drudge, plain and simple. No longer a comic, no longer a fighter; I had to work because there wasn't enough income to make ends meet, so I took whatever odd jobs I could find. I remember having a paper route with 330 houses, and I worked in a gas station. My brother, who was six years older, had five different jobs at one time. For about the first half of our high school career, we walked roughly three miles to and from school. (Uphill, both ways, as the joke goes, but the distance was true.) Mom managed to find us a place nearer to the school (with the aid of a relative), so that helped. As I recall, I wasn't much of a discipline problem in high school; that guy who finally taught me a lesson, coupled with the long hours of work, adjusted my attitude. I didn't do much for enjoyment, though; it was either school work, or job work, and there weren't many hours left in the day beyond that.

With some encouragement from Mom, I went on to college. My father, mother and sister all graduated from Westminster college, but I started at Penn State - the Dubois undergraduate center. Though I didn't have any time to savor it, I loved the outdoors, and I really wanted to become a forest ranger. Practically everybody I knew advised against this, saying there was no money to be made as a forest ranger, and that I should follow a business curriculum. And so it was, Mom guided me into Westminster college for the second year. Again, as far as my memory serves me, I don't recall college being much different from high school. I commuted to school because I couldn't afford to stay there. I remember that the home we lived in then was nine miles from the college. Back in those days, if you had to be at class in half an hour, you could put your thumb up and someone would always stop. I got a job at the college, and worked long hours outside class in order to get by. I cleaned windows, emptied garbage cans, hauled coal, broke stone for the roads... for about thirty cents an hour. The only real difference I remember about college is that we were growing up... I'd hear my friends talking about where they went on the weekends, or what beer they drank, and I became more aware of the fact that I didn't go away on weekends and have fun like many of the others. I didn't date much, for the same reasons that I didn't spend much time partying. I made it through college as an average student, pouring it on toward the end as the realization began to set in that I'd soon be out in the "real" world. Again, the timeline becomes important here; I graduated from high school in 1938, and came out of college in the spring of 1942. At that time, it had become obvious that war duty was on the horizon.

While I was in Westminster, they offered a flight course in which you could solo a Piper Cub at the New Castle Airport. (The Piper Cub is a small single engine airplane, carries two people - easy to fly. Known even today as a classic, there are many still flying.) They also offered courses in navigation and field procedure. By taking this, I could get credit toward my degree, and it wasn't math or economics, or whatever. It was done during school time, as a part of the school study. To a young lad who had no money or time for leisure activities, this was pure recreation, so I took it. I can't even say that I always dreamed of being an aviator. Rather, for a guy with no money and no time to himself, soloing a plane seemed a great way to rise above it all, even if briefly. I came out of the effort having soloed a cub, with a few hours flying time, and also with my eyes wide open. One morning near the time of our final flight test, I went to practice some spins, which were a necessary part of the test. To enter a spin, we took the plane up over a road (to give us a directional landmark). To actually put the plane into a spin, you generally chop the throttle, pull the stick back, kick the rudder, and you're in a spin. What you then do is spin around one, one and a half, two turns, then recover and come out in the same heading; that's called a controlled spin so someone evaluating you from the ground knows that you're doing it on purpose. So, on this morning, I ascended to 3,000 feet, chopped the throttle and did the other stuff, and put the little cub in a spin. Then the engine quit. I'm all alone in the airplane... I saw a little fog bank down below, with some cars going along, and thought to myself, "I'm gonna die today." Well, not quite. I remembered my flight instructor, Frank Farrone, telling me if the engine ever cuts out, stick the nose over (dive the airplane) to windmill the prop (the airflow over the propeller will actually cause it to turn the engine, in an effort to start it again). So I did. In doing this, I found out the little cub flew almost as well without an engine as it did with one. So I descended gradually in circles. I never did get the engine started, but I made a decent dead stick landing (dead stick means with the engine off) on the runway. I coasted to a stop, and a car came over to me, with my instructor in it. He said it quit because I chopped the throttle too fast.

So I went up and did it again, only this time I pulled the throttle back very slowly and repeated the procedure just as the instructor said... And the engine quit just like it had the first time. Same procedure again, I circled down and landed silently, coasting to a stop about 20 feet from where I had 20 minutes earlier. This time, it wasn't only Frank Farrone in the car, but also the airplane's owner, who was giving Frank hell for sending me up again because I could have damaged the poor little cub. So the two of them took it up to about 5,000 feet, and repeated the test. Again, it cut out. Again, they managed to get it back on the ground in one piece. I heard them speak to each other in harsh words, then the airplane's owner departed.

I said to Frank: "What am I gonna do? The CAA instructor is supposed to be here this afternoon. What's he gonna say when he sees that I've had two dead stick landings?"

Frank replied "He's probably gonna see that you've survived them and hand you your license right there on the spot! No, seriously, you'll have to take your test just like the others, but walking away from two dead sticks will work to your credit, not your detriment."

O.K., so the CAA instructor came. There were four of us taking our tests that day, and the instructor sent us all up with directions to do pylon 8's around a smokestack, some touch and go landings, then each of us was to proceed to a certain sector and at a certain time, do a spin. The instructor would then watch us at our given times. So I went up and started to do the maneuvers.

Now, for this flight, I had drawn a seatpack, as opposed to a backpack. The seatpack is a parachute you sit on, and the backpack rides behind you. I proceeded to do all the maneuvers without difficulty; pylon 8's around the smokestack were no problem. The touch and go landings were easy. I climbed to my designated sector, and at the proper time proceeded to do my spin. I cut the throttle and applied full rudder. When I pulled the stick back to do the spin, the presence of my seatpack under my rear end wouldn't let the stick come back all the way, and the forgiving little cub refused to enter a spin. I tried this 3 or 4 times, squirming frantically in my seat trying to shinny the parachute back, but ended up with the same results. So I gave up, and landed the airplane.

I can still remember thinking to myself, "Gees, after landing this thing safely twice this morning with no engine, I'm gonna fail in front of the CAA instructor because I can't make it spin."

As I got out of the airplane and headed toward the others on the ground, I saw one of my buddies who had positioned himself behind the CAA instructor. This buddy was waving his hands at me and putting his index finger up in front of his mouth as if to say "Keep your mouth shut." So, I approached the CAA man silently, thinking of how I was going to explain what happened (or, what didn't happen, as it were), and he asked me how it went. I replied "Pretty good, sir," and with that, the instructor signed my papers. I grabbed my buddy, and we started to walk away together. As we got out of earshot of the instructor, my friend whispered to me, "He never even looked at you! He asked me how your spins were, and I told him you did O.K." And that was that.

By now the reader has no doubt noticed that military training has yet to surface in this picture I'm painting. Let me break into that just a little... While I attended Westminster college, I spent six weeks during the summer of my sophomore and junior years at platoon leader's school at Quantico, Virginia. The deal was for us to do this, then spend another six weeks after graduation, and we would be commissioned as second lieutenants in the Marine infantry. Military service was something I had always kept in mind as a possible path to pursue; sort of a safety net. I began my senior year in college in the fall of 1941. Remember that the Japanese bombed Pearl Harbor on December 7, 1941, so the need for fighters of all types went through the roof. Anyway... before I graduated from Westminster, a Navy Lieutenant J.G. (Junior Grade – a rank classification) came to the campus in search of candidates to join the Naval Aviation Reserves. Because I was listed among names who already had some military training at that point (and the pilot's license probably didn't hurt, either), this Lieutenant J.G. sought me out with a "deal." The deal was for me to find nine of my buddies to sign up, and he would get us out of taking our exams, and out of writing our theses for graduation. He said he'd arrange it with the Dean of Men so we would be all set. [Didn't this sound too good to be true??] Now, remember all my hard labor during school. Again, I didn't have time or money for parties or socializing. I didn't spend time with the basketball players or football players, but I knew many of them. Let's just say that my janitorial duties during those years involved me finding many papers (and carbon copy sheets) in wastebaskets which might have helped lots of those guys pass their exams... So these guys listened when I had something to tell them. I told them the story, and eventually managed to talk six or seven of them into doing it. They twisted whatever arms they had to, and I managed to end up with the required nine total. We all met with the Lieutenant J.G. and signed on the dotted line. From there, we were to go to the Philadelphia Naval yard and get our physicals, then we'd be all set for after graduation. So about a week later, this Lieutenant J.G. came back, and I asked him to review the deal as a means of reassuring myself. The reply was "Well, Bob, a few things have changed…"

"W--Wh--Whatt has chhhanged?"

"Well, I think you're still gonna have to take your exam, and I think you're gonna have to write your thesis."

"Oh, gees! I'm in real trouble. I'll be dead by tonight when the guys find this out."

He said "Don't worry about this." And the Lieutenant J.G. got us all together, and told us: "I've made arrangements with the Dean. You'll take your exam and write your thesis, but don't worry about it. You'll get by."

Doesn't this sound fishy? Well, times were what they were, and everyone was waving the flag for the boys to go become cannon fodder. We went in to take our final exams, and we wrote our theses. There were lots of misspelled words, and "t's" not crossed and "i's" not dotted. We were allowed to use our books, and we were allowed to talk. I ended up graduating from college with all A's and one B. According to the agreement, we didn't attend the Westminster graduation (this was April, 1942), but instead, went straight to Pennsylvania for our physical exams at the Naval Air Corps. (I might add here that we were the first group of fliers to join the U.S. Navy as a unit from Western Pennsylvania, and we all eventually made the cut.)

Military Training

We transferred to the Philadelphia Navy yard on April 23, 1942, and it was a day or two after that when we were given our physical exams. I'll never forget this little side story... We were all standing there in line in the physical examination room, stark naked. There were the ten of us (me and the nine other athletes who would have torn me apart had this deal not come together.) Standing first in line ahead of us, there was also another guy whom we did not know. He was reading a book, and he asked me to hold the book when the doctor started looking at him. Doc said to him "Now bend over and spread your cheeks." (Of course, this was so he could get a look at the young man's southern parts to make sure nothing unauthorized was living down there.) In response to the doc's request, this bookworm bent over, stuck both his pinky fingers in his mouth, and pulled it wide open to give a good look at his teeth. The Naval doctor let out a bunch of expletives, ending with "Ahh! I don't believe this. Where did we get this one? Step off to the side..."

We ten from Westminster all passed our physicals later that day. I had a little problem with my eyes; my vision was excellent, but I was just a little cross-eyed. The doctor sent for a tool which was nothing more than a stick, and I practiced and practiced with this thing for 6 weeks, moving it in and out away from my face, focusing on it with my eyes. This helped to strengthen my eye muscles so I wasn't so cockeyed. I was given the exam again and passed with no problem.

The Westminster graduation came around shortly. By that time, we had already been at the Philadelphia Navy Yard for about a month, going through "elimination base." Essentially, they were giving us a certain amount of training, and if we didn't demonstrate what they thought was sufficient beginnings of a military flyer, we were "out."

Back at Westminster, Captain Eddie Rickenbacker was to hand out our diplomas, and Mom was there to accept mine for me. As the story goes, she came up to get my diploma, and said to Capt. Rickenbacker, "You must know my Bob... He's a flyer, too." Of course, Rickenbacker didn't know me from the man on the moon. He replied with something cordial along the lines of, "Oh, yes, yes that's right," and I got a phone call in Philadelphia shortly after, with an ecstatic Mother McClurg telling me, "Captain Eddie Rickenbacker knows of you !"

Let me go through the military specifics once more, because Uncle Sam's standard operating procedure isn't always easily understood. The deal I had in college where I went six weeks during sophomore and junior summers allowed me to enter the Marine Corps as a PFC (private first class). Then another six weeks (the training we took at the Marine base in Quantico, Virginia Platoon Leaders School) made me a Marine second lieutenant. But you can't take Navy flight training as a Marine... You can be commissioned a Marine at the end. Funny thing about that, too... I completed my training at the Philadelphia Navy yard, and exited then technically as a Naval seaman second class. But they don't just give you your papers and tell you to go to the Naval reserve signup... During that transition, you are technically detached from the Marine Corps as a private first class, with papers and everything. People could simply walk away, with their military service officially fulfilled and documented. To make sure this didn't happen, they put two Naval MP's on one side of me, and two Marines on the other side, and marched me from the Marine Base over to the Naval reserve signup place and enlisted me. Then, I was a Navy seaman second class, ready to start Naval flight training. Why can't you simply go through Naval flight training as a Marine? Just don't ask the Navy people. I wonder how many people were on the committee that dreamed this all up!

O.K., so now we're all in the Navy. Because I had taken that Marine training during my Westminster days, they made me squad leader of our group. So now little McClurg, who had talked these other guys into this whole deal, was ordering them around. "Hup, two, three, four, Hup, two, three, four... Left face, right face," and so on. We went through another period of "elimination base" at the Philadelphia Navy yard. Again, this was spring 1942. The U.S. had declared war on Japan, and the war movement was getting into full swing. We basically did what we had to do, and completed the training. It was a whirlwind that lasted about eleven weeks; the purpose of the Philadelphia experience was mainly to identify the potential "fly boys," and sort everybody into the multitude of other possible positions.

As a side note here, I'll mention that the Navy Yard wasn't just for training. There was all sorts of stuff going on there, from refitting ships to testing new top secret equipment. We were given strict orders that when we had liberty, we were not to walk anywhere in the Navy Yard unless we were told to do so. Well... We were denied leave one weekend, so of course we decided to walk around the Navy yard. We came across a chain link fence, behind which was a Japanese Zero. We figured it must have come from Pearl Harbor, and they had it there to do some checking on it. As we inspected the plane, we noticed that the propeller said on it "Philadelphia Navy Yard," and we couldn't get over that. Looking back, I can't be sure whether Uncle Sam actually supplied those parts to the Japanese in previous years, or (more likely) the prop was damaged in the downing of the plane and they refitted it with an American one to get the thing airworthy again. But we blabbed it to all of our buddies that the Jap plane had a U.S. made prop on it, and this eventually made it back to the people in charge. We caught all hell for looking where we shouldn't have. As I remember, we paid for our infraction with several hundred pushups, then a trip to the baseball field. Why to the baseball field, you might ask? I'll tell you... They made us strip to our underwear and pick up cigarette butts for about an hour in the early evening, when the mosquitoes were at their worst.

The next step after Philadelphia was Cadet training at Pensacola, Florida, but we could only get that far if we first got "upchecks" on our flying from Philly. So the last hurdle before getting out of Philadelphia was to make the grade on this test. We checked out in N3's, which were two-seater open cockpit biplanes. The guy I got for my evaluation was nicknamed "downcheck Dalton." Dalton was a Marine captain, and I tried to gain his favor by making sure he knew I had signed up in the Marines a long time ago.

Now, one thing you never do is fly over the Navy Yard. You fly around it, but not over it. Guess what McClurg did first thing after takeoff on the check flight. Dalton grabbed his stick and rattled it back and forth (the sticks in both seats are linked together), knocking my knees until they ached. We flew to this field in Camden, NJ, and Dalton got out. He shouted to me over the engine noise, "Well, I don't know. If you wanna fly this thing so bad, go ahead, take it up and kill yourself." I was so elated that he was still going to let me solo after buzzing the Navy yard that I kicked the plane around to taxi out, and blew gravel all over him. I remember sitting there in the plane, shaking my head, thinking, "I'm gonna get an upcheck now, for sure." We were supposed to make two touch and go landings, no more. I made four. The plane was fun to fly, and I enjoyed it. By the fourth one, Dalton was waving his arms, beckoning me to make the thing stay on the ground this time. He got in, said "I got it," and without more words he flew us back to the Navy Yard. I got out, and tried to get his chute for him. Again, "Naw, I got it," was all he said, and he disappeared. I found out what really happened was that Dalton had been out the night before. He was so disgusted with me that he just put his parachute in the rack and left for the day.

On the following morning, I was listed on the flight board to fly! So they gave me a plane, and I went out to another adjacent field, made three or four landings and practiced some flying in the air. When I brought the plane back, the seaman second class in charge of the flight board said, "Captain Dalton wants to see you."

When I found Dalton, I caught hell for taking an airplane out without authorization to do so. I told him that my flight was on the board, and that I had only done what I was scheduled to do. Then he remembered... In his hurried exit on the previous day, he had not checked me "up" or "down," so the scheduler assumed that I was a "go," and this just aggravated Downcheck further. "We'll see about that..." was his reply (now, he was madder than hell), and he set out to make my life difficult. But he almost signed his own doom... I had flown the plane without damage, and demonstrated the ability to take off, fly, and land repeatedly without problems. Remember that these were difficult military times, and they needed pilots; it was hard for someone to justify "scrubbing" a pilot who could fly an airplane. "Downcheck Dalton" wound up appearing in front of the board, reprimanded because he hadn't done what he was supposed to. "Downcheck" Dalton sure didn't care for Bob McClurg, but I was on my way to Pensacola, just the same. Phew!

Early August, 1942: O.K. We're on to Pensacola for about seven months of flight, instrument and navigation schooling. Pensacola wasn't a sorting process; once you were there, it was pretty much known that you had a flying career ahead of you, so long as you paid attention and didn't do anything dumb. Exactly what type of flying career remained to be determined... Now, everyone wanted to be a fighter pilot; that was top shelf. Not everyone got to be a fighter pilot. At that time, the way they determined whether you got to be a fighter pilot was... If you had a good gunnery score... If you had good aerobatics scores... If you could navigate well... If you were lucky... Some of the boys would become TBF (torpedo bomber) pilots. Some would become SBD (dive bomber) pilots. Some would be PBY (flying boat, search and rescue) pilots, and some would become instructors. Nobody I knew really wanted to be an instructor; we all wanted to get into the fight. In Pensacola, we learned to fly mostly the SNJ (same as the army plane AT6). We also flew OS2UY's. We took radio school, navigation school, gunnery school, and learned field carrier landings (where we landed on a strip the size of a carrier deck, but it was a piece of land). After the Pensacola training was nearly over, our names all appeared on a board under what category of pilot we were endorsed for. I remember searching the board for my name, wondering where it would be. I had done well in gunnery and navigation, but I still couldn't believe it when I saw that my name was up to be a fighter pilot. So that was the route I took. After completion of work at Pensacola, I was commissioned a second lieutenant in the Marine Corps on February 2, 1943. Next, it was on to Opa-Lacka field in Miami for some (but not nearly enough) fighter training. This training (or lack of it) would become my Achilles heel in the not too distant future...

It was at Opa-Lacka air base that I was introduced to a fighter plane made by Brewster Aircraft, called the F2A "Buffalo." It was also at Opa-Lacka that I was introduced to raw military style death, first hand. One of my initial memories of checking in at Opa-Lacka (in fact, one of the most vivid memories from my entire service career) is that of a friend's crash. I didn't witness the crash, but I witnessed its effects. He went to Opa-Lacka two weeks before I did, and he crashed and burned in a Brewster Buffalo. I wasn't allowed to actually see him, but I got a look through a first floor infirmary window with the help of another friend of mine, clasping his hands together and stooping over to offer me a lift. There lay my buddy in a hospital bed with clean white linens all around him. He looked like a burned baked potato.

Maybe now is the right time for a quick "crash course" in airplanes (no pun intended). Without going into too much detail, an airplane is built on a wing; you move the wing through the air, and it generates lift. Then, to make the thing fly, you put a motor on the front which spins a propeller, which generates a pulling force on the front of the airplane (just as if someone hooked a rope on the front to tow it). So, the engine pulls the plane through the air, and when it goes fast enough, the wing's lift is more than the plane weighs, and it becomes, as we say, "airborne." in other words, it flies. They add some other controls so we can direct the thing up or down, and side to side, and roll one way or the other, and we have an airplane which is steerable. You could theoretically put a set of wings on a Sherman tank, then add some control surfaces (rudder, elevator, etc.) and if you put a big enough engine on it, you could indeed get it to "fly." This is not to discredit the airplane designers; to get all of this stuff done elegantly is a real design feat, and an art. It is what distinguishes ships like the graceful F4U Corsair from the F2A Buffalo, but I'm getting ahead of myself a bit... The point I wish to make here is just this: it definitely does matter how the stuff is all arranged. It does matter how smooth everything is, and how it all works together. The Brewster Buffalo was an airplane in the academic sense; it had a wing, and all the appropriate control surfaces. Also, it had an engine that would pull it fast enough so that its wing would create more lift than it weighed, so the thing would "fly," as in "become airborne." But...

For starters, it wasn't very aerodynamic at all. That means it didn't slip through the air; it didn't slice its way through the sky smoothly. Nope. Rather, it sort of plowed its way through the sky, sort of skidded along. This meant that it was difficult to keep the nose of the airplane heading where you pointed it. This becomes a very significant problem when you're trying to do something like line a target up in the gun sights and stay on it. Another poor trait of the Buffalo was the fact that it had short, stubby wings, so there wasn't much wing in the Brewster to keep you in the air. You had to have the engine pulling you along at a pretty good clip, just to stay in the sky. Combine the short wings with the fact that the plane wasn't very aerodynamic, and now consider what occurs if the engine should happen to quit: the heavy drag slowed it down quickly, and again there wasn't much wing, so when it did slow down, the Brewster tended to fall out of the sky like a brick.

This was a big cause of death for the inexperienced (and sometimes just plain unlucky) cadets flying them. Our trainer Buffalos only burned low octane gas, instead of the high octane stuff they were supposed to have, because all of the high octane was being sent to the various war zones. I remember when I got to the field, the first thing I saw upon getting out of the transport plane was a big black smoke column off in the distance. They told us it was burning tires, but I later learned that it was the smoking wreck of the buddy I mentioned a few paragraphs ago. I remember, too, when I first checked in to the barracks at Opa-Lacka; it was just about empty. I saw some guys way down at the other end, so I approached them. As I got closer, I saw that one was in a full body cast. Two had arm casts, and one had a leg cast; all playing poker. After some greetings and exchange of stories, I learned that they were all victims of engines which had cut out during takeoff or landing. Burning the low octane gas caused the high performance engines in those planes to have major problems if the pilot failed to do certain things to keep the engine's internal parts "cleaned out." Eight people died of such a fate while I was there.

I had my own experience with this one day, as I was practicing spot landings with an F2A "Buffalo." I was coming in for a landing at about eight hundred feet, and the thing quit on me. True to the Brewster fame, I started to fall like a stone. I thought to myself "this is it, I'm the next one." I frantically got the booster pump going, and managed to get the engine back to life with about thirty feet of altitude to spare. As another quick tangent here, the booster pump was known as the "wobble pump," because a plane would be viewed by others to "wobble" as the pilot frantically pumped the lever while doing his best to hang onto the controls. And this wasn't specific to Brewster aircraft, either. Anyway, I managed to get the thing down in one piece, and taxi it out of the pattern. The problem was widespread, but I still had trouble convincing the field instructor (who was not pleased that I had made an unauthorized landing) that the thing had really cut out on me. Fortunately, the guy behind me in the traffic pattern witnessed my trouble and spoke up about it. Whether this Navy instructor believed me or not, he wasn't very sympathetic, and gave me the option to fly the plane back to the airfield we came from a few miles away. The truth was that I didn't want to fly the thing anywhere, but I figured I'd get washed out if I refused to take it back, so off I went. They told me to circle the airfield as I climbed, to about five thousand feet. The other airfield wasn't far away, so if I got up high enough, I could "coast" over there and make a dead stick landing. I climbed and climbed, concentrating on the engine sound all the way up. All I could see in my mind was those guys in the casts back at the barracks, and my buddy - the baked potato. I brought the Brewster in hotter than hell (very fast to keep airspeed in case the thing quit), and touched down without a hitch. I continued to fly those things, sweating every second of the way. Aerobatically, the Brewster was everything they say it was; awful. To make a good gunnery run with a Buffalo was next to impossible; on the cockpit gauges, you couldn't keep the needle and ball anywhere near each other, which generally means that you were never actually going where the nose of the airplane was pointed; you were usually in a skid of some sort. Trying to follow a moving target (like an opposing plane), and at the same time hit it with the Brewster's gunfire, was also next to impossible. But somehow, I managed to pass the tests and accumulate twenty-one hours of time in the things without auguring myself into the ground anywhere. My negative comments about the Buffalo said, I will also offer the information that other countries that used the F2A Brewster Buffalo thought they were just great. Then again, they didn't have access to some of the other aircraft to compare them to.

I finished Opa-Lacka in the end of March 1943, and then went on to Norfolk to do field carrier landings. They didn't have enough fighters for us to do the qualification run in fighter planes, so we flew mostly SNJ's again. We had to make about nine successful field carrier landings, evaluated by someone on the ground. If you made nine good landings there, you went out to the carrier USS Charger, which was anchored at Norfolk. That's right... The carrier wasn't even moving. It was stationary, and if the wind was right, they did the landing trials. (It's easier in some ways to land on a carrier that's headed into the wind, because the carrier's speed and the windspeed help the airplane to fly, so you can slow down more (relative to the carrier) before the airplane "stalls" and falls out of the sky). Anyway, I went out in the SNJ with another buddy of mine in another SNJ. I remember coming in for one of my landings on an approach which I thought was pretty good, but the landing signal officer (LSO) waved me off. I checked my gauges and altitude, and thought to myself "I'm dead on here, what's this guy waving me off for?" It was when I came back around in a turn and looked out the side of the cockpit that I saw my buddy piled into the barrier at the end of the carrier deck. He wasn't hurt badly, but I had to circle for a few minutes while they cleaned up the mess.

I made my nine landings, then they put him in my plane, and he made his landings. We then flew back to land together in my plane, and this is another story...

We flew back in my SNJ with my buddy "Cal" in the rear, piloting. As fate would have it, he groundlooped the thing on the landing (it wasn't a good day for Cal. Groundlooping is sort of like spinning out in a car. It generally means getting out of control and going off the runway, sometimes catching a wingtip on the ground.) We had a few tense moments together before anyone got over to us, as Cal said he was going to tag me for the ground loop. We went back quite a way together, but it took me a few minutes to figure out that he was joking. He ended up taking the "credit" for the incident, and life went on. That's how things were in those days. There's also a joke that goes with this; any American who wrecks five of his own planes is considered a Japanese (or opposing force) "Ace"... and indeed, we did have some fliers graduate with that distinction. We had guys in night flying missions fly into each other and die. It was grim, but it was part of life. The planes we flew weren't the greatest, because the best equipment was all being sent to the war zones. We took our chances, and made do with what was available. That's just the way things were. As unlucky as I like to think I am sometimes, I was then one of the lucky ones, and I made it through everything. On to the next adventure...

After "The Norfolk incident," we were given thirty days leave. From late April to late May 1943 was my last opportunity to go back home and visit Mom before regrouping in San Diego, where we were staged for transfer to wherever they wanted us to go. It was pretty well known at the time that you went from the West coast to the South Pacific, and from the East coast to the war in Europe. Also, South Pacific was mainly Navy and Marines, and the European war was mainly Army and Air Force. So, I was off to the South Pacific. By this time in San Diego, our confidence was up; we had made it through the rigors of flight training and were on our way to enter service somewhere. This is what we all wanted, what we had worked so hard for. While waiting to go into combat, I did have some time to reflect on things and wonder inside, "What have I gotten myself into?" There was fear of the unknown, but there was also a great sense of adventure, excitement, and desire to serve our country. As a bunch of fresh young Marine aviators, I can't say that we feared the Japanese at all; everyone was eager to join the fight.

Journey To The South Pacific

Logbook:
Arrived at Camp Miramar, San Diego May 26 1943

There, my name was put in a pool of pilots to be drawn from for all sorts of purposes. Overall, our confidence was up; we had made it through the rigors of flight training and were on our way to enter real service somewhere. This is what we all wanted, and I was going to be a fighter pilot! I had also begun to enjoy something that I hadn't had previously, ever: camaraderie with others doing the same things I was. No longer was I the custodian while others slept. No longer was I the late night and weekend study, while the rest of the crowd enjoyed recreation. I was right there, ready and willing to have the same fun everyone else had. Most of us ended up in San Diego a few days early, and this is where I really began to emerge from my shell. Prior to San Diego, I had never ever stayed in a hotel room; I couldn't afford to, much less travel anyplace where a room was required. We enjoyed our time roaming around and seeing what there was to see. We enjoyed the freedom.

It was on our journey from San Diego to Hawaii that I had another revelation as I learned about the world outside of Pennsylvania; there was an inconceivable amount of ocean out there! Our journey from San Diego to Hawaii went from May 26 to June 2 1943, aboard the USS Henderson. I remember many long hours spent looking out the sides of our boat (uh, ship), mouth agape, marveling at so much water. One item of entertainment was the flying fish; at night, we saw these things, which had a phosphorescent glow as they caught the moonlight on the water. We floated over about two thousand miles of that water, and eventually arrived at Hawaii.

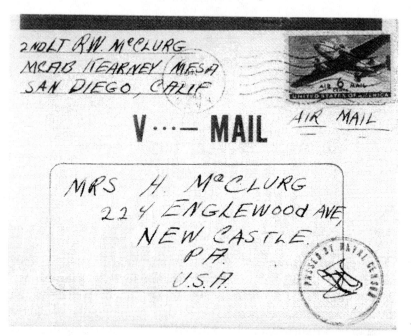

Postmarked June 3, 1943. There was no "Mrs. H. McClurg;" mother's name was Martha. The "H" was a simple code to indicate "Hawaii" because we couldn't reveal our location in the message; the mail censors would either cut it out or kick it back altogether. (McClurg collection)

Arrived at Hawaii June 2 1943

When we came upon Hawaii, I remember that we were all interviewed by a colonel. He looked through my log book and asked me how I got there. I said "By bbb... uhh, sshhip, sir." (Referring to a floating vessel as a "boat" is akin to farting in church when you're talking to a Navy man.) He said "Naw, naw, that's not what I mean. How did you get here with a log book like this? You've only got twenty-one hours in a fighter." I said "Sir, I don't cut the orders," and the colonel promptly informed me that I wasn't going any further with my log book the way it was; he didn't plan to let me leave Hawaii until I logged at least a hundred additional hours in fighters.

I had the afternoon to reflect a bit... two thousand miles away from the West Coast of the US, and about another twenty-five hundred miles away from my home state of Pennsylvania... All that aerobatic training... All that gunnery practice... The carrier landings... I wondered if I was going to get more fighter time, or spend the war ferrying supplies around Hawaii for Uncle Sam. My days as a fighter pilot seemed over before they began. But the military was a very busy institution at that time, and things didn't always happen as planned; paperwork didn't get generated as it should have. I remained just another one of the flock, and when morning came, I quietly slipped aboard the transport plane, off the island of Hawaii, and on to the next link in the chain, an island called Palmyra, with everyone else. I almost think I had developed a sort of divine, slippery quality; I had squeaked through once again, just as I had through my college exams and thesis, my solo of the little Piper Cub, just as I did past "Downcheck Dalton."

Heading away from Hawaii was a series of steps, now aboard a transport plane, from remote island to even more remote island. I was headed essentially southwest, ultimately to end up in the New Hebrides area, which is south of the Solomon Islands, where I was to see combat in a few weeks.

First from Hawaii was about 1000 miles to Palmyra, which is located in the area known as Polynesia.

Arrived at Palmyra June 6 1943

From Palmyra was another eight-hundred mile jaunt to a place in the Phoenix Islands called Canton. What I do remember is all those many hours droning away in transport planes; we flew mostly in Douglas R4D's (which were military versions of the DC-3). Their interiors had all the comfort features of small boxcars. They were "transports," mainly for cargo, and any seating inside usually appeared to be an obvious afterthought – perhaps just a few crude seats made from canvas and tubing. Quite often there was no seating at all, and we just made ourselves comfortable amidst whatever cargo was there; canvas bags were good to lie on, and wooden crates were not. Remember that this was 1943, and aircraft had no such things as a "fasten your seatbelt" light, much less seatbelts themselves, or luxuries like air conditioning or heat. To extend the flying range, they installed extra fiberglass fuel tanks inside the cabin, where we rode. These tanks always had leaks either in the fiberglass joints or in the pipes connecting them. Remember also that these old planes flew at about one-third the speed of today's airliners; I spent many hours looking out the window, staring down at endless open water as the engines droned on, all the while smelling strong gasoline vapors from the cabin fuel tanks. It was almost impossible to avoid being sick after many hours exposed to such thick fuel odors. Because of this, it was common for us to be sick and vomiting for the last half of most of the flights. The gas smell seemed to tattoo itself on us; once you had spent a few hours amidst the odor, you reeked of it for days, even after showering.

Arrived at Canton June 7 1943

From Canton we flew another six-hundred miles or so and crossed the International Date Line shortly before landing on the island of Funafuti. There is an initiation of sorts which occurs when crossing the international date line, but we didn't experience this on our outward journey. I would have the initiation ceremony about a year later on my return trip; maybe they just do it to you when you're on a ship. Funafuti... now there was a place. I can't describe where it was by including it with a group like the previous ones. If someone needed a definition of "the middle of nowhere," Funafuti was it. There were other islands nearby, but no civilization to speak of. I don't mean to discredit the area by calling it "middle of nowhere." There was a certain unspoiled appeal to it, but for me, it was overshadowed by desolation.

Arrived at Funafuti   June 8 1943

From Funafuti, we made one last very long flight (about 1400 miles), and landed on the island of New Caledonia. We had flown for so long that I was numb. It was the one leg of the journey where I hadn't been so bored toward the end; I was more worried that we might run out of fuel after having been in the air so long! One of the first things I noticed after extracting myself from the airplane was a big snake which crawled past my foot. That was my introduction to the South Pacific; the first of many pesky creatures that I would have to learn to watch out for.

Arrived at New Caledonia June 10 1943

We were all exhausted from the day's flight (and from the previous day after day of droning along), and didn't do much before turning in for the evening. I had a stomach ache and a light head from the gasoline fumes. I was informed that the bunk I would sleep in that night was occupied 48 hours ago by a guy who was killed. I don't even remember how he got killed; but I do remember lying awake in that bunk, exhausted, unable to sleep. In retrospect, this was the first time that the actual reality of death in war had hit me. It was no longer something we heard and read about; it was the guy who had been on this cot two days ago. Heavy fighting was happening in the area a few hundred miles north of where I was. I was roughly four thousand miles southwest of Hawaii, which meant that I was about sixty-five hundred miles away from home. I thought about the Lieutenant J.G. who had gotten me (and a few of my buddies) into this deal. I thought about my mother. Somehow, getting home didn't seem as simple as just retracing the jumps I had made in the past few days. Instead, I just lay there and wondered what was next, and whether I'd ever make it home across all of that water. So much water, the likes of which I could never have imagined by myself in a hundred years! I felt as if I had a one-way ticket. Finally, exhaustion took over and put me to sleep.

Daybreak eventually came again, and I awoke, much clearer in thought, and once again, ready to go. The next (and final) hop was to New Hebrides, an island called Espiritu Santo. This was combat oriented area, with a fighter strip code named "Buttons."

Arrived at Espiritu Santo June 11 1943

Postmarked June 19, 1943. Mother's name was Martha. The "N.H." was code for New Hebrides. (McClurg collection)

At the point of our arrival on "Buttons," we were really just a bunch of miscellaneous or "replacement" pilots. None of us had enough fighter credentials to even be considered for service in combat flights where enemy contact was anticipated. I, with my twenty-one hours of time in the Brewster "brick," was probably among the least qualified of us all. Again, most of the other pilots had well in excess of a hundred hours of fighter time. I spent my early days on New Hebrides (fighter strip "Buttons" at Espiritu Santo) serving fill-in as needed. As my log book has it these many years later, I did the following stints:

- I spent some time in the old VMF-214 from June 16, 1943 to July 19, 1943. (This was really the old VMF-214 squadron number being used for fill-ins. At that point, I believe the pilots who used to be VMF-214 had all succumbed to malaria.)
- I then served in VMF-124 for officially four days from July 23, 1943 to July 26, 1943.
- Next, I joined VMF-112 from July 27, 1943 to August 31, 1943.

I had heard about the Corsairs, even seen them. But I had yet to fly one. We still flew our hours in the SNJ trainers and other miscellaneous aircraft. We spent the first few days at "Buttons" doing routine training and familiarization, flying if and when we could get access in order to accumulate whatever hours we could. Flyable aircraft (of whatever type) were a commodity like most things. In order to receive flight pay, we needed to rack up a total of four hours per month in any combination we could. The only real stipulation was that whatever we flew had to burn gasoline, so kites weren't quite good enough. I quickly realized the label I had been assigned, as nobody wanted to fly with me because I had so few hours logged flying fighters. I suppose I can't really blame any of them; it all came down to protection in a fight, and they all wanted to have as much experience associated with them as possible in the event that someone might be the one shooting a Zero off of their tail in combat. I got used to not having much company in the early days at Espiritu Santo. I was really a loner then! As alone as I was, I did have a couple of friends. One was Don Moore, another fisherman who I spent time with whenever we could get away. The other was a guy named Chris Magee. Both Moore and Magee were seasoned pilots, and they knew what I was going through. Their encouragement helped to keep my spirits up, and although I didn't know it then, time would find me flying fighters right along side them. I continued to fly whenever I could get access to an airplane. In the meantime, I had the opportunity to get a closeup look at the new Vought fighter we had heard about; the F4U Corsair. Corsairs seemed to exude all of the qualities I had heard about them; they just *looked* fast, even sitting there parked. They were so smooth, so clean. They looked mean, too, with three holes for bullets to come out of each wing. Those were .50-caliber Browning machine guns. Six of them. And one more thing about the Corsair; it was HUGE. Absolutely immense for a fighter, viewed from any angle. The propeller was gargantuan when compared to any other fighter I could think of at the time. We joked about the intimidation factor that must have represented by itself; could you imagine being a Jap pilot and seeing something with a huge propeller arc like that coming at you?

I remember feeling the desire to fly one, but also feeling the depression at wondering whether I would ever actually get to do it. Ah, but it wasn't all dullness and drab... I hadn't been on New Hebrides for much more than a week when I was approached by a serious, purposeful man who sat down with me to review my log book and discuss what might lie ahead. He, too, shook his head when he learned of my lack of hours at the controls of fighters. But his reaction wasn't to turn away from me. He knew that the only way to fix my situation was to do just the opposite; fly fighters. We began repetitive cockpit checkouts in the Corsair. Don't even start the engine. Just sit in the thing, and go through the checklist over and over. Learn where the different knobs and gauges are in this bird. Learn where they are to the point where we didn't have to think about it because it was second nature. The F4U, like all fighters, could be a handful to fly, and if a pilot had to first think of where to find a particular knob when he needed it, he was finished before he had begun. This was true to an extent with all airplanes, but perhaps a bit more so with the Corsair.

My reward was a first flight in the Corsair, and it happened on June 25, 1943; exactly two weeks to the day after my arrival at Espiritu Santo. (Those studying my log book dates will note that this flight was made during my first stay with VMF-214, about 10 weeks before I was to return to that same squadron as one of a group who would become the "Black Sheep.") That first F4U Corsair flight was made possible and supervised by that same serious, purposeful man who had reviewed my logbook; Greg Boyington. You might think my memories of this would be exhilarating and glorious, but they weren't. My thoughts were more along the lines of respect and thanks; respect for a huge, powerful bird that was quite obviously a thoroughbred. Thanks for two reasons; first, for the opportunity to fly it. Second, for it letting me get through the initiation flight in one piece. A friend of mine, who I remember now only as "Shorty," also took his first Corsair flight on that same day. His initiation ended in a large cloud of black smoke at the end of the runway, followed by a funeral. He was the second friend of mine to die in an aviation accident. My first Corsair flight was not completely uneventful, either; it ended with the mechanics picking some palm fronds out of the landing gear and inner wing area of the plane I flew (airframe # 02195, for the record); I had just barely made it off the field. This was due to caution; we had been warned over and over not to try and lift the airplane off the ground too early in the takeoff roll; the big engine had so much torque that it would simply flip the plane over if you weren't moving fast enough. I had held the thing on the ground long, all right; so long, in fact, that I didn't leave myself enough room to get comfortably above the trees.

But I was one of the lucky ones... landed with only a few pieces of palm tree stuck in my plane, and Boyington shook his head. As you know by now, I was used to having people shake their heads at me; Downcheck Dalton, the colonel at Hawaii, now Boyington. He said: "Kid, you fly like a big bag of piss. You're never going to make it home unless I teach you something." I always remembered that. But he kept me at it, and he taught me well.

I think one of the things that kept me in was my gunnery ability; I had since the Pensacola days demonstrated a good ability to hit what I shot at. And the truth was that although I might not have been an artist of the skies, I hadn't had any serious crack-ups either. I flew and flew, accumulating hours in the Corsair little by little.

I flew my first combat mission on the afternoon of July 19, 1943, during which two Japanese "Betty" Bombers were shot down. The Japanese bombers were coming out of Rabaul and bothering our supply ships near dusk, when there was low likelihood for them to encounter Allied aircraft. Our objective was to bloody their noses so they might think twice about harassing our supply transports so regularly. I was flying fourth position in a division, and didn't do the shooting, but saw the events unfold from my ringside seat in the air. Witnessing the downing of an enemy aircraft for the first time was an unnerving thing. All I wanted to do was touch down at home base again, but I was to have some action of my own...

We were well into the sunset hours on our return flight. Daylight was getting scarce, and things took a turn for the worse as I became separated from the rest of the group after encountering some dense cloud formations. I knew I was headed in the correct general direction for "home," but I became increasingly unsure of my navigation as time passed. The tension mounted as I scanned the compass and my watch and whatever scenery I could see outside the canopy. After a while, I began to see orange flashes in front of me. Unfortunately, the flashes turned out to be flames licking their way out of the engine cowling on my own airplane! I slowed the motor down to ease its labors, and fortunately it continued to run just fine. But the fire remained. At about that same time, as if this were all an orchestrated hoax, the darkness and cloud formations I had been contending with became a rainstorm. I continued to fly along, skidding the airplane back and forth, side to side, in hopes that the extra rain passing through the engine cowling might help rid me of my unwelcome orange lights. The flames flickered out, then returned. Out again, then returned, over and over. Just as I came through the other side of the rain squall, luck smiled on me once more; I saw an airfield. Actually, luck smiled on me twice, and here's why... There were very specific procedures for approaching one of our airfields in the dark. The correct approach involved coming in at a predefined altitude, on a certain "line" in the sky, with a couple of very specific, deliberate turns mixed in. This was done to identify the pilot without question as "friendly," else our anti-aircraft batteries were instructed to blow the incoming plane into tiny pieces. I did none of that. I squinted and strained and managed to find the strip, and landed on it. I think I might have even made a downwind landing (opposite the direction a pilot is supposed to land), just happy to get on the ground. By some stroke of luck, the graceful Corsair managed to get itself parked without further fire. By a similar stroke of luck, nobody shot at me while I was coming in. All I can figure is that they must have recognized the sound of the engine and known it was "friendly," though every one of our procedures probably would have instructed them to make Swiss cheese out of me. As I finished taxiing the airplane in, I had one final surprise for the evening; I was mildly shocked to discover that the airfield I had landed at... was the same one I departed from. I had managed to get back to where I was supposed to be, though I don't think my heart slowed down to normal pace until well into the next morning !

I continued to fly such missions through August of 1943, with short assignments to different squadrons as I mentioned a page or two ago. But Boyington had been up to other things besides charitably helping a bunch of under qualified lads out of their "light duty" pilot careers. Boyington had previously been a Flying Tiger; he was an ace (that means he shot down five or more enemy planes), had tasted combat, and considered it his purpose to do more of the same. While we were grinding our teeth trying to learn the finer points of the fine Vought F4U Corsair, Boyington was grinding other things – whatever he had to grind – to get himself the necessary components to make up a fighter squadron. During those couple of months (July and August '43), Boyington was using whatever connections and means he had to assemble a squadron. His moves included everything from paperwork to the executives for "on the books" acknowledgment of this, to coordinating things for which there were no formal procedures. There were negotiations and forays to the bomber strip to "procure" parts for the beat-up Corsairs we were to train in. I want to be very clear with statements like the one I just made; as many know, and as I will cover in the coming pages, Greg Boyington was many things. But he wasn't a thief. Our parts scavenging missions often involved stripping parts from totaled aircraft. Other times, things had to be done "off the books" simply because military procedures didn't provide the means to accomplish what needed to happen.

The Corsairs we flew were actually shot-up birds that came back from combat areas further up the line. Many were considered below the standards required for reliable combat duty. Some were stripped for parts to make others fly. All sorts of deals were made to get enough of them in flying condition so we could train. Some of the planes were really bad, to say the least. Sometimes now I have to laugh when I see a Corsair at an air show or in a museum; they are always shiny and perfect. The only thing that shined on the Corsairs we flew was the pilot's sweating forehead. The chosen military paint was not high gloss to begin with, but the planes we flew were weathered to a further flat finish, with all the markings showing an obviously high degree of wear and tear.

Eventually, Boyington got what he wanted; he managed to assemble enough of everything to make a squadron. Boyington finally got paperwork cleared to make use of a squadron number which had previously been disbanded because (I think) the majority of its pilots had fallen ill with malaria. This was VMF-214, and it was officially reactivated under the command of Gregory Boyington on September 7, 1943. I was ecstatic to be chosen for service with VMF-214. Finally! A long-term assignment to a squadron! I had 73.1 hours of flight time logged in the Corsair when the squadron became official. With the twenty-one hours in Brewster "bricks," this was still far less than most of my soon-to-be cohorts, who generally had at least a couple hundred hours by that time.

First Combat Tour

As I write this book, the researching and recreating of times sixty years in the past has not always been easy. However, our combat tours are proving to be among the most straightforward for me to put together. This is partly because I am a packrat and saved just about everything I ever had, partly because my log books are full of notes, partly because I have access to the original VMF-214 combat reports (made by our intelligence officer, Frank Walton, during the war as the events unfolded), and partly because, perhaps, these are some of the most stark, vivid memories I have.

This writing is intended as a stand-alone account of my own life and times with the Black Sheep, but I should mention again that two other members of our squadron wrote books years ago. Our skipper, Pappy Boyington, wrote his own autobiography in 1957, *Baa Baa Black Sheep*. I think it was a best-seller then, and it has been re-printed since. Aside from telling his "war story," I think Pappy's writing was very well done and worthy of reading even for those not specifically interested in the Black Sheep. Additionally, our intelligence officer, Frank Walton, published his book entitled *Once They Were Eagles* in 1986. It is an excellent view of our life in wartime, and it contains interviews with most of the Sheep well after the war, as we were pursuing our lives.

Unfortunately, repeating some of the information from Boyington's and Walton's books is unavoidable, but I will include things pertaining to myself that they didn't. Writing about the Black Sheep has continued even through the past couple of years. There is a difference between the writings of Boyington, Walton and myself when compared to writings of those outside the squadron; we were there, in the flesh.

Rather than launch into our flight missions and combat narratives, I think it is best to start at the beginning. Before fighting, we had to eat and sleep, and establish ourselves in an encampment. We were, without a doubt, in a totally different environment. Palm trees and sand. There was dirt because I remember shoveling it for things like foxholes, but it was a sandy sort of dirt. Every waking moment was filled with reminders that this was not "home" as I knew it; all the trees and vegetation looked different. The sounds of the birds and other creatures were all different. Some were beautiful, and some were unwelcome, especially as we tried to fall asleep at night. We all underwent major dietary changes. Water was no longer plentiful. Most often, our drinking water was made by desalinating ocean water, and it didn't taste very good. (We just used it, and relied on others to come up with the stuff.) Breakfast consisted of coffee, toast and powdered eggs. We didn't have cream, and rarely had sugar, which is why most of us just learned to drink it "black."

Nearly everything we ate came from cans or out of boxes in powdered form. We ate lots of SPAM, and beans appeared at meals late and early. We had rice and bread, and canned yams. One major thing lacking in our diet was variety; we quickly got used to eating the same food, day in and day out, although we did get fresh mutton (sheep) from Australia. I was one of the fortunate ones because I happened to like the stuff. Mutton was one of the few things which had a fresh, distinct taste. It had a strong, musk flavor. Some of the other guys absolutely hated it.

We lived in huts which were sort of hard framed with plywood from the ground to about 3 or 4 feet up, with a tent-like cap on top. There was usually one light bulb in the center. Inside were our cots, with miniature tents of mosquito netting over each one. We slept in (or on top of) sleeping bags on the cots. Being too cold was not much of a problem where we were.

South Pacific weather was highly changeable. It was generally warm and very humid, but the sky could cloud over and rain like hell in an hour or so, and often did. This made living on the island inconvenient, but was also dreaded by us as pilots because we never knew what the weather would be like when we tried to return from wherever it was we had been. (The only thing worse than trying to nurse a shot-up fighter back to home base was to try and do it in a rainstorm.) Sometimes the weather was so bad that it would be difficult to even find the island we were trying to return to, and, indeed, pilots were lost because of this alone.

Huts were typically set up in groups. This hut is typical of the size and construction we used. Exact date and location unknown.
(Bourgeois collection)

Processed water was not used for bathing; for that, we waded into the surf. That water was as plentiful as could be, and of course we could bathe in it as often as we wanted to. The surf was also fairly warm. This all worked pretty well until you got a blister or sore somewhere - and remember that the humidity gave rise to a great assortment of skin conditions because nothing ever dried completely. Then the saltwater would sting like crazy. Some of the guys got smart and collected runoff water from their tents, but we quickly discovered that this couldn't really be used for anything because the tents were treated with some sort of chemical for waterproofing and anti-fungus. I used some of that "tent water" to shave with once; my eyes swelled shut for about 2 hours. We simply got by with whatever we could.

As I try to paint this picture, one important thing must be noted; don't think of us as a bunch of fighter pilots marooned on an island with some airplanes. Although there were no women, there were actually many men. There were the Sea Bees who constructed the strips and set up camp for everyone. There were the cooks who took care of our eating. There were the mechanics who maintained the motor pool and worked miracles with our warbirds. There were parachute riggers who packed (and repaired) our chutes. There was the security and intelligence section, who handled information and organized foot patrols to keep us safe. We pilots all roomed together, about four to a hut, in our little area, but there were hundreds of military men of all sorts on the island.

I got friendly with the Sea Bees, and much horse trading went on. I remember that they built me a little chair and table to sit at. This might have been made from materials found in the jungle, or from an old pallet, but served our purpose. I think I was the only one on the island with a deep sea fishing rod. I loved to fish, and for some reason I brought one from the states. I could have sold that thing for a fortune many times! For a short time, I also had one of very few radios on the island. It was a little portable thing. (In those days, a portable radio only weighed about 25 pounds, and "portable" meant mainly that it could be carried by one person.) I say "for a short time," because we got the thing working and listened to a very scratchy Tokyo Rose telling us "Yankee go home" for about 2 nights. On the second night, the generator sped up uncontrollably and blew out all the light bulbs it was connected to, along with all the tubes in my radio. So much for that.

McClurg and another serviceman with barracuda, red snapper and tuna caught fishing from shore. Catch of the barracuda prompted a ban on swimming in certain areas at certain times of day. (McClurg collection)

Desolate as it was, the island was still a new place for a bunch of Marines in our early twenties, and we spent much of our free time in the early weeks exploring. We were warned to be watchful for booby traps and snipers. The island was only a few weeks out of Japanese hands, and there were rumored to be some isolated Japanese warriors still running around. Some of our men did find bodies of dead Japanese soldiers, which made for some interesting photos and collectibles. We also heard stories that the Japanese would stand a skull atop a stick in the ground, with what appeared to be a gleaming gold tooth waiting to be found. These were traps, as most often the ground in front would be mined, or maybe the skull itself would be connected to the trip wire on a hand grenade. I never encountered such a trap myself, but I heard of them.

Heier and Alexander with Japanese skulls found while hiking, sometimes set on a table as a hat-holder. (Bourgeois collection)

I'd like to touch on two informational items while I have them in mind. We will see reference to a place called "Kahili". This is also often spelled "Kihili", and I believe the more proper reference for the South Pacific place is the latter. The former seems to have more reference to the area of Hawaii, however we have chosen to leave the spelling this way because it originally appeared so in the combat reports. Secondly, about the Japanese "Zero" aircraft. "Zero" is a generic term of reference and can mean any enemy aircraft. The allies divided enemy aircraft into the categories of fighter and bomber, assigning specific American male names to the fighters and female names to the bombers. The famous Japanese fighter was called a "Zeke", but this isn't synonymous with "Zero". To say "I saw a Zero, and it was a Zeke" makes complete sense. You could also say "I saw a Zero, and it was a Sally." The informed listener would then know you saw a bomber. But to say "I saw a Zeke, and it was a Zero" is redundant. "I saw a Zeke, and it was a Sally" is nonsense.

Onward to the job at hand; a squadron is made of people. Following are the names of the participants in our first tour as VMF-214. The list below is who we refer to as the "original" Black Sheep. A history of each one can be obtained from Walton's book.

```
Major Gregory Boyington,  Commanding Officer
Major Stan Bailey,  Executive Officer
Captain Robert Ewing,  Flight Officer
1st. Lt. Frank Walton,  Intelligence Officer
Captain Jim Reames,  Squadron Doctor
```

```
Captain George Ashmun        1st. Lt. James Hill
1st Lt. Robert Alexander     1st. Lt. Chris Magee
1st Lt. John Begert          1st. Lt. Bruce Matheson
1st Lt. John Bolt            1st. Lt. Harry McCartney
1st Lt. Henry Bourgeois      1st. Lt. Don Moore
1st Lt. Robert Bragdon       1st. Lt. Robert McClurg
1st. Lt. William Case        1st. Lt. Paul Mullen
1st. Lt. Warren Emrich       1st. Lt. Ed Olander
1st. Lt. Don Fisher          2nd. Lt. Virgil Ray
1st. Lt. Denmark Groover     1st. Lt. Roland Rinabarger
1st. Lt. Ed Harper           1st. Lt. Sanders Sims
1st. Lt. Walter Harris       1st. Lt. Bernard Tucker
1st. Lt. William Heier
```

The squadron was comprised as one might think, of more experienced pilots combined with less experienced ones. Of all, I remained about the tail end where experience was concerned. Boyington was a veteran in the truest sense of the word, having already shot down at least six planes in his service with the A.V.G. Those claims happened to be Japanese planes like what we were to encounter, so Boyington afforded us all the further benefit of first-hand experience fighting the same opposing force we were to fight.

Henry Bourgeois was another whom I would refer to as a "core" Black Sheep; Henry happened to travel to the South Pacific with Boyington, and assisted in the early days of forming the VMF-214 that was us. Robert Ewing was also a core pilot, as were Begert, Case, McCartney and Mullen. I'd like to reiterate one thing; through the media, the Black Sheep have been portrayed as a gang of misfit, violent, law breaking individuals who shot down a bunch of Japanese airplanes, almost as a secondary thing whilst satisfying our own lusts and fighting among ourselves. That may have been convenient to make an interesting media story, but it really wasn't that way. The squadron was, indeed, composed from a bunch of pilots with miscellaneous backgrounds, but some did have very valid combat experience, and those (named above) were placed as section leaders to mentor the others. None were displaced as a result of disciplinary problems.

Allow me to break out of the story line here for a minute, to step out and outline some goals and limits of this writing... I am able to accurately reconstruct my combat tours from my log books. The voluminous data must be reduced in some way, and I have chosen to do the following: I will cover the combat tours here in chronological order. I am fortunate to have access to photocopies of the original combat reports. Where my combat scores occur, I will present the actual combat reports written by Frank Walton in our tents during the hours immediately after the action happened. The reports will be presented just as they exist in the (now declassified) military archives. To my knowledge, the combat reports have not previously been presented. Because there remains so much interest in Pappy Boyington's past, I have chosen to include the combat reports from any days when Boyington scored, as well. Of course, some of the days for scores of Pappy's and my own are the same. Lastly, as a tribute to those Black Sheep who weren't as lucky as I was, I have chosen to include the reports of any of our squadron's losses. Some of the items in the VMF-214 combat diary were written as press releases, and the tone is apparent.

As noted in the end of the previous chapter, the reformed VMF-214 containing the names mentioned above was officially activated under the command of Greg Boyington on September 7, 1943. Not to belabor the point, but I want to make this very clear; VMF-214 existed previous to "us," and called the "Swashbucklers", through August, 1943. When I refer to the "first combat tour," my reference is to our first combat tour with (myself) and the other pilots who would become known as the Black Sheep. You as the reader will be prudent to note that our "first" tour was actually the second or maybe third, etc. tour of VMF-214. By the seventh of September, 1943, we had taken time to think of a name for ourselves. As you may have read elsewhere, "Boyington's Bastards" was really the first moniker suggested, but this was not well accepted; it was 1943, and "bastard" was still a bad word, one that you didn't print freely in the press back home. In keeping with the misfit theme, someone suggested "Black Sheep," and it seemed to fit well. I do remember that once we came up with that name, all the other stuff like the squadron insignia fell into place almost immediately.

The squadron insignia: to my knowledge, this hasn't ever been well detailed, but the symbol was designed mostly by Bill Case, and was itself originally intended to be an enigma. We took a coat of arms, and ran the banner backwards from upper right to lower left; this implied illegitimacy or "bastard," so you see that the "Boyington's Bastards" part has really been there all this time, just in a subtle way.

The Black Sheep coat of arms from a decal image. (McClurg collection)

At the top, we placed the gull winged image of our trusty steed, the Corsair. With that, we placed an intentionally sway-backed ewe "Black Sheep," and a ring of what was supposed to be thirteen stars, to signify lack of luck (The Black Sheep itself is the thirteenth star.) I think the coat of arms and backwards bar with the sheep idea came first, then the Corsair was added, then maybe the thirteen stars. The Black Sheep name went on to survive even until today. However, some of the future Black Sheep pilots of the 50's and maybe 60's decided that a forlorn looking swayback ewe sheep was not macho enough for the flyboys, and they changed it to a ram with big horns and an arched back. This is generally loathed by us, the "original" Black Sheep.

That said, let's get back to the story line. For most of us, the official organization of the squadron didn't change much. We had been flying whenever we could to gain flight time, and most of us had been on a few combat missions to escort bombers or reconnaissance planes, even if we hadn't been in a dogfight. September 7, then, was not a major point of change for us. That date brought mostly happiness at having some more stable definition to our Pacific theatre service. If nothing else, we knew that we had a cohesive group and would be consistently flying missions. We trained through September 12, 1943, which was the official start of our first combat tour.

At that point, I had no idea how fast my life was really moving, no idea that I would experience a victory and another loss all within the next few days. I didn't fly on September thirteenth. On the fourteenth and fifteenth, we flew missions escorting B-24's to a place called Kahili, the Japanese airstrip on Bougainville Island. I flew another mission on the sixteenth, escorting SBD's and TBF's (small bombers) to Ballale island. This mission contained six divisions of four Corsairs each :

Boyington	Ewing	Begert
Fisher	McClurg	Hill
Ray	Mullen	Ashmun
Harris	Emrich	Magee
Bailey	Case	McCartney
Alexander	Rinabarger	Matheson
Bolt	Bragdon	Olander
Tucker	Groover	Harper

For example, the first division consisted of Boyington, Fisher, Ray and Harris. Fisher flew wing on Boyington, Harris flew wing on Ray.

The mission of the sixteenth was an afternoon mission, to escort small bombers to hit the airstrip at Ballale. The way they usually did this was to have the bombers fly at the lowest altitude, with three layers of cover above them, stepped at three higher altitudes. For this mission, the bombers flew at 13,000 feet, with cover above them at 15,000, 17,000 and 21,500 feet. We flew the highest cover. This was quite an initiation for me, as complete pandemonium broke loose just when the bombers got on target. Japanese planes were waiting near our altitude and above, and they seemed to come from everywhere.

I liken it to shaking up a bunch of bumblebees in a jar. Instantly, there are planes everywhere, doing all sorts of turns and climbs and dives. The clouds can offer some protection because you can fly into one to hide from someone, but they offer similar safety to your enemy, and they create blind spots because you never know what is waiting for you behind (or in) any particular cloud. Flying into a cloud in such situations always presented the risk that you might collide with another guy who had the same idea.

There was so much buzzing and turning and firing going on, I didn't know where to look first. The real answer was that I had to look everywhere, because the threats to me weren't limited to only one place. Just as the guy I was flying wing on pushed over to make a run on someone, I spotted a far-away airplane directly in front of me, coming head on. The clock was ticking, and slow thinkers didn't last long where I was at the time. I began to squint at the airplane, trying to discern whether it was friend or foe. Then the oddest thing happened: it looked as if he was flashing his landing lights at me. In a split second, I knew it was a friendly plane, signaling to me. In the next split second, as I began to think about looking over my shoulders for someone on my tail, it all clicked. That plane coming at me had just finished sending one of our aviators into the ocean. Those weren't landing lights at all; he was firing at me! The sinking feeling came over me, and my mouth began to dry as my pulse raced. My guns were charged, and I sent some lead back his way. Remember that this all happened within a fraction of a minute. My aim was true; I saw little pieces come off his airplane. By that time, we had gotten to within a few seconds of passing each other. Then I saw heavy smoke start to come from his engine cowling. He was going to pass me on my left, just as an oncoming car passes you on the U.S. highways. The Japanese plane began a shallow descent, and I banked my plane completely sideways and got a quick look into his cockpit as we passed. I saw the pilot fighting flames coming from his instrument panel. At that point, I knew he was done. Next was a look around for other threats, or others in need of my help, or other opportunities. I saw none. I couldn't find Ewing, the plane on whom I had flown wing. As a matter of fact, I didn't find anyone at all. The air had become empty just as fast as it had become full. All I saw were little specs way off in the distance. I headed home with gusto. I wanted to report my score, but I think I wanted to get away from where I was even more. So much was going through my mind. I remember thinking to myself that I'd take whatever ribbing for being one of the first home, so long as I got there in one piece. As it turned out, I was next to last at the strip. I landed with my tongue feeling about the size of a pear, got out of the plane, and went immediately to a palm tree to take a leak. I think I must have stood there urinating for about half an hour. Our skipper gave us a little scare, coming in over an hour late. He got so low on gas during his fight that he stopped at another strip to refuel. It turned out that he shot down five planes on that one mission alone; yes, Boyington was, indeed, something very special. Ewing was never heard from again.

So it was, all in the course of a few minutes of combat. I had my first score. I had that awful feeling of knowing that a man I had gotten used to seeing around camp wouldn't be there any more. Everything was heightened. Never had I been so glad to get out of a Corsair back at home base, and never had I wanted so much to get back into one and do it again. Maybe Boyington's hour delay should have concerned me more than it did; I was so distracted by the experience I just had that I really wasn't able to give him much thought. Anyway, he showed up before I had regained enough composure to really register it all.

Everything about our combat was documented as well as possible, often right down to the amount of ammunition expended in a mission. Two common forms of this documentation are the "combat report" and the "narrative account". Although the two different reports often contain similar data, one sometimes covers information not recorded in the other. In the interest of completeness, and at some risk of repetition, I have chosen to include both the combat report and the narrative account for any given mission, if they were available to me.

Following is the official military combat report from that mission. They aren't all this long; remember that this was our first mission. Frank Walton (our intelligence officer and writer of the reports) was eager to do his work. You'll see that he was also eager to make sure everyone knew that we worked well as a squadron, perhaps to justify our continued operation so we wouldn't be relegated to the miscellaneous status from which we were assembled.

COMBAT REPORT

DATE : 16 September 1943.

TIME :   Takeoff 1300, rendezvous 1350, over target 1450, pancake 1605 – 1630
NATURE OF MISSION : Strike escort.

PLACE : Ballale.

Forces engaged : OWN : 24 F4Us of VMF-214:

BOYINGTON	EWING	BEGERT
FISHER	MCCLURG	HILL
RAY	MULLEN	ASHMUN
HARRIS	EMRICH	MAGEE
BAILEY	CASE	MCCARTNEY
ALEXANDER	RINABARGER	MATHESON
BOLT	BRAGDON	OLANDER
TUCKER	GROOVER	HARPER

ENEMY: 30 – 40 Zeros (Zekes and Haps)

RESULTS : ENEMY LOSSES:
     Major G. Boyington – 5 Zeros
     (4 Haps and 1 Zeke)
     Lt. D. H. Fisher – 2 Zeros (Zekes)
     Lt. J. F. Begert – 2 Zeros (Zekes)
     Lt. R. W. McClurg – 1 Zero (Zeke)
     Lt. R. A. Alexander – 1 Zero (Zeke)
     Lt. H. A. McCartney – 2 Zeros (Zekes)(Prob.)
     Major S. R. Bailey – 1 Zero (Zeke)(Prob.)
     Lt. W. N. Case – 1 Zero (Zeke)(Prob.)
     Lt. V. G. Ray – 1 Zero (Zeke)(Prob.)
     Lt. C. Magee – 1 Zero (Zeke)(Prob.)
     Lt. E. L. Olander – 1 Zero (Zeke)(Prob.)
     Lt. B. J. Matheson – 1 Zero (Zeke)(Prob.)

     OWN LOSSES:
     Captain R. T. Ewing – missing.

ALTITUDE: 21,500 ft.

NARRATIVE ACCOUNT:
At 1300, 6 divisions took off for escort of TBFs and SBDs striking Ballale. All 24 planes got off the ground in 7 minutes.

Rendezvous with the bombers was made on schedule (1350) over Munda and the formation circled between Kolombangara and Vella Lavella, then swung up the slot bearing to the west; the bombers at 13,000 ft. A flight of P40s was acting as close cover at 15,000, a flight of F6Fs provided medium cover at 17,000. The formation circled to the right of Shortland and the bombers began their run W to E across Ballale. It was 1450. At this time 30 - 40 Zeros spilled out of the clouds. The fight spread out all over the sky for 150 to 200 square miles at all altitudes and continued for 30 minutes. Major Boyington hit the jackpot with 5 Zeros (4 Haps and 1 Zeke). Lts. McClurg and Alexander each got 1 Zeke; Lt. McCartney got 2 probable Zekes, and Major Bailey and Lts. Case, Ray, McGee, Olander and Matheson 1 probable Zeke each. LTs. Fisher and Begert 2 Zekes each.
Most of the flight pancaked at 1605 - 1630 excepting Major Boyington who landed at 1755.

REMARKS:
Captain Ewing failed to return. The last seen of him was when he lost his division as he pushed over into a sharp diving turn preparatory to making a run. His plane was #127.

Our pilots observed Zeros of several colors, some black, some brown, some mottled green and brown and others greenish brown.

They reported an excellent pattern of bombs on the target, one hitting an AA position to the SW of the strip and one in the center of the southern portion of the strip.

Sixteen pilots stood ground and scramble alerts until 1300.

McCartney and Matheson practiced ground strafing from 0845 - 1000

*   ACTION REPORT   *
MARINE FIGHTING SQUADRON 214
RUSSELL ISLANDS, 16 September, 1943

"ZEROS SPILLED OUT OF THE CLOUDS"

"Zeros spilled out of the clouds," said Lt. J. F. Begert in describing the action over Ballale on September 16, in which the red hot pilots of Major Greg Boyington's Marine Fighting Squadron engaged 40 Zeros and shot down 11 sure and 8 probable in their first contact with the enemy. The fight spread all over the sky for an area of 200 square miles and lasted 30 minutes.

Major Boyington, a former Flying Tiger, hit the jack pot with 5 sure Zeros to his credit in the action.

It was one o'clock in the afternoon of September 16 when Major Boyington taxied to the center of the white coral runway, gunned the motor of his Corsair, and sped out over the blue waters off the Russell Islands. Twenty Three others of his squadron followed him off with machine like precision, the twenty-four pilots getting off the ground in seven minutes.

His squadron had landed in the combat zone only 2 days before and were afraid all the Jap planes would be gone before they could get into action with them. They found out there were plenty for everyone.

Although most of the boys were brand new to actual combat, all division leaders were veterans of dozens of tangles with the tricky Japs and all had Jap planes to their credit.

This was to be a strike on Ballale, Jap strong point and A/A position lying between Kahili and Faisi, strong Jap land-and-sea-plane bases, respectively.

Squadron 214 was to act as high cover for a flight of Avenger torpedo bombers and Dauntless dive bombers.

The rendezvous was made on schedule—at 13:50, over Munda.

The bombers were at 13,000 feet, with Squadron 214 at 21,000.

A flight of Warhawks provided close cover at 15,000, while a flight of Hellcats were at 17,000 as intermediate cover.

The striking force of more than 100 planes—One of the largest assembled in the Solomons area, moved northward and circled to the right as the bombers started their dives across the island from west to east at about 1500.

It was then that some 40-50 <u>Zeros spilled out of the clouds</u> onto the 24 Corsairs.

From this point on it was a mad scramble, with 214's squadron handling themselves like old hands, although it was the first taste of battle for 16 of them.

Twenty-two year old Lt. R. A. Alexander was one of the new ones. He was flying wing on Major S. R. Bailey, Squadron Executive Officer, who was in his third tour of duty in the combat area.

Major Bailey and Lt. Alexander dived toward a circling hive of twenty Zeros, selecting one and coming in on a quarter pass. The Zero split-S'd out to the right and the Major followed him down with Alexander on his wing down to 10,000'.

At this point Alexander saw 3 Zeros preparing to dive on them, so he pulled up and circled at 10,000 feet to chase them off the Major's tail.

Bailey followed the Zero down, firing until he went into the clouds, smoking.

Bailey just stuck the nose of his plane out of the clouds when a Zero dove on him, firing from long range, causing him to duck back into the clouds. This happened 5 consecutive times, so finally Bailey flew on instruments toward Vella LaVella.

Coming out in the clear, he continued on when he saw a pilot in a chute with a Zero making passes on him, attempting to machine gun him as he was helplessly dangling there.

Bailey dove at the Zero, which pulled up into a tight loop and got on his tail. The Major dove out at 300 knots and headed for Vella LaVella. After pulling away he circled back and saw another Zero, made a run on it,

and heard the rat-tat-tat of bullets on his plane and
saw <u>3 Zeros on his tail</u>. He dove away and nursed his
bullet riddled plane home.

Alexander at 10,000 feet made a run at the 3 Zeros
and swung away as they scattered. Then he went
hunting. He did not have long to look. He saw 2 Zeros
in section about a thousand feet below him.

The wing man was trailing slightly and was about 100
feet to the right, slightly stepped down.

Alexander dived in on them, making a direct stern
approach on the wing man. Going at 240 knots he closed
on them at a fair rate of speed. Waiting till he saw
the huge red meat balls, he started spraying the wing
man from about 200 yards. He saw the bullets pierce
the cockpit, tail, and mid fuselage. Little pieces
flew off the Zero and it began to smoke just forward of
the cockpit on the right hand side.

Alexander continued to fire till he passed over the
Zero's right wing. Looking into the Jap's cockpit as
he passed over within 50 feet of him, he saw flames
come up from under the instrument panel and immediately
fill the whole cockpit, making it look like a <u>movie
kill</u>.

By this time the leader was 500 feet ahead, so,
knowing the wing man was through, Alexander cut across
in front of the flaming Zero and sighted in on the
leader, who did a slow split S to the right, out and
down.

Looking up he saw 4 Zeros in echelon with the leader
peeling off for an overhead pass on him, so he nosed
over and dived down, turning to the right.

Seeing his tail was clear he began to climb again
toward a big melee above him. On getting close enough
to recognize them he saw that they were all Zeros
(about 16), circling and slow-rolling among themselves.
This was no place for a lone Corsair pilot so he dived
and left them to their play.

Lt. Wm. N. Case, leading one division of Corsairs
(4), was at 20,000 feet when he first sighted 7 Zeros
at 16,000 starting to attack a flight below them. His
division rolled over and dove on the Zeros. The leader
saw them coming and pulled up with his wingman.

All 4 of the division got in short bursts at the Japs, pulled up sharply and turned back to the right, and rolled over into an overhead run as they passed under the Corsairs.

Picking out one, Case corkscrewed down hill with him for two turns, both pulled out together and lined up on parallel courses about 40 yards apart, with the Jap to Case's right. The Zero was a Hap—dark brown mottle with greenish shading.

By this time Case had lost his second section, but his wingman, Lt. R. W. Rinabarger, was still with him. Climbing to regain altitude, Case saw one burst of tracer go over his left wing but couldn't tell where the firing was coming from.

Taking sharp evasive action they shook their attacker and surveyed the situation. They were at 17,000, 10 miles south of Ballale—the bombers were in their dives.

Rinabarger reported, "Nine Zeros, 9 o-clock and up" and Case then saw them out to their right beginning their runs. The two them spread out about 200 yards apart, flying a level, parallel course with the Zeros still high at 9 o'clock.

In spite of their numerical superiority, the Zeros failed to press home the attack, making only short, ducking, ineffectual passes at the two Corsairs.

The two Corsairs gradually pulled away from the Haps until they observed slightly to their right and 2,000 feet below, 4 Zeros attacking 2 Corsairs.

As one of the Corsairs dived out of trouble, Case and his wing man dived on one of the Zeros, getting in a no - deflection shot. The Jap plane smoked, pulled up sharply, rolled over and split S under, leaving a black trail of smoke.

Case rolled and spiraled down behind him, losing his wingman in the dive. Rinabarger had mistaken the other Corsair for Case and joined with him.

Case lost his Zero when he pulled out sharply under him, so he pulled up to get some altitude. However, one of the other Zeros made a high stern run on his tail, so he dove away, going straight down from an

altitude of 14,000 feet to 6,000 feet in a vertical
dive!

By this time the bombers were rallying directly under
him for their return trip.

Seeing a Hellcat, Case joined up with it and started
home. He saw a straggler in trouble, waggled his wings
and turned back to make a pass with Case following.
The Hellcat made a sharp beam run, firing, but missed,
and the Zero turned into Case; and the two planes, Jap
and American, came at each other with guns blazing.
Four of Case's guns quit firing, but he continued his
head on run.

It was the Jap who pulled out in a chandelle to the
left, and Case pulled sharply to the right and rolled
over on him in an overhead pass. The Jap rolled under
and spiraled down with Case spiraling down with him
still with only 2 guns firing.

At 4,000 feet Case began his pull out, leveling off
at about 1500. The Zero had disappeared.

Case then pulled back up to 5,000, directly behind
and east of the formation of bombers.

Looking around for someone to join up on, he saw low
on the water a straggling Hellcat at an altitude of 50
feet with a Zero making a high stern run on him,
pulling up before he reached him.

Case made a beam run on the Hellcat, forcing the Zero
to pull off.

Climbing back to 2,000 feet, he noticed far behind a
string of bullet splashes in the water. Looking
further back, he saw another Hellcat about ½ mile
behind the first one, with four Zeros making stern runs
on it.

Just as Case swung to help, the Hellcat smoked and
dropped sharply into the water from about 100 feet and
disappeared beneath the surface. There was no sign of
life.

Case then turned and joined up with the other Hellcat
for the trip home.

During the scramble, Lt. Rinabarger saw a "daisy chain" when he saw a Corsair with a Zero on its tail, another Corsair on the Zero's tail, and another Zero on the Corsair's tail, all about two hundred yards apart.

Rinabarger dove to make the fifth in the little flight but the last Zero pulled away as he dove.

Lt. Begert was leading one division of Corsairs at 17,000 feet when the skies rained Zeros.

One came across his bow, followed by a Corsair. The Zero slow rolled to the right, rolled on his back and pulled through with the Corsair unable to follow. Begert peeled off and got in a short burst at the Zero (a ZEKE, dirty brown in color). He burst into flames from the under side of the engine and all along the belly. The pilot bailed out.

Begert's wingman lost power and fell behind.

Thirty seconds later another Zero (ZEKE) came across his bow followed by a Corsair and the same maneuver was repeated---the Zero slow rolling over and pulling through so sharply the Corsair could not follow. Opening fire at about 50 yards, Begert gave the Zero a short burst. The Zero rolled over on his back and Begert rolled with him firing all the way through and he caught fire along the sides from the cowl as they were inverted and the Zero headed down for the long crash plunge into the sea. .

Lt. Begert looked for the bombers, found a Corsair to join up with and assisted in the escort home.

Lt. Henry McCartney, leader of another division of squadron 214 was at 19,000 feet when he saw four Zeros (dark, brownish green ZEKE's---with what looked like a ¼" orange stripe around the roundel) coming up at them about 1,000 feet below, struggling for altitude. His division made a high side, diving turn pass on the leader who began to smoke, quit and then received another burst with observing the result.

Pulling up, he saw another Zero on the edge of a cloud bank. McCartney made a beam run, gave him a short burst and he popped into the clouds.

Making a 300 degree turn, he saw four more Zeros about 1,000 feet below them---made a beam run, looked in his mirror, and saw a Zero on his tail. McCartney did a split S with his division anticipating him and staying with him during the maneuver.

Rolling out, he saw three more Zeros, dove on them and saw his tracers going into one, which began to smoke as they went by.

By this time they were over Poporang at 14,000 feet so he took his division down to the slot till he located the formation of bombers and covered them back to Munda.

Capt. Robert T. Ewing started a run in a diving turn to the right with full gun. He crowded over toward Lts. Paul A. Mullen and Warren T. Emrich, his second section, who were on his left. Lt. Robert W. McClurg, Capt. Ewing's wing man, crossed over to try to get into position, but the three of them were going too fast for him, so he lost them.

Capt. Ewing continued to crowd over toward Lt. Mullen, evidently trying to get into position to fire. Mullen kept sliding over 'till he saw a Zero in a steep dive on a Corsair below. He cut under Ewing, made a pass at the Zero and got in a short burst. Mullen and his wing man, Emrich, made a 130 degree turn to the right and looked for Ewing's Corsair but couldn't find it.

Lot's of Zeros were above and below them. One made a run. They made a sharp diving turn to the left, breaking free.

Still couldn't see anything in the sky but Zeros.

Apparently these two were the last who saw Capt. Ewing, as he did not return from the flight---although he was not in any trouble when last seen.

Lt. Mullen saw one plane do a snap roll and then dive on two Hellcats and pull off to the left without his show of maneuverability having frightened the Hellcats Pilots as he had perhaps hoped.

Lt. E. L. Olander was in Lt. McCartney's division. He got in a good burst at a Zero (ZEKE, dark brownish green) and saw his bullets going into him. Nosing over, the division went down under the Zeros in a diving turn to the left.

Starting to turn, Olander found a Zero on his tail, spraying the division. McCartney nosed over and they dove from 13,000 feet to 7,000 feet before they could shake him.

Coming back to Vella LaVella with the bombers, Olander's electrical system began to smoke and he debated landing at Munda but finally headed on to his base.

Lt. McClurg pulled out at 21,000 when he lost his division and looked around. He saw off to his left a single Zero (ZEKE) (brown rust color, brilliant red roundel, round wing tips) in a slow roll, lying on his back.

There was another off to his right---at about his same altitude.

Behind the second Zero was a Hellcat or Corsair, some 500 yards behind and 300 feet below the Jap.

The first Zero was firing at a Corsair or a Hellcat---which went down in a vertical dive, caught on fire and went straight down.

When the Zero recovered, he rolled out level to the left—at which time McClurg and the Jap were in a head-on position coming straight at each other at the same altitude, about 400 yards apart. McClurg saw puffs of smoke come from the Zero's wings as the Jap fired at him. McClurg gave him a continuous burst and the tracers seemed to cross right in front of his motor, apparently having no effect at first.

McClurg gave him another burst, a short one, and the Zero immediately rolled to the right and dropped into a diving turn with black smoke streaming from the front of the plane. Passing over the Zero in a vertical bank, McClurg could see the mottled brown color of the Zeke, lighter on the bottom than on the top. At this time flame burst from the engine and shot back to the cockpit. This entire action took place in about 30 seconds.

Major Boyington, veteran of eight months with the A.V.G.'s, was leading Squadron 214's first division.

He was scissoring with Lt. Don H. Fisher, his wing man—who was contacting the enemy for the first time.

Major Boyington circled sharply to the left with Lt. Fisher circling about 200 yards behind him.

At this time a Zero (Zeke, round wing tips, brown, big greenhouse), came in from the left, crossed between Fisher and the Major and circled in making a starboard quarter pass on the Major.

Fisher fired a burst at the Zero and he went into a slow roll to the left. At the top of his roll, Fisher gave him another burst _____ the cockpit and he began to flame and then exploded.

Fisher looked around for the Major and saw a Corsair come in with a Zero on its tail. Fisher gave him a short burst and missed.

The Zero pulled up into a slow roll to the left.

Fisher gave him a continuous burst as the Zero was on his back; He scooped his slow roll and began to smoke heavily. Then he fell off on his left wing and spun down in a tight spiral with black smoke pouring out.

Fisher followed him down for a thousand feet, firing, until a thin streak of flame showed. At this time he was down to 4,000 feet.

Fisher climbed back up, found the bombers, and headed for home.

Major Boyington was leading Corsairs over a fleecy layer of clouds at 20,000 feet, directly over Ballale, when he heard the "Tally-ho". He couldn't see any, so he dove down through the clouds. Passing below them he saw a layer of 30 Zeros milling about in a huge circle over the point where the Avenger bombers and Dauntless bombers were going in.

In a short turn to attack, Major Boyington lost his flight and his activities for the next forty minutes were such as to make flying history.

A Zero (HAP) came up along side of him, waggled his wings, and pulled ahead, passing within 100 feet, showing the huge red roundel on his fuselage as he went by.

Boyington flicked on his gun switch and gave him a long burst from 50 yards. The whole cockpit burst into flames, he rolled over to the left and went straight down, crashing into the water about 10 miles southeast of Ballale.

Looking for his flight, he could see only one Corsair, which was firing into a Zero about 200 or 300 yards off to his right.

Circling to his left he found two other Corsairs and joined up with them, called on the radio and took the lead, turning toward Kahili. The two Corsairs left him and he continued on just under the cloud layer toward the circling Zeros.
There were nothing but Zeros on both sides and in front of him, so he pulled up through the cloud layer and circled, gaining altitude, going up to 24,000 feet.

Headed toward Vella LaVella, he spotted Zeros at 10,000 feet, making passes at the dive bombers which had started for home. They were making high stern passes on the bombers, pulling up short of gun range.

He selected one, (a HAP) and made a diving high stern run on him, opening fire from 300 yards, closing fast.

The Zero exploded completely as Boyington was about fifty feet from him---causing the Major to throw up his arm to protect his face from flying debris and sustaining dents in the engine cowling and leading edges of his wings.

He turned right and climbed back into the sun to 18,000 feet and saw two Hellcats flying a tight formation on the right flank of the bombers at about 19,000 feet.

A Zero (HAP) pushed over and opened up on the section of Hellcats. He could see the tracers going past them Their formation was so tight they couldn't maneuver except to turn slightly toward the bomber formation.

The Zeros overran the Hellcats and pulled up to 10 or 11,000 feet.

Boyington dove and caught him on the rise as he climbed—opening fire at 300 yards and holding his finger on the trigger he kept on him as he went up into a loop, over onto his back and burst into flames as the Major passed under him. The Zero completed his loop and headed down.

Boyington headed back into the sun to 17 or 18,000 feet. By this time he was 1/3 of the way back to Vella LaVella.

Zeros which had been pursuing the bombers home were leaving the formation and coming back in pairs at about 5 or 6,000 feet.

Boyington saw what he thought was a single at about 6,000 and, knowing he'd have too much speed in a regular dive, went down on him in a throttle-back glide. The Zero saw him and began to make a gentle turn to the left. Boyington, an old hand at aerial combat, knew this was too easy so he looked around for the catch—and found it—the bait's wingman was off to the right waiting for Boyington to make a pass and sucker in.

Instead, the Major made a head-on run at the second Zero (HAP) opening fire at about 300 yards and holding the trigger all the way as he tried to pull up.

As the Major passed under him, he could see pieces flying off the Zero's cowling. The Major pulled up in a chandelle to the left intending to make another run on him and saw that he was smoking badly. Boyington flew back toward him, (towards Ballale) climbing and the Zero went about ten miles in a flat glide smoking and then crashed into the water.

Unable to see the other Zero, Boyington climbed back into the sun---deciding he'd done a full day's work and not wanting to crowd his luck too far.

However, at 10,000 feet, he spotted a pair of Zeros which were almost abeam of him and 3,000 feet below--- they turned toward him evidently thinking he was a cripple.

As a strong offense is the best defense, Boyington then made a head on run on the leading Zero---he pulled out to the right so Boyington continued his run on the second Zero (HAP), opening fire at about 600 yards, slightly abeam---the Zero smoked but the Major was short of both gas and altitude so he headed for home, climbing to 10,000 feet.

He then saw a single plane fairly close to the water (about 3,000 feet) going towards Vella LaVella. He first thought it was a Zero and then saw two planes going in the opposite direction (towards Ballale) circle and make a pass at the single. He saw the tracers going past him.

Low on gas from his long runs at high speed, and his dives and climbs during his engagements, nevertheless, he made a run in the two Zeros, opening fire at extremely long range to drive them off the friendly plane.

One Zero pulled straight up into the air with Boyington following him and holding his trigger down all the way.

The Zero slow rolled, going practically straight up and then burst into flames, leaving the Major on his back, in a spin, at 10,000 feet.

The Zero crashed into the water and Boyington looked for the Corsair (which had been attacked) in order to join up but it was no where in sight.

The Major then headed south again, much lower on gasoline and pancaked at Munda with 10 gallons of gas and only 30 rounds of ammunition.

The strike was very successful, the Avenger and Dauntless bombers plastering the entire island with bombs, hits being particularly noticed on the runway and in dispersal area around it. The bombers made their drop at about 1500 or 2000, attacking from East to West.

A/A on the whole was light, primarily from South end, some from the South West end of strip.

However, the A/A stopped when the run started.

Several colors of Zeros were noted---some HAP's and some ZEKE's; some were dark brownish green; some were predominately black---partly camouflaged.

Others, Army type camouflaged mottled brown green; Plain brown, lighter than others, looked very new; Some were brown, looked like a P-40, wing looked like a NELL;

Some had a ½" orange ____d around the red roundel on the wings.

New pilots might take note of some of the tactical points brought out in this action. Many are already known, but will certainly bear repetition.

Paramount, of course, is the matter of maintaining division and section formations. It's usually the single and stragglers that get picked off.

Look out for the too easy shot when you know the Zero sees you---he probably is suckering you in for his partner.

The best run at Zeros is, of course, the stern run--- although you can always get the best of them in a head on run. They don't have the guts to press it home.

Don't open fire too far away in a <u>stern run</u> as their extreme maneuverability enables them to split S out on you before any damage can be done. <u>Hold your fire till at close range.</u>

<u>In a head on run</u>---open fire at <u>long range</u> since you are closing much more rapidly.

Often you can recognize Zeros by their acrobatics when you can hardly see them. They apparently do slow rolls to impress our pilots; however, one good burst will end his acrobatic career.

The best defense when a Zero is on your tail is to nose over and dive---they never or rarely follow you. In diving, get your nose down fast and maintain your airspeed. If you're firing in a climb and your ship begins to <u>mush</u>, nose over and get down before the Zero flips over onto your tail and gets in a long burst before you can get up any air speed.

If you have a good defensive formation of four planes, all the Zeros in the world won't touch you. A division should fly in two sections, abreast, separated by about 400 feet for ordinary defensive tactics. If attacked, the attacked plane noses down and turns into the attacking plane.

Ordinarily, if alone and unable to join up--- <u>head for home</u>.

Of paramount importance in heading for home, whether alone or with your division, <u>be sure to maintain your</u>

altitude. You lose your initiative when you lose your altitude.

Too many pilots head directly home at low altitude after a strike. If they have been intercepted, the Zeros usually follow the flight partly home to pick off stragglers and cripples; and you're easy meat when you're down low.

If you're alone you should circle the direct line course home and thus avoid the returning Zeros.

If you're in formation stay on the course but at sufficient altitude to initiate an attack on returning Zeros.

All strikes should have a rally point where the bombers and their escort can reassemble for the home trip after the strike. Sometimes they have this point but it is not communicated to the fighter cover.

All in all the action was eminently successful—good bomb hits and the box score for Marine Fighting Squadron 214 in its first contact with the enemy :

Enemy Losses : 11 Zeros sure (7 ZEKES - 4 HAPS)
              8 Zeros probable (All ZEKES)

Our Losses :   1 Pilot missing.

Report submitted by : FRANK E. WALTON, JR.,
                      First Lt., USMCR,
                      Intelligence Officer.

...And that's what the combat log for our first contact with the enemy looks like. It was an invigorating day. We all felt good because our first contact with the enemy had left them with their eyes well blackened; nineteen of them probably didn't report for supper that day, against one of us missing. Unfortunately, the "one of us" missing happened to be the guy I flew wing on. The wingman was supposed to cover his partner, and I felt terrible about this. But nobody criticized me for it. All hell breaks loose when a battle of that size happens, and that's just how it is. Ewing was never heard from again. Nobody saw him in trouble. Problem was that nobody saw him after his first dive – we were all busy with our own affairs at the time. Our guess is that he was shot down and landed in the water, possibly dead on impact or drowned. It is possible that he could have been captured and died in a prison camp, but somehow I don't think so.

Our learning came very early on. Everything the pilots told Frank Walton was noted, reported, and analyzed. The background tapping of Walton's typewriter was soon a familiar sound . One thing we learned very early was that the Japanese had an affinity for flying in circles of four or more planes, way up high. (If you're flying in a large circle, no enemy can dive in on you without your squadron mate getting a shot at him.) We noticed that they flew in such circles, and tended to send one of their flyers down as bait; when somebody made a run on the Japanese pilot, his buddies above would then swoop down and try to get all over us. They also loved to hide in clouds, and they made good use of the sun, flying directly out of it to attack whenever possible. The idea was that the glare of the sun made it nearly impossible to see them coming until they were very close. Boyington was onto this, and he taught us to hold up a thumb into the sun, to block the bright spot and thus be able to inspect the sky for unwanted specks that could be deadly if undetected.

We had our own events at "home," too. The Japanese sent "Betty" bombers just about every night at all hours to harass us so we couldn't sleep. Night patrols were soon organized, in which a lone Corsair would loiter up in the sky, waiting for the visitor. I read in our combat log that on the twentieth, Begert was knocked down by the concussion from one of the "Betty's" bombs as he ran to the revetments to get in his plane on a scramble. I don't remember if it was exactly that same evening or not, but I do remember once diving into a foxhole full of other people during an air raid and knocking head-on into someone. I saw stars for half an hour, and had a welt on my head the size of a golf ball. There's another foxhole story; the heavy rains we often received would sometimes fill foxholes with 2 or 3 feet of water. When you're seeking refuge from bombs, you don't worry too much about getting wet by diving into a foxhole. As the story goes, wearing only boxers, Pappy and our squadron doctor, "Doc" Reames, both scrambled into a wet foxhole one night during a raid. Shortly thereafter, Doc seemed to go crazy, jumping and splashing all around. It turned out that a small green chameleon had found its way into Doc's shorts. We got used to that sort of thing. They came awful close a few times, but the Japanese never got our tents with those bombs. They were more intended to steal sleep from us (which they did).

Henry Bourgeois in a foxhole. Exact location unknown and may be a previous combat tour of Henry's before VMF-214. A foxhole could be a simple dirt hole dug in the ground, or could be a significantly fortified installation like the one shown. (Bourgeois collection)

We also experienced our fair share of operational problems; remember that we weren't flying brand new Corsairs. The ones we had were "hand me downs," just like our squadron number was, just like most of the stuff we worked with was. Sparking electrical malfunctions in the cockpit soon became nothing to write home about. Coughing engines were also too common. Getting into a dogfight was horror enough, but there aren't any words I can use to convey the feeling that goes through a pilot when the engine sputters just as he's adding power on the "tally ho" to enter a battle. Yes, that happened. This wasn't because the F4U was unreliable. Actually, the Corsair was known for just the opposite. The plane could take a terrible beating and still get us home. Another piece of trivia about the F4U is that I think it was the only aircraft ever to receive a citation of merit from the armed services. (They issued merit citations to people, but not pieces of equipment.) I believe a

Corsair in some squadron endured something like 100 hours of combat flights with only routine maintenance. Personally, I think there were many other pieces of equipment that should have received merit citations (such as the small military "Jeep"), but that's another subject.

After my first score on September 16, I flew missions again on the September 20, 21, 22, 23, 24, 25, 26, and 27. Denmark Groover ("Quillhead") was wounded on September 23, and Roland Rinabarger ("Rollie") was wounded on September 26, but both managed to limp their planes home. We weren't so fortunate on September 27, as my mission was a search mission for our Lt. Walter Harris. Following is the official combat report...

ACTION REPORT
MARINE FIGHTING SQUADRON 214,
MUNDA, 27 September, 1943.

"TEN CORSAIRS BATTLE 50 ZEROS"

Twelve Corsairs, of VMF-214 were scheduled to provide medium and high cover for 27 Liberator bombers in a strike on Kahili, September 27th.

However, the information came late so that only two flights got off the ground on schedule. Lt. Henry M. Bourgeois, leading one of the flights, found that his instruments [malfunctioned], so he and his wingman returned to base, leaving only 6 Corsairs as medium and high cover for the 27 Bombers.

Rendezvous was scheduled for 1135, at 18,000 feet, over Wagina Island, however, the bombers had already taken off when the six Corsairs arrived, so that the fighter plane pursued them all the way to North Choiseul, before catching up.

Major Greg Boyington had been instructed that he was to take his division up in a fighter sweep if he got off late.

He was off late so he took his flight of Lts. D. H. Fisher, W. N. Case and Walter R. Harris, up the slot at full power, climbing all the way---hoping to knock down or disperse any Zeros which might be waiting for the bombers.

He reached the Kahili Strip at 1205, ahead of the bombers and passed over it at 25,000 feet. The strike was scheduled for 1230.

Looking up---he saw, at 35,000 feet, a twin tailed ship heading north across the field emitting intermittent twin streamers of black smoke.

Thinking this was a signal for the Jap fighters to take off the strip---he nosed down to 10,000 feet, in order to knock down any fighter planes taking off.

However, only two planes were on the field, probably dummies.

He received no A/A of any kind.

Climbing back up, he saw two groups of Zeros (one group of 8 and one of 12) coming at them from the southeast.

Circling to one side and still climbing, he got on top of the Zeros and nosed down for a pass. In the dive he lost his wingman, Lt. Don H. Fisher. Attempting to open fire, he found his guns jammed, so he pulled up, rejoined the remainder of his flight and cleared his guns.

Climbing again, the three planes turned over again in a divisional run on a column of Zeros (ZEKE's) and each selected a target---there were plenty for everyone.

Boyington opened fire at 200 yards, tearing pieces out of the tail of his target, while Case's Zero flamed and headed downward, burning brightly. Boyington's Zero slanted down at about a 30 degree angle and crashed in the water off the Kahili strip. Boyington, in a cloud, following the Zero down, almost crashed in the water himself.

Climbing back up to reenter the flight, he found that it had moved away and was lost in the clouds---so he turned his plane homeward, hoping to join up with someone.

Lt. Fisher, looking for his flight, saw a Zero passing below him, and made a high side pass sieving one wing tip and the fuselage behind the cockpit of the Jap plane. The Zero split S'd out and dived downward.

Through the corner of his eye, Fisher observed Boyington turning left and headed toward him.

Just below Fisher's Corsair, a Zero crossed his bow from right to left.

Nosing over in a diving turn, Fisher made a high side stern run on the ZEKE, opening fire at 75 yards and holding down the trigger as he flattened out. The Zero smoked and headed for a cloud.

Coming out of the cloud, on the tail of the smoking Zero, Fisher found that another burst was not necessary, as it slanted downward, crashing into the water just off the shortlands.

He patrolled there for time looking for someone to join up on. During his flight, he saw one Jap plane explode and two others burn.

He finally called his flight leader who told him to return to his base, which he did without incident.

Lt. J. F. Begert, leading his flight of Lt. J.G. Hill, Capt. G. M. Ashmun and Lt. C. L. Magee, had also joined Lts. S. S. Sims and D. J. Moore. They were over the Bombers at 23,000 feet, as they neared the southeast tip of Bougainville. At this time, a squadron of Zeros attacked them from the southeast and they veered off to the east and down.

Climbing back up to position, the flight got lost in a storm and battled it for fifteen minutes, finally coming out into the clear near the Treasury island.

By this time, Sims and Moore had become separated from Begert's flight.

A dozen Zeros blocked Begert's path to the bombers but he took his flight up and across, scissoring all the way and the Zeros never pressed home an attack.

He stayed there all the way back to Vella LaVella, weaving over the bombers.

Sims and Moore were alone just southeast of the Shortlands when they were attacked by 12 to 15 Zeros. One came in for a stern pass at Sims and Moore throttled back and went wide momentarily---and then dove on the Zero, giving him a long burst, and then

turned back and joined Sims. Looking back, he saw the
ZEKE burning as it fell toward the water.

Sims, by this time, was low on gas, so he dived under
the bombers, throttled back, and headed for Vella
LaVella.

At this time, it appeared to Moore that Zeros were
still bothering the bombers, so he turned back to
protect their rear, staying with them all the way to
New Georgia.

Lts. Case and Harris came out of the storm in the
vicinity of Treasury Island and headed toward Vella
LaVella. The route back was apparently free from Japs.

However, Case looked back and saw Zeros attacking the
bombers. One bomber was smoking.

"Harris, we've got to go back!" he radioed and the
two Corsairs turned back to fight the Zeros off the
formation of Liberator Bombers.

Climbing as they went, the two Corsairs scissored as
40 Zeros (HAP's) made pass after pass on them.

The Zeros drew off and then went down and began
making low wide passes on the bomber formation.

Pulling around in an over-head, the two Corsairs
drove the Zeros off momentarily, but at that time, a
Zero made a run on Harris' tail.

Case turned into him, but a 20mm exploded in his own
left wing and 7.7s went by him in a hail so that he
slid under Harris and came out in formation on the
right.

He looked for Harris, but he was gone.

Another hail of bullets hit him so he dived down to
evade the attacker.

Finally free, he looked a long way back to see four
planes heading toward the water and thought it might be
Harris with Zeros on his tail. Later he saw a splash
as a plane went into the water---this was 25 to 30
miles southeast of Treasury Island.

Case climbed up and scissored over the bombers until
one called him :

"Corsair, you're losing gas and oil, <u>get the hell home</u>!"

Case headed for home with oil streaming past his bottom vision window.

Pancaking at Vella LaVella, he found a 20mm shell in his left wing, 20mm shrapnel in his accessory section and 7.7 holes in his air duct and oil tank.

A new oil tank was installed at Vella LaVella and he took off for his home base, pancaking at 1630.

Case reports a beautiful job of wingman done by Harris against <u>tremendous odds</u>.

SCORE: <u>OUR LOSSES:</u>
         1 Plane and pilot missing.

         <u>ENEMY LOSSES</u> : Four (4) ZEKE's.
         Boyington 1 ZEKE.
         Case   1 ZEKE.
         Fisher   1 ZEKE.
         Moore   1 ZEKE.

         Report submitted by: **FRANK E. WALTON,**
                         First Lt., USMCR,
                         Intelligence Officer.

COMBAT REPORT
DATE: 27 September, 1943.
TIME: Takeoff 1105, over target 1230 (approx.), pancake 1330.
NATURE OF MISSION: High cover for B24 strike.
PLACE: Kahili
FORCES ENGAGED: OWN: 12 F4Us of VMF-214:

BOYINGTON	BOURGEOIS	BEGERT
FISHER	HEIER	HILL
CASE	HARRIS	ASHMUN
SIMS	MOORE	MAGEE

         ENEMY: 50 - 60 Zeros.

RESULTS:
ENEMY LOSSES: Boyington - 1 Zero (Zeke)
                Fisher   - 1 Zero (Zeke)
                Case   - 1 Zero (Zeke)
                Moore   - 1 Zero (Zeke)

OWN LOSSES: Lt. Harris - missing in action.

ALTITUDE : 20,000 feet.

NARRATIVE ACCOUNT:
   Three divisions took off at 1105 to act as high cover for B24 strike on Kahili. Poorly organized. No word to here until 15 minutes before takeoff. No time to get planes selected.   Some flights late.   Rendezvous scheduled with 27 B24s at 18,000 ft. at 1135 over Wagina I.   Boyington, off late was instructed to take his flight directly up as a fighter sweep. Bourgeois' instruments froze and Heier returned with him, leaving only 6 planes at high cover for 27 B24s.   These six caught the bombers just before they reached target, then were attacked by 15 - 20 Zeros (Zekes) and dove into clouds to shake them.

   Boyington observed twin tailed plane crossing the Kahili strip at 35,000 ft. emitting twin intermittent streams of black smoke 300 yards long, some sort of a signal.   Thinking it was a signal to the fighters to take off, Boyington dove down on to the strip - intending to knock them off as they took off. However, there were only 2 planes on the field and those looked like dummies.   Encountered no AA.   This was at 1210 before the strike which was scheduled at 1230.   He climbed up to 20,000 and attacked 20 Zeros - his flight getting 3 Zekes. There were 50 - 60 Zeros in the sky.

   Moore downed one Zero, shooting it off Sims tail.

   Harris is missing in action.   He was last seen when he and Case were alone and attacked by 20 Zeros, Case being hit by 20mm. and 7.7 and his oil line severed. Case dived out and when he looked for Harris he was gone.   Looking back, he saw 4 planes heading down and thinks Harris was one with Zeros on his tail.   Later, he saw a plane splash in the water. This was 20 - 25 miles SE of Treasury I.   Case and Sims made emergency landings at Vella LaVella.   Both brought their planes into base later in the day.

   The bombers went in on the target at 21,000 feet from E to W. Because of the confusion - swamped with Zeros, the fighter pilots were unable to observe the bombing.

   Mostly Zekes observed early in the action, Haps later.

Pancaked - 1330.

27 September, 1943.
  0540 - Bourgeois, Heier, Sims, Moore, Begert, Hill, Ashmun and Magee on dawn patrol till 0735 at which time they were vectored to Vella LaVella to cover beached LST which was to be removed. Vectored for bogey over Diamond Base. Left at 0800, pancaked at 0810. LST is at mouth of Naroai River.

  1540 - Bailey, Alexander, Bolt, Tucker, Mullen, Emrich, Bragdon, McClurg, McCartney, Matheson, Olander and Harper took off as escort for "Duck" on alleged search mission for Harris and P40 pilot reported down this morning 20 - 25 miles SE of Treasury I.

  Pilot of "Duck" talked to Lt. Case, who told him where he last saw Harris. Instead of searching this area, "Duck" pilot flew around Vella Gulf - some 50 - 60 miles SE of reported location. Naturally no results.

  McCartney's flight was vectored to Ganongga I. On a bogey and sighted a twin-engined bomber at 28,000 feet over SE tip of Ganongga - unable to get up to him. Pancaked at 1730.

  1700 - Boyington, Case, Moore and Sims scrambled off on bogey. Negative. Pancaked - 1900.

  Air raids missed us tonight till 0400. Then had half a dozen planes over. All clear at 0500.

One thing to note here on the story of Case's plane being shot up; this is the difference between the Corsair and the Zero. The Zero was much lighter and more agile. But the Corsair could take a pounding; Case's plane got all shot up, he flew it to a friendly base, had some parts replaced, and flew it home. Had a Zero been hit like Case's plane, it would have been at the bottom of the ocean. But they managed to get Harris. It took two or three of them, but Harris was gone. One could devote lots of thought wondering why or how it could have been avoided. Doing that works to confuse the mind. We never really accepted things like that; when one of the Sheep came up missing, anything that was seen to do so much as flinch was obliterated in the next few missions. But Harris was still gone. As the song went, "Ten thousand bucks going home to the folks;"

Harris was gone. I thought again of my slumber in the cot a few weeks ago, which had been occupied by "someone" two days earlier. Now it was more clear, closer to home. Ewing was gone, now Harris's cot would be empty. The atmosphere at camp changed when someone was lost, almost like dark weather closing in. Things got quiet, and tempers became short. Only passing days and more missions would dull the sense of loss. Unfortunately, passing days and more missions often renewed those same feelings. I flew missions again on September 28, 29 and 30. How I wish I could forget September 30, 1943...

30 September, 1943.

0530 - a dawn patrol of Bailey, Alexander, Bolt and Tucker. Acted as dawn patrol and task force cover. On station at Visu Visu Pt. At 0540 - left ships off Lever Pt. At 0730 and went on barge strafing search.

Found 4 boats off Sosoruana I. At 0740 at Ropa Pt. Bailey radioed instructions, "Don't fire till I give the word." Went down and recognized our own PT boats and immediately radioed, "Don't fire, they're our own boats." Alexander went in and was firing. He possibly accidentally tripped his trigger, eased off the stick at the burst and then didn't pull out in time - crashing in flames on the beach. Next thing Bailey and Tucker knew - Alexander's plane had crashed on the beach in flames, sliding under the brush and a huge column of smoke was coming up. Bailey and Tucker circled the spot but could see nothing but smoke. The PT boats pulled out about 1 mile off shore. Flight pancaked 0800.

PT BOAT REPORT OF ACTION OF 30 SEPTEMBER:

FORCE: Four Boats on Patrol

After a routine and uneventful patrol in lower Kala gulf, boats departed for base at 0510 after the DDs had departed from the vicinity. At 0535 when on course 040 degs. T, seven miles off shore and abeam of the Okopo river, a barge was sighted ½ mile off Waugh Rock headed north. Speed was increased and a course laid to skirt the minefield in order to intercept the barge. Contact was lost with the barge and at 0602 it was decided to search the northern coast of Kolombangara. Boats proceeded on course 230 about one mile off-shore and, when abeam of Rei Cove, boats reversed course and came to 400 yds. off shore. The 126 leading, the 124, 116, 189 following in that order. The 126 came to about 300 yards and proceeded to strafe the barge. At 0754, the 126 having just finished its run, three planes were sighted coming in low around the shore from the NE tip of the island. The planes were immediately recognized as F4Us and the gunners were so informed. As soon as the planes had been sighted, the 126 ordered full speed ahead, full right rudder and the American Flag was waved, all actions in accordance with standard recognition procedure. Upon sighting the boats, the two outboard planes appeared to recognize the boats and swung northward, wagging their wings. The inboard plane continued its run and opened fire on the 126. Due to the movement of the 126, only its stern was under fire. Ensign Dailey, on the after gun was hit, as well as Ross, a gunners mate, who was knocked overboard. A small fire was started in the engine room and it was determined that the engineer, Paul, had been killed instantly. After the plane had opened fire, a short burst was fired at the plane by the starboard forward twin 50 Cal. The plane was hit and went into a slow turn and landed 200 yds. Behind Ropa Pt., exploding when it hit. It was determined that Dailey had been killed instantly. A thorough search for the missing gunner was negative.

Boats departed for base at 0810.

NOTE : This is an unofficial report.

[Note to the reader; this information is from the combat report files. The moniker "unofficial" was intended to indicate that the report had not yet been fully organized according to military procedure of the time. In other words, the indication was made to acknowledge that the information was in raw form.]

STATEMENT OF STANLEY R. BAILEY, MAJOR, USMC,
re: STRAFING PT BOATS ON NORTH SHORE, KOLOMBANGARA.

At app. 0740 on the 30 September, 1943, I left station and started to return to the base.   In accordance with our usual custom we started an immediate let-down from 16,000' and headed for the Northern tip of Kolombangara to look for possible hidden Jap barges.

Half -way through Kula Gulf I placed my division of three planes in column in order that all might be able to search and cover the area effectively. It was shortly after this that I spotted four objects that looked like barges. They were close in to the beach, the nearest one app. 70 - 75 yards out, and seemed to us to be dead in the water. At that time I put out the information on the radio not to fire until I had given the word.

Then recognizing the objects as our own PT boats and seeing the crews waving I immediately said on the radio, quote; don't fire as they are our own PT boats, unquote. Both messages were received and understood by Lt. Tucker, the man directly behind me, in ample time. Lt. Alexander, the third in column, and I had been in excellent radio communication earlier in the hop. I then started to weave and wobble my wings.

Just as I passed abeam and between two of the boats I saw tracers surrounding one of the boats. I opened up and called for someone to stop firing.
Immediately, I pulled up into a climbing turn to see what damage had been done. As I did so I saw a large flash of flame and then a column of fire and smoke from the beach.

The PT boats by then were underway and proceeded at full speed to a point app. three to five miles off the NE shore. As only two of us pulled up I knew then what had happened. I circled hack over the spot but could see nothing but a black, burned swath under the trees directly on the beach, and scattered pieces of debris still burning.

I then returned to the base and pancaked at approximately 0800.

S. R. BAILEY,
Major, USMC

STATEMENT OF FIRST LIEUTENANT B. L. TUCKER
CONCERNING PT BOAT INCIDENT, 30 SEPTEMPER, 1943

At approximately 0740 we left our station over the task force. We headed for the North coast of Kolombangara as it was customary for us to make a sweep around Kolombangara after each patrol, in search of barges.

As we let down, Major Bailey put us in a column and called us saying, "Don't open fire until I give the word."

As we drew nearer the coast of Kolombangara I saw four boats inshore, the nearest seemed to be approximately 75 yards out. As we drew nearer I identified them as our own PT boats and turned off all my guns. At about the same time Major Bailey called up and said,

"Hold fire, they are our own PT boats."

As we drew nearer major Bailey started rocking his wings and I did likewise.

As I was abreast of the boats looking over to the left side, I saw someone who seemed to be dressed in blue denim standing on the bow of one PT boat waving at us. At the same time a hail of tracers hit the boat and I saw the person on the bow throw up his arms and fall.

At that time I didn't think he was hit but that he dropped to escape the tracers, which seemed to cover the boat completely.

This all happened in a split second as I was traveling very fast. I pulled up over the trees in a left turn to join up on the Major. I glanced back to pick up the third plane but did not see him, so I figured he was in my blind spot directly behind me.

As the Major and I swing around, I saw smoke rising from a point about 15 or 20 yards inshore. At first I thought it was a fire started by the PT boats, and then it dawned on me that it was the third plane. The Major and I circled about twice and came close inshore. I could see none of the plane at all because of the foliage. I joined up on Major Bailey and we returned to base at approximately 0800.

B. L. TUCKER
1st. Lt. USMCR

30 September, 1943,   (Cont'd.)

0545 - Mullen, Emrich, Bragdon, McClurg, Boyington, Fisher, Case, Bourgeois - task force cover. On station 0600. Picked up ships near Visu Visu - left off Bakelai Opening at 0800. Mullens's flight went over Kolombangara on return and observed 4 PT boats ½ mile off shore and saw smoke(from Alexander's crash, apparently) rising from about 50 or 75 feet into the brush. Pancaked 0830.

0930 - Begert, Hill, Ashmun and Magee on task force cover. Picked up on bearing of 060 from base - left at 070, at 1145, almost to Segi. Pancaked at 1200.

1110 - Bourgeois, Heier, Moore, Mullen, Emrich, Bragdon and McClurg scrambled on bogey.

Bourgeois' flight observed 40 - 50 Zeros (Zekes) at 15,000 (he was at 21,000), climbed to 24,000 reaching that level at the same time as the Japs, the Japs climbing 9,000 feet while the Corsairs climbed 3,000. Continued to climb to 27,000' and Japs quit climbing but chased them to Kolombangara. Moore said he saw at least 3 bombers with them, down low. No other friendly planes in sight. Pancaked at 1230.
1330 - Bailey, Ashmun, Begert, Bolt, Bourgeois, Case, Heier, Fisher, hill, Magee, Moore, Ray, Sims and Tucker took off for Russells I. via Scat. Pancaked 1430.

1630 - McCartney, Matheson, Olander, Harper, Mullen, McClurg, Emrich, Bragdon - took off and flew to Russells in F4Us. Pancaked at 1645.

Air raid alerts all night, 1900 to 0400.

SUBMITTED BY :   FRANK. E. WALTON, JR
                  First Lieutenant, USMCR
                  Intelligence Officer

OFFICIAL: GREGORY BOYINGTON
                  Major, USMCR
                  Commanding.

And that is what the reports look like which emptied Alexander's cot. It is unattractive, but friendly fire was the cause of many casualties on both sides. As the above report indicates, friendly fire happened with the Black Sheep, too. It isn't something a bunch of hot fighter pilots like to acknowledge, but it is part of reality, part of the truth. Being such, it is part of this book. Now allow me to tell you a little more about this ghost of a fighter pilot named Robert Alexander; he was one of the best. A natural. Note something from the report; although it was a fatal mistake to strafe, Alexander had made one run on a small boat and covered it squarely with gunfire. That isn't easy to do. Before that terrible event, Bob Alexander was the envy of many of us. He could fly a Corsair as if it was a custom tailored suit he wore. He was vibrant, aggressive. An excellent marksman. I remember when we were doing night training weeks before; most of us were happy just to stay in the air without colliding and then get the plane back on the ground in one piece. But Bob Alexander was beyond that. He was doing loops and rolls on those night flights. Not reckless, but just totally comfortable and in command of his flying machine. I think it was with Bob Alexander's death that I really began to have the feeling of fate; the feeling that it was somehow a game of luck. Surely if it were simply the most talented who survived, Alexander would be here today. It was just his time. Someone called him to go. By the same token, that same power must have chosen for me to stay here this long for some reason. This is stepping a bit forward in time, but some of us Black Sheep went back to Alexander's crash site about six weeks after the event, to find him and give him a proper burial. This is mentioned in Pappy's book, and I was one of about five of us who went. After six weeks in the jungle, we found mostly bones. But we buried them just the same, using one of Alexander's Corsair's prop blades as a headstone. We laid Alexander facing Tokyo so he could watch as the rest of us fought on. I took a picture of Alexander's grave, which I don't think has ever been seen by outside eyes.

Robert Alexander's grave site. The writing on the propeller blade reads
Bob Alexander 1st Lt. USMCR VMF 214 SEPT 30 1943
(McClurg collection)

Time check: Remember again that this was the beginning of
October, 1943. We were flying the hot Corsair F4U, though the
ones we flew were battle weary "hand me downs" and not the
"cream of the crop." In 1943, no aircraft had the advanced weather
instruments which are so common today; the stuff simply wasn't
available. We had engine instruments to tell us various things about
how the engine was running. We had what were called "navigation
instruments" to tell us things about what the airplane was doing in
the air. These included instruments which told us how fast the air
was passing over the airplane, how high the airplane was and
whether it was going up or going down. There was also a turn and
bank indicator which indicated how the airplane was turning. Of
course, there was also a compass which indicated magnetic heading.
Beyond that, we had transmit and receive radios for communication

and a "friend or foe" transponder which was used to help identify friendly aircraft. A pilot could count on having all this stuff work properly at the same time on only about half of any missions flown. Our speculation was that Alexander's radio receiver or headset had quit at just the wrong time on the unfortunate event of September 30. I think he never heard the call identifying the boats as friendly, and I am pretty confident that he was killed by the boat's return fire; a shallow glide into the brush (or water), as Alexander had done, is almost always a sign of an unconscious pilot. Anyhow, one thing we didn't have was storm finder satellite networks or other military planes charting weather and beaming the information to us on secret frequencies. So when the weather got bad, the flying generally stopped. And that is exactly how it was for the first three days of October, 1943. I actually didn't fly a mission again until the sixth, but Pappy was back in the air on the fourth, shooting Japanese planes full of holes. October fourth's action is important for a few reasons, as I will comment later. First, here is Frank Walton's account from our combat reports:

```
WAR DIARY, VMF-214
- - - - - - - - - - - - - - - - - - - - - - - - - - - - - -


                    C-O-N-F-I-D-E-N-T-I-A-L:

COMBAT REPORT

DATE:      4 October, 1943

TIME:        Take-off 1115; Rendezvous 1155; Strike
             didn't materialize.

MISSION :    Medium  cover  for  SBD's  on  Malabeta  Hill
             strike.

RENDEZVOUS:     10,000 feet over SE tip of Rendova.

FORCES ENGAGED:
             OWN: 6 F4U's, VMF-214.

             Boyington  Begert
             Case       Hill
             Fisher     Ashmun
             Emrich     Magee

             ENEMY: 30 Zekes.
```

CONTACT:
          Altitude :   26,000 feet.
          Location: Moila Point.
          Time   :   1330.

RESULTS:
          ENEMY LOSSES: 3   Zekes   shot   down   by   Major
          Boyington.
          OUR LOSSES   :   None.

NARRATIVE ACCOUNT:

At 1115 Boyington, Fisher (pancaked 1230 – motor trouble) Case, Emrich (pancaked 1130 – motor trouble) Begert, Hill Ashmun and Magee took off to act as medium cover for SBD's on a strike on Malabeta Hill AA positions NW of Kahili. They reached their rendezvous (10,000 feet over SE tip of Rendova) at 1155, 20 minutes early. Orbited until 1230 without sighting the bombers, then heard one bomber call another and say that they were going home. Unable to contact by radio, so went north to look for bombers.

Fifty to Sixty miles from Kahili they saw dust clouds as fighters left Kahili strip. The six Corsairs contacted 30 Zekes at 26,000 feet over Moila Pt. At 1330. Made run on [___]

the first division of Japs, continued in a circling pass and Major Boyington shot down 3 Zeros in one 360 degree pass, taking less than 60 seconds for the job. One was a flamer, one crashed on land; One parachuted out.

Captain Ashmun, separated from the flight, attempted to join a formation of B-24's leaving the Kahili strike, but was attacked by P-38's, even after he had showed his belly to them and another plane had radioed:

"P-38, that's an F4U you're firing at!"

However, no damage was done, and all our pilots pancaked at Munda at 1425 for refueling. They left at 1533 and pancaked here at 1620.

Walton makes an interesting note in one of the itemized sheets associated with this action report, which I think is worth including here :

Our F4Us were planes sent down from Munda with too many hours for operation from there – yet we had to operate them from here, 126 miles further. Zekes can't get nose down and dive with the F4U – safe in making pass and continuing in dive.

The action report continues...

3 ZEROS IN 60 SECONDS

Major Greg Boyington, fighting squadron commander of VMF-214, led two divisions of his outfit off from the Russell strip at 1115. The eight planes were Corsairs which had seen so much combat service in the front area, from (Munda), that they had been returned to the Russells for major overhaul.

Now, still without their major overhauls, they were taking off on a trip 135 miles farther than they would have had to make had they remained at Munda.

The 8 Corsairs were to act as medium cover for a strike by 20 Dauntless dive bombers on Malabeta Hill – a strong AA position NW of Kahili airdrome.

Two of the 8 wheezing planes had to return to base because of a multitude of mechanical difficulties, so Major Boyington led the other 6 worn Corsairs to the rendezvous point – 10,000 feet over the South East tip of Rendova.

Arriving there at 1135, twenty minutes early, the six planes flew in lazy circles through the clouds – awaiting the arrival of the bombers.

However, no bombers appeared, so at 1230, the Major decided to take his flight up the slot in an effort to locate them – and, failing in that, hoping to run across a few Zeros.

He was successful in the latter desire – 50 miles S of Kahili they could see clouds of dust rising from the Kahili strip as the Zeros rose to meet them.

Ready for a fight, the little flight of Corsairs drove in to meet the climbing Zeros.
There were 30 of them climbing in flights of 4 and 5.

Boyington took his flight down in a high stern run on the right hand of one of the first four as they were beginning a right hand climbing turn.

Coming down from 3,000 feet above, Boyington almost over ran the Zero after opening fire at 300 yards, so he chopped back on his throttle, skidded sideways, settled back on the Zeros tail, opened fire again and chopped the Jap's tail to pieces.

The Zero spun in.

Wheeling around, Boyington came in on the second plane in a high port quarter pass. After a very short burst, the Jap popped out of his cockpit, parachuting to safety. The chute was a light tan color like raw silk. It streamed out 6,000 feet before it opened.

Continuing on, Boyington came in on the tail of a third Zero - opened up with a long, no deflection burst - boring in till the Zero flamed from the right wing root and went down.

At this time tracers began to whip over him so Boyington nosed over and dove, having bagged 3 Zeros in less than 60 seconds.

Shaking off the pursuing Zeros, Boyington pulled out at 10,000 feet and climbed back to rejoin his flight.

Captain Geo. M. Ashmun, separating from the flight, climbed to 25,000 feet over Ballale and attempted to locate the other Corsairs.

He observed a B24 strike on the Kahili strip - with a good pattern of bombs W and N of the runway.

At the time Ashmun observed what appeared to be one of the phosphorous aerial bombs - a huge explosion occurred in the sky at his level but between Fauro I. and Kahili.

The explosion was accompanied by a huge cloud of white smoke with 5 or 6 large white streamers emanating FROM THE CENTER. He could observe no planes in the

vicinity, nor was there any land underneath on which an
AA battery could have been located.

Ashmun saw the B24s with P38 Lightnings as cover for
them, circle Fauro I. and headed toward them to assist
in escorting the bombers home.

As he neared the bombers, two P38s detached
themselves from the cover and headed toward him.

He rolled over and showed his belly to the P38s in
order to assure recognition, and then circled on the
flank of the bombers.

As he did so, tracers from one of the P38s whistled
over his head. A voice over the radio called, "P38,
that's an F4U you're shooting at".

Ashmun weaved about violently, showing the P38s every
part of his plainly-marked plane and then settled down
again on the bomber's flank.

Once again tracers flashed over his head, so he nosed
down and headed for home.

At Munda, where all the Corsairs pancaked at 1425,
one P38 pilot said, concerning the incident, "Well, I
didn't know there were going to be any Corsairs
around."

Another P38 pilot said, "Some of our boys are kinda
trigger happy."

This incident, coupled with the recent incident where
the commander of an F6F squadron made a firing run on a
member of his own squadron, makes one wonder if a pilot
should regard every other plane in the sky as an enemy.

All Corsairs left Munda at 1533 after refueling and
pancaked at the Russells at 1630.

Lt. Emrich couldn't start his first airplane - tried
another and could only get 2150 revolutions out of it -
pancaked at 1125.

Lt. Fisher returned with an oil leak, pancaking at
1240.

Weather was clear over Kahili but a solid front from 3,000 to 4,000 ft. up was in evidence over Malabeta Hill.

The hit and run attack method was again successful in this encounter.

The Zero can't dive with the F4U. In a diving stern approach it is safe to continue on past the Zero as he can't get his nose down to dive with you.

The Zero's superior maneuverability makes it suicide to attempt a dogfight with him, particularly at low speed.

(REPORT PREPARED BY)	(APPROVED BY:)
Frank E. Walton	Gregory Boyington
1st Lt., ACI. VMF-214	Major, C.O., VMF-214

And that closes October 4, 1943. Boyington added three more flags to the side of his fuselage, for a total of nine (not including the six or so with the A.V.G.). That is a good lead–in to reveal this fact; we never, ever flew with decorative flags on the side of our planes. We did have planes that we flew repeatedly, but we did not have specific airplanes assigned to specific people. Maintenance work, breakdowns, and scheduling simply did not allow for that. We mostly hopped in an airplane and flew it. Sometimes the plane we hopped into for a mission wouldn't start, and we'd hop out, run off to another plane, hop in, etc. The airplanes seen in many of the Black Sheep press photos were indeed the actual planes we flew. We generally applied the Japanese "score" decals to the fuselage temporarily, and chalked on names or nicknames. The stuff came off after the pictures were taken. Someone made a joke about the terror that must have been experienced by a Japanese rookie pilot (which is what they had most of later in the war), after seeing a Corsair full of "score" decals (as Pappy's would have appeared later in the war) whiz past in a dogfight. The other side of such a joke is that any Corsair so full of "score" decals would surely have been the one they made certain to finish, which is exactly why we didn't keep "score" decals on the planes, regardless of who flew them.

Date and location unknown. A shot up Black Sheep Corsair. Significant
battle damage did not prevent the F4-U from bringing its pilot back home.
(Bourgeois Collection)

Looking back over the action of October 4, some very important
things are becoming evident; combat and scores are becoming a
more relaxed, standard thing. Largely thanks to Pappy, VMF-214
was becoming accustomed to combat, and getting good at exploiting
the weaknesses of the Japanese planes and tactics. Combat wasn't
boring by any means; we Black Sheep were beginning to show
ourselves as a capable group when it came to fighting the enemy;
something we all wanted so badly to demonstrate, happy as we were
to have been taken out of the "replacement" pool. Because the
bombers VMF-214 was supposed to escort were not found at the
agreed rendezvous point, October fourth's action was also one of
the earliest manifestations of Pappy's brain child, the "Fighter
Sweep." This was aggression, Pappy style, in which we had the
opportunity to go calling on the Japanese ourselves, with no
bombers to watch. Pappy would go on to promote and plead for the
ability to do this stuff, in the interest of blatantly confronting the
Japanese Zero and exercising our F4Us and tactics on them. Lastly,
we can see in Frank Walton's combat report of October 4 the
frustration at having worn fighter planes to work with; we really
wanted new shiny stuff, but we all knew that we were lucky to even

have the "hand me down" units. We all would have done anything to get first rate equipment, but I think we all knew it wasn't going to happen.

After Pappy's action of the fourth, I flew missions on the sixth, and the tenth through the sixteenth. Pappy had another score on the fifteenth...

WAR DIARY, VMF-214.
- -

C-O-N-F-I-D-E-N-T-I-A-L

COMBAT REPORT

DATE: 15 October, 1943.

    MISSION: Medium cover for B-24's on Kangu hill supply dump.

    TIME: Take-off 1045-1120; Rendezvous 1123; Strike 1215.

RENDEZVOUS: 18,000 feet over Simbo Island.

FORCES ENGAGED:
    OWN: 12 F4U's, VMF-214

        Bourgeois Olander Boyington
        Heier Matheson   Tucker
        Sims   Bolt   Case
        McClurg Harper Emrich

    ENEMY: 12-15 Zeros.

    CONTACT:
    Altitude: 12,000 feet.
    Location: Between Kahili and Ballale
    Time: 1200.

RESULTS:
<u>ENEMY LOSSES</u>: Case.......2 Zeros
        Emrich…..2   "
        Tucker…..1   "
        Boyington..1   "   and 3 Probables.

      Total 6 Zeros and 3 probables.

<u>OUR LOSSES</u>:   None.

NARRATIVE ACCOUNT:

Bourgeois' and Olander's flights took off to act as high cover for B-24 strike on Kangu Hill Supply Dump area, Kahili, at 1045.   Low cover was provided by 8 F4U's from VMF-221; high cover by 16 P-38's from Cactus.

Rendezvous was made on schedule at 1123 and 1800 over Simbo Island, just south of Ganongga Island.   The formation was supposed to proceed directly to the target, however, instead, zig-zagged back and forth, arriving at the target 15-20 minutes late of the scheduled time of 1200.   Consequently, Boyington's flight, which took off late to act as a fighter sweep to protect the bombers' tails on the return trip, arrived over the target before the bombers.

They saw clouds of dust on the Kahili strip as the Zeros took off to intercept—but they never allowed them to reach altitude in order to attack the bombers.

Approximately 21 B-24's made bomb runs, approaching the target at 22,500 feet along the Bougainville coastline from Moila Pt. Toward the Kahili strip, and concentrating their bombs in the area between Kangu Hill and the beach.   About forty to fifty percent of their bombs fell in the water—probably necessary because of the proximity of the target to the beach. Four to five fires were observed in the target area.

As the bombers passed over the target, low cover was at 24,000 and hight cover was at 26,000 feet.   The formation circled to the left in a wide sweep outside the Shortlands (west of Shortlands), and headed down the slot for home.

Twelve to fifteen Zeros attempted to come up underneath the bombers, but were engaged at 12,000 feet by Boyington's flight, and the enemy never got within 8 to 10 miles of the bombers.

Major Boyington's flight intercepted the Zeros over the area between Kahili and Ballale, making their first contact at 1220, at 4,000 feet.

In the ensuing scrap, the four Corsairs shot down six Zeros (Zekes), and probably destroyed three more. Major Boyington is credited with 1 positive and 3 probables. Lt Case shot down 2. Lt Emrich destroyed 2, and Lt Tucker nabbed 1.

AA fire was medium and inacurrate. Bomber cover made no contact and all our pilots pancaked safely, Bourgeois' entire flight returning early when three of the four pilots had mechanical difficulty.

                    *   *   *

(AIRCRAFT ACTION REPORT)

Two divisions of Corsairs took off from Munda at 1045 L to act as medium cover for B-24 strike on Kangu Hill supply area and Kahili.

Rendezvous was made on schedule,1123, Simbo Island, 18,000 feet.

The formation proceeded in a westerly direction, then headed E and continued to Zig zag until they passed over Shortland Island, then headed N E along the Bougainville coastline.

One division of Corsairs, led by Major Boyington, took off at 1115 to act as fighter sweep to protect tail of returning bombers.

The strike has been scheduled for 1200, but the bombers did not arrive until 1215 or later. Consequently, the fighter sweep arrived over the target before the strike.
Boyington's division orbited Kahili and saw the bombers make their drop. Then they observed Jap fighter planes taking off. They dove down and made their first contact at 4,000 feet, halfway between Ballale and Kahili.
In the ensuing scrap, this division tangled with 10-15 Zeros; shooting down six and probably destroyed 3 more. It was Major Boyington's 16th Jap plane.

The enemy planes never had a chance to get up to the
bombers as they were engaged far below them.

It is recommended that such a fighter sweep be sent up
early on every strike to engage the enemy fighters. An
additional sweep should go out to protect the bomber's
tail on the return trip.

Maintenance of our planes continues to be bad, three of
the four planes in Lt. Bourgeois' division having to
return to base because of various mechanical
difficulties. Lt. Heier had carburetor trouble. Lt.
Sims' high blower failed to function, and Lt. Bourgeois
had a half inch of dirt on his gas filter.

REPORT PREPARED BY: APPROVED BY:
Frank E. Walton, Jr., 1ˢᵗLt. Gregory Boyington, Major
ACI. VMF-214   C.O., VMF-214

    Although the above action report duplicates the combat report, I
chose to include it because it mentions two significant things; we
continued to have problems with our airplanes. The planes were
tired warhorses to begin with, many in need of overhaul. As if that
weren't bad enough, the South Pacific conditions were getting to
them. The high heat and humidity was gunking everything up so it
wouldn't work right. And the coral dust which was everywhere was
also finding its way into our fuel tanks, which caused things like
clogged fuel filters and hence engines which couldn't make their
maximum power because they couldn't get the fuel they needed.

    Now is a good time for another little tidbit of information about
the Corsair's engine. One of the biggest problems with putting such
a huge engine in that airplane was keeping it cool enough, and part
of what cooled the engine was a small amount of unburned fuel in
the form of a rich (lots of fuel) combustion mixture. Given this,
when a fuel filter got gunked up and restricted the fuel flow, the
engine didn't just fly slower. Rather, it often tended to overheat…
Just what every pilot wants to have happen as they go to full power
for a dogfight! That said, I think it's only fair to add one more
thing: the problems we encountered were environmental and
nothing to do with the design or manufacture of the equipment
itself. In fact, the Pratt & Whitney engine in the Corsair was one of
the finest engines ever made. Gunked up, shot up, those engines
would pull us back home many times, often to the amazement of
crew and mechanics.

"Cappy"

Location and date unknown. Pappy climbing into a Corsair. This was likely a posed photo, taken with a personal camera at the same time other photos were being taken. (Bourgeois collection)

Perhaps, though, the most important thing mentioned in Walton's combat report of October 15 was the fighter sweep; this was more evidence of the success from Boyington's change in tactics. Pappy had implemented his concept of "fighter sweep" again, in which our fighters didn't stay limited to protecting bombers. By applying Pappy's idea and doing things just a little differently, we got to go engage the opposing fighters before the bombers arrived. By doing this, we got to scrap with the fighters and leave them either shot up, out of fuel, or at least severely distracted by the time our bombers showed up. This took the opposing pressure off of the bombers and allowed them to concentrate on their targets. And it worked. On that day, according to our reports, the Japanese chef served those pilots twelve to fifteen breakfasts, and only three to six lunches. Pappy's score on that day was his tenth, and so made him an ace twice over, if you don't count the six scores he was credited while with the A.V.G.

While we're on the subject of Pappy, let's cover a couple other things... It is fairly well known that Pappy was a drinker. I won't deny that. I'd go so far as to say that Pappy's drinking caused him an awful lot of problems. I never knew of him flying drunk, but he sure did spend many of his ground hours "pickled." This is where imagination and sometimes desire to view things in certain ways have taken over when recounting. While it is true that things were less structured when we fought in the 1940's, it wasn't a "free for all." As pilots, we were an item of which there was not enough, and they invested an awful lot of training in a pilot. I have also mentioned that our warbirds were not exactly in plentiful supply, either. Logically, and further for those reasons, the squadron doctor had definite authority and absolutely would not let someone fly drunk. Pappy suffered from something else which presented a much more serious risk of grounding him, though. It is not well known that he had narcolepsy—sleeping disease. He often had a difficult time staying awake when forced to do monotonous things for over an hour or so. Monotonous things, like, say, drone along in a Corsair behind a bomber formation. Of course, reporting such a thing could easily have gotten him shipped stateside, and we couldn't have that. So Pappy used to improvise... One thing he did was to take a little pinch of the cigar he so often chewed on and stick it in the corner of his eyes. The sting would keep him squinting, and keep him awake. Unfortunately, this would also make his eyes bloodshot, which looked like evidence for the drinking stories even when they were not true. (A modern day fighter pilot would be immediately "washed out" if such a condition were detected. I wonder how many "Pappys" they have washed out?)

Well, Pappy was on a roll. He was to have some more success on the seventeenth, and I was part of the flight that time...

WAR DIARY, VMF-214.
- -

C-O-N-F-I-D-E-N-T-I-A-L:

COMBAT REPORT

DATE : 17 October, 1943

MISSION: Fighter sweep over Kahili Airfield

TIME: Take-off 0815; Rendezvous 0820; Strike 0915.

RENDEZVOUS : 22,000 feet over Kahili

FORCES ENGAGED:
Own : 16 F4U's, VMF-214

Boyington	Olander	Begert	Bourgeois
Moore	Matheson	Hill	Heier
Case	Bolt	Ashmun	Mullen
McClurg	Harper	Magee	Tucker

ENEMY: 40 Zeros.

CONTACT:
Altitude: 10-15,000 feet.
Location: Shortlands-Ballale area.
Time: 0945

RESULTS:
Enemy Losses: Boyington...3 Zekes.
Heier.......2 Zekes and 1 probable Hap.
Tucker......2 Zekes.
Magee.......2 Zekes.
Olander.....1 Zeke.
Matheson....1 Hap.
Bolt........1 Zeke.

McClurg…..1 probable Hap.

TOTAL : 12 Planes and 2 Probables.

(11 Zekes, 1 Hap and 2 probable Haps)

Our Losses: None.

NARRATIVE ACCOUNT:

At 0815, Boyington, Olander, Begert and Bourgeois'
divisions took off with two divisions from VMF-221 to
act as a fighter sweep to Kahili. One of 221's planes
could not get off the ground. Begert and Bourgeois, of
214, had to return because of electrical system failure
and sinus attack, respectively.

The remaining 21 planes proceeded over Vella Lavella
for a direct course to Kahili with the division from
VMF-221 at 6,000 feet and ahead to act as bait to draw
the enemy fighters off the field. The rest of the
formation flew at 22,000 feet.

The formation reached Kahili at 0915 and made a lazy
circle over the field. The Jap fighter planes began to
take off in two's and three's, joined up and split into
two groups—one circling out over north Choiseul and the
other out west of the Shortlands.

Two divisions went down in big, sweeping "S" turns,
while the remainder of the formation made a lazy figure
"8" turn over the strip.

AA was of medium intensity and was thrown up at the
Corsairs from both Kahili and Ballale. Most of the AA
was low. One or two peculiar-looking bursts were
observed coming as high as 20,000 feet. They were
tremendous black puffs from which there came three
long, red streamers. They apparently came from
Ballale.

Approximately 40 Zeros, mostly Zekes, with some Haps,
were engaged by the Corsairs. The ensuing melee was
scattered all over the sky, from Kahili to Ballale, and
from Fauro to the Short-lands.

VMF-214's pilots shot down 12 Zeros and probably
destroyed 2 more. All our pilots returned safely,
Lieutenants Matheson, Harper and Moore having their
planes shot up extensively, and Harper having to make a

belly landing in a heavy tropical storm when his wheels wouldn't come down. Harper did a beautiful job of landing. Harper was wounded in the neck and Matheson in the legs—both slight wounds.

Because of the heavy weather, the remaining pilots were instructed to pancake at Vella Lavella, and did so. They returned later in the day.

*   *   *

AIRCRAFT ACTION REPORT

At 0815 16 F4U's of VMF-214, together with 7 F4U's of VMF-221, took off from the Munda strip on a fighter sweep to Kahili. The formation was led by Major G. Boyington of VMF-214. 2 of VMF-214's planes had to return early; 1, piloted by Lt. J. F. BEGERT, was pancaked immediately because of electrical trouble, the other, piloted by H.M. Bourgeois, returned from Vella Lavella, suffering from sinus attack.

The remaining 21 pilots went up toward Kahili, climbing, reaching an altitude of 22,000 feet as they passed over the Kahili strip at 0910.

One division of VMF-221's planes were down at 6,000 feet as bait to draw the enemy fighters off the strip. The higher planes passed over the southeast tip of Bougainville and circled lazily to the west.

The enemy fighters began to take off the strip as the Corsairs circled the area. They took off in twos and threes.

The Kahili strip was green, and very difficult to see—apparently camouflaged.

Major Boyington took two divisions down in big sweeping "S" turns.

AA of medium intensity was coming up from the area around the strip, most of it low. Some peculiar AA was observed, possibly aerial bombs. They were big, black puffs of smoke, as big as their airplane, and had 3 long red streamers. Came up to 20,000 feet, and it was apparently shot from Ballale.

Major Boyington took his flight down to 10,000 feet, where they made their first contact with 15-20 Zeros—

All Zekes. The remainder of the formation contacted 15 Zekes at 18,000 feet over Ballale. These had apparently circled in from N. Choiseul. At this time another 15 or 20 Zeros came down from 22,000 from west of the Kahili strip.

From then on—for 40 minutes—the 21 Corsairs battled 40-50 Zeros all over the sky in an area ranging from Kahili to Ballale and from Fauro Island to the Shortlands (about 375 sq. miles), They fought the Zeros right down to the water until the remaining Jap planes turned tail and headed for home, when the Corsair pilots, low on gas and oxygen, headed for Vella Lavella.

In the scrap VMF-214 pilots shot down 12 Zeros sure, and probably destroyed 2 more, without loss to themselves. Major Boyington got 3, making a total of 13 in the past 31 days.

Lt. Harper, hit by 7.7mm and 20mm, which destroyed his hydraulic system, had to make a belly landing at his base when his wheel would only come part way down. In spite of the fact that ceiling and visibility at the strip wre Zero, due to a heavy storm, he set his plane down beautifully and slid to a stop without injury to himself.

Lt. Matheson, his left wing and left elevator seriously damaged by 20mm, and with 7.7mm's beating a tatoo on his armor plate, nursed his tattered Corsair back through the heavy tropical storm to his base and set it down without mishap—another tribute to the ruggedness of the F4U.

The remaining planes of the strike wre instructed to pancake at Vella Lavella, and did so.

All VMF-214 pilots took off an hour or so later, and pancaked here without incident.

The Zeros were very cautious in the fight: Individuals would not attack individual Corsair pilots.

Several planes were seen to burn, several crashed, and 2 Jap pilots were seen to bail out.

REPORT PREPARED BY   APPROVED BY
Frank E. Walton, Jr.,   Gregory Boyington,
1st. Lt., USMCR, ACI VMF-214   Maj. USMCR CO, VMF-214

The overall outcome was similar to that of before; our tactics were being honed, and we were having success. It wasn't exactly a turkey shoot, as two of our men were wounded in combat and a total of three are indicated as being pretty well shot up—this was serious business. But when all was said and done, all our boys came back from the mission. The Japanese, however, would have about fourteen extra lunch trays in their mess hall that day. Pappy ended up with three more scores. I am credited for a probable Hap on that day—I sent one down smoking, but wasn't able to watch whether it hit the water or limped back to its strip, and nobody else could vouch for me.

We began to note something else, though, about the Japanese. We couldn't be sure, but it seemed as if the Zeros we encountered were becoming less offensive and more defensive. Several of our pilots noted that they had to pursue the Zekes more to get them to fight. A Zeke wouldn't challenge a Corsair one-on-one. We were getting used to fighting while outnumbered two, three or four to one. The difference in planes was showing, too: while the Zeros could outmaneuver us, it took only one decent shot to splash one into the water. The Corsair, on the other hand, was like every Japanese barfighter's worst nightmare: he could smash on an F4U seemingly forever and it would still fly. Indeed, we did have to junk a few of them when they returned home. But WE junked them, not the Japanese. It was getting so that the Japanese could count on losing a bunch of their aerial hardware when we were around, and we would do our best to keep it that way...

October eighteenth was also a good day for us, and for me especially. Good for more reasons than one, and I have no problem remembering this particular mission after all these years... It began with humor, and ended with horror...

I flew as Pappy's wingman while we escorted bombers to Ballale. As usual, we flew for some time, then met the bombers at a rendezvous point, and proceeded to the target. We flew to the rendezvous points at economical power settings in order to save fuel for the fighting. In a Corsair, this was throttled way back, usually at around 160 MPH. At that speed, it was easily possible to fly with the canopy open, depending on what altitude we flew at (higher was too cold to leave the canopy open). It could actually get boring after a while, watching the water, waiting to arrive.

On this particular day, I noticed that Pappy's plane was making some erratic moves in the air as we flew along, almost as if he was encountering turbulence.   But I knew that he wasn't hitting turbulence, because the rest of us were there and we were flying straight and level. I maneuvered a little closer, above and ahead of him so I could look down and slightly rearward, into his cockpit. It turned out that all the erratic maneuvering had occurred as Pappy was relieving himself into his canteen cup.

You see, the airplanes were equipped with a little tube which was attached to the control stick. The tube, known formally as the "pee tube," led down and out through an opening in the belly of the airplane. We had long funnel attachments (designed to put the male anatomy into) which we could attach to the hose to relieve ourselves in flight.   But there was a problem...   In the humid jungle environment, and with the dust from the coral runway strips, those tubes gunked up in no time at all. Of course, no self respecting mechanic would clean one out, so they stayed that way. With a gunked up "pee tube," it would simply back up when used, and the pilot's urine would overflow the little funnel device and drip down into the bottom catacombs of the airplane. That is, until you got upside down in a dogfight. This is why nobody used the "pee tubes," and hence why Pappy had gone to all the trouble to fill his canteen cup. Now this should be obvious, but I feel obligated to state it anyway: of course we didn't drink from the canteen cups. We drank directly from the canteen.

So there sat Pappy, with a cup full. He dumped the cup out the right side of his bird, but held it up too high, and it promptly splashed back in, all over him, face, goggles and all. Remember that we were in radio silence while en route, so no words were spoken. As my teeth began to show in a wide grin, Pappy leaned forward as if into me, pointing with his left index finger. Not a word needed speaking. I could hear him in my mind; "McClurg... Don't you DARE say a word..." (As a side note, I've seen this same antic written elsewhere, allegedly about a different pilot in our squadron. It may be that the same thing happened to others. One thing's for sure; I was there and it was Pappy!) What happened when the action started made me forget all about the antics on the outbound journey...

I remember that I was flying at fairly high altitude: twenty-four or twenty-five thousand feet. Our bombers started their runs. Some

Zeros were spotted way off in the distance. We throttled up toward full power. As I did this, my cockpit became very quiet. The engine stopped making its powerful whine, which I would just as soon have continued to hear at that particular moment. I began to descend, the choice having been made for me by gravity. In that situation, the only way to maintain control of the airplane is to point the nose down like you're diving, to keep the airspeed up. This also gets wind going past the propeller, which will actually turn the engine and sometimes offer a chance to get it started, as I had mentioned some chapters ago in a different situation. Of course something must have made it quit in the first place, so the chances of a re-start weren't great. All the while, I was falling out of the sky, from twenty-four thousand feet or so, down, down, down. A quiet cockpit like that allows what seems like an eternity to think... so I thought. I thought about where to put down so I might have the best chance of being picked up by some of our boys. I figured water was better because the land below was infested with Japanese. I thought to myself, "This is it! This is the day I go in, with the enemy all around me!" I figured for sure that I would be strafed in the water if I landed there. Still falling, propeller still turning over erratically. As I got down to about ten thousand feet or so, my engine began to sputter occasionally. Down to about five thousand feet, my engine was running again, although roughly. I had hopes, but still believed that I was "going in." It was about that same time that I spotted two Zeros flying in formation at around three thousand feet. Resigned that I was going to get wet, I decided that I would try to take a couple of the enemy with me. From fairly long range, I came in behind the rearmost of the Zeros and began firing while I was still above them. Because I still had an altitude advantage, my gunfire into the wingman went through him, and beneath the front plane. Fortunately for me, they were both highly inattentive. The wingman crashed into the water without much ceremony at all, and I proceeded to repeat the process on the leader of the two, with the same results. This all happened within half a minute or so. I don't think they ever saw me coming, and this was my good fortune. Just after that, I began to feel rattles on my ship; I was taking fire from someone else wearing a red meatball.

By the time I was down that low, my engine had begun to produce some power, but was still coughing badly and would not allow me to get up much speed or climb; I was resigned to limping home. I didn't find anyone to join up on, and fortunately whoever was pounding on me... stopped. They either gave me up for gone or got chased off by a big brother, or perhaps ran out of ammunition. I managed to limp the plane home safely, with the engine sputtering all the way. On final approach, my landing gear seemed to deploy just fine. It was when the mains touched down on the strip that I knew all was not well. One of my tires had been shot out, and I couldn't retain control of the aircraft as it slowed down and the flying surfaces lost their influence. I ended up off the runway, coming to a rather abrupt halt in a revetment. That I had shot down 2 Zekes was not on my mind. That I had almost been "erased" was all I could think of. My closest brush with death, yet something had again seemed to deliver me home. It turned out that I was the only one on that flight to score. I think this was because the others stayed with the bombers, and because the Japanese in the air avoided tangling with our flight. Had I not almost fallen out of the sky, I might not have encountered the two planes I did. As it happened, I was ridiculously lucky that both the Zeros I fell onto weren't paying attention, else I'd have been a goner for sure. (Note: I have seen something written elsewhere about me having a negative stigma after groundlooping a Corsair during training. For the record, I never groundlooped a Corsair in training. I suspect it was this mission, with some confusion, that might have led to the errant comments. This is another good example of how even something well researched can contain inaccuracies. People have a large tendency to take the printed word as gospel. Again, I was there!)

WAR DIARY, VMF-214.
- -

COMBAT REPORT   C-O-N-F-I-D-E-N-T-I-A-L:

    DATE: 18 October, 1943.

    MISSION: Medium cover for SBD strike on AA positions in Ballale.

    TIME: Take-off, 0900; Rendezvous, 0930; Strike, 1025.

  RENDEZVOUS: 1500 feet over Rendova.

FORCES ENGAGED:

    Own: 12 F4U's, VMF-214.

Boyington	Begert	Olander
McClurg	Hill	Matheson
Case	Ashmun	Mullen
Emrich	Magee	Harper

    Enemy: 2 Zekes.

CONTACT:

    Altitude: 2,500 feet.
    Location: Over Fauro.
    Time: 1100.

RESULTS:

    Enemy Losses: 2 Zekes shot down by McClurg.

    Our Losses: None.

NARRATIVE ACCOUNT:

Boyington, Begert and Olander's divisions took off to act as medium cover for a SMD strike on AA positions on Ballale. Coordinated in the strike were 27 B-24's covered by 16 P-38's, and 12 TBF's covered by 8 New Zealand P-40's and 12 F4U's. Other SBD cover was provided by 24 P-39's.

The bombing was the best the VMF-214 pilots ever saw. The AA positions around the perimeter of Ballale were well hit. TBF bombs crossed the runway, and the bombs from the B-24's walked right down the Ballale runway.

The SBD's made their drops from 1,500-2,000 feet over the target at 1025. Fifteen Zeros were observed over Moila point, SW of Bougainville, but did not close. Eight to ten others were seen over Fauro Island at 7,000 feet. AA fire was of medium intensity and accurate.

Lieutenant McClurg's motor cut out on him at 26,000 feet over Ballale and he nosed down, attempting to get it started. He got it running but it was running roughly at 15,000 feet and he hit Choiseul, thinking he was going to have to make an emergency landing.

Passing over Fauro, he observed two dark slate grey
Zekes with rusty red meat balls at 2,500 feet, in front
of him. He slid down on them and knocked down both in
one continuous run—both going into the water without
smoking or burning.

Lieutenant Begert reports that he observed a large
cloud of dust on the west end of the Kahili strip as
though a number of planes was taking off. However, as
there were no planes on the Kahili strip, he wonders if
this might be done as a ruse to make it appear that
planes were taking off.

Lieutenant Emrich pancaked at 1010, sick, and the
rest of the pilots landed safely at 1145.

*   *   *

(AIRCRAFT ACTION REPORT)

At 0900, 3 divisions of F4U's from VMF-214 took off to
act as medium cover for an SBD strike on AA positions
on Ballale.

Assisting in the SBD cover were 24 P-39's close down.
Coordinated in the strike were 12 TBF's, covered by 8
P-40's New Zealand, and 12 F4U's from VMF-221 --- and
27 B-24's covered by 16 P-38's.

Rendezvous with the SBD's was made at 0925, 12,000 feet
over Baniata Pt., Rendova.

The formation proceeded directly up to Wilson Strait to
Fauro Island, turning L and coming back to Ballale from
N to S.

They were over the target at 1025, going down to 1500-
2000 feet for their drops.

VMF-214 Corsairs, circling Ballale at 22,000 to 25,000
feet, observed 15 Zeros at their same altitude over
Moila Pt., S.W. of Bougainville. The Zeros did not
close.

Eight to ten other Zeros were observed over Fauro
Island at 7,000 feet.

AA was medium intensity, accurate. Lt. Mullen observed
what he thought to be a TBF crash in the water 1 mile

off the west tip of Ballale. No one had time to get out.

Our pilots report and excellent all around job of bombing done by all striking planes. The B-24's bombs walked right down the length of the strip.

Lt. McClurg's motor cut out on him over Ballale and he nosed over, attempting to get it started. He got it going, but running rough, at 15,000 and headed for Choiseul, thinking he was going to have to make an emergency landing.

Passing over Fauro Island, he observed two planes out in front, at 2,500 feet, climbing. They were dark, slate colored Zeros (Zekes), with rusty, red meatballs.

McClurg slid down on them and they apparently never saw him coming.

Coming in at high 6 o'clock on the wingman, McClurg opened fire at 800 Yards and saw his tracers dropping under the Zero. He kept the trigger down, closed, eased back on the stick, and pulled his fire right through the fuselage of the Zero.

The Jap plane circled slightly to the right, nosed over and crashed into the water, just off Kasiki Island.

Continuing on his run, Mc Clurg turned slightly to the left - throttled back to keep from over-running, and came down on the section leader from high 6 o'clock. He opened fire at 250 Yards and again pulled his fire through the cockpit. The Jap plane nosed over and crashed into the water. He heard someone call on the radio, "Did you see those two planes go in?"

Neither plane smoked or burned, indicating the pilots were probably both killed.

His motor again quit on him so McClurg nursed his plane over to Choiseul and followed the coast down, expecting to have to make a water landing at any time. However, he was able to pancake at his own base without mishap.

Lt. Begert reports that he observed a huge cloud of dust on the W end of Kahili strip, as though a number of planes were taking off, although there were no planes on the strip. He wonders if this might be done

```
as  a  ruse  to  make  it  appear  that  planes  were  taking
off.
```

```
REPORT PREPARED BY:            AUTHORIZED BY:
Frank E. Walton, Jr. 1ˢᵗ. Lt.  Gregory Boyington, Maj.
ACI  VMF-214                   C.O., VMF-214
```

A couple interesting things about the combat report here, which further illustrates how different writings are different memories... The combat report mentions me throttling back, which I am sure I didn't do. I wish I had the need to throttle back in that instance! Also, the combat report doesn't mention anything about my landing incident. So long as there were no major injuries and the plane was salvageable, things like that (and there were many of them) didn't often make it onto paper; it wasn't considered part of the combat interaction with the enemy.

I can't even claim that we knew it at the time, but our persistence was wearing down the Japanese. With the comparative strengths at 1:1, the Japanese were beginning to shy away from confrontations. They preferred to fight us when they could lure us into a skirmish where they had a superior numerical advantage or a sucker punch, and would almost never come near us when we outnumbered them. (That said, the truth was that we rarely outnumbered them). As the Allies kept fixing things day after day such that the Japanese were always feeding their squadrons more breakfasts than lunches, this meant that the Japanese couldn't sustain fights for too long with themselves in the numerical advantage.

I was starting to feel "on top of the world" for another reason by this time, too. I started as an outcast within the Black Sheep—nobody jumped at the chance to fly with McClurg in the early days because I had so few fighter hours. And, as I have mentioned, I can't say I blamed them. But I had a few scores under my belt now. People would talk to me. And I was actually flying combat as the wingman of the C.O. I don't think I was getting an ego problem; I was just so happy to have gained the acceptance of the guys.

The combat report above was for the morning flight on October 18, 1943. During an afternoon flight, Pappy flew again and scored another Zeke...

WAR DIARY, VMF-214.

- -

C-O-N-F-I-D-E-N-T-I-A-L:

COMBAT REPORT

DATE: 18 October, 1943.

MISSION: Fighter sweep to Kahili.

TIME: Take-off, 1530; Rendezvous,   1535;
                        Strike, 1550

FORCES ENGAGED:

Own: 12 F4U's, VMF-214

Boyington	Begert	Olander
Tucker	Hill	Matheson
Case	Ashmun	Mullen
Sims	Magee	Harper

Enemy: 20 Zekes

CONTACT:

Altitude: 6,000 feet.
Location: Between Kahili and Ballale.
Time: 1550

RESULTS:

Enemy Losses: Boyington.... 1 Zeke
              Olander...... 1 Zeke
              Magee........ 3 Zekes
              Hill......... 1 Zeke
              Case......... 1 Zeke
              Mullen....... 1 Zeke
              Harper....... 1 probable Zeke.
              Sims......... 1 probable Zeke.

TOTAL: 8 Zekes, 2 probable Zekes.

Our Losses: None.

NARRATIVE ACCOUNT :

Twelve F4U's, led by Major Boyington, took off at
1330 on a fighter sweep to Kahili. Joining up over the

strip, they headed for Vella Lavella and were joined
there by 8 F4U's from VMF-221.

The 20 planes proceeded up to Kara airfield, circling
at 15,000 feet and receiving AA fire of medium
intensity—low at first and then extremely accurate.
They circled Kara once and then circled Kahili twice,
receiving more and closer AA all the time.

At first none of the 60 planes on Kahili took off,
then about 20 did take off and climbed as Major
Boyington took his formation down in big "S" turns to
11,000 feet to meet them.

The fight started at 1450 at 6,000 feet half-way
between Kahili and Ballale and ranged down to 2,000
feet. A few black Haps were sighted and 1 Tony—brown
with white stripes and white tail.

Lieutenant Case received a 7-7 shell through his
helmet, splitting his scalp for about an inch. The
bullet lodged in his gun sight.

Lieutenant Tucker, separated from the rest of his
formation, could not relocate them because his radio
failed to function. He went down low over the
Shortlands looking for strafing targets.

Tucker made a west to east run across Shortland
Island, between Faisi Island and Korovo Point,
thoroughly strafing a bivouac area containing tents and
personnel. He continued on and strafed a gun
emplacement, expending 1,400 rounds of ammunition in
the run. After he was one half mile past the AA
positions, he saw big splashes in the water under him
as the heavy shells fell short.

All our planes returned here safely and pancaked at
1745.

This was Major Boyington's fourteenth Zero since 14
Sept.; Lt. Magee's seventh and two probables, and Lt.
Case's eight. Lieutenant Tucker reported he thought he
saw tanks on Moila Pt.

It wasn't easy by any means. Many of us had dysentery, which
is a South Pacific form of laxative. Runs to the latrine are frequent
in a man with dysentery, and if the path isn't perfectly clear... That
same man ends up in the surf, doing some "spontaneous laundry."

Fortunately, there were no ladies on the island with us. Unfortunately, there were no ladies on the island with us. We all had foot fungus, too. Skin would crack and bleed. With feet in such condition, trips into the salt water were exercises in pain. But we were succeeding. Even if we didn't quite understand the full degree at the time, we were doing it. We took our lumps, but our pilots tended to come back from their missions. The Japanese, I imagine, were encountering a surplus of clothing. We had made it. We weren't worried about being replacement pilots any more. Difficult as it was sometimes, we had settled in to life as a squadron. We were a group, and we were doing our group duty. Perhaps now is a good time to let on a bit more about the lighter side of life during non-flying hours. It wasn't all drudgery...

Date and location unknown. Leisure time while not flying. Upper left is McClurg. Rear of Doc Reames's head visible upper middle. Lower L-R is Sims, Fisher, Bolt, Mullen. Pappy is at end of table. Olander at lower right. (Bourgeois collection)

There were local natives who did our laundry for a small fee. They kept the laundry separated by adding small stitches of colored thread inside; one red stitch was Smith, while two red stitches was Jones, etc. There was something at the top and center of the coconut tree which produced a very tender cocunut-tasting substance. It wasn't the same as coconut meat, but tasted similar and was considered a sort of candy of the South Pacific. We also hunted lobsters. This required at least 2 people working as a team: at night, one person would take a torch and challenge lobsters near the water's edge. A second person with a burlap bag tied to the end of a pole would position themselves nearby. The lobsters would always retreat from the light of the torch. They would walk backwards, into the open mouth of the burlap bag. They were vivid green and huge, but tasted just like the "American" lobster we know of: delicious. Toward the end of the combat tour, we also had a pig roast. A wild pig was caught, and a fire pit was dug and lined with rocks. A huge layer of palm fronds was placed above and below the fire. The moisture from these would steam the pig over many hours. You might think the meat from a wild pig would be tough, but cooked this way, it melted in your mouth.

Date and location unknown. Begert (L) and Ewing begin a pig hunt. (Bourgeois Collection)

After the mission of October 18, 1943, we were just days away from completing our first combat tour. At about four o'clock in the morning on October 19, 1943, Pappy entered our tent, asking

"Which of you clowns wants to go with me to Kara for a little going away present?" As I remember, there were more than enough volunteers. Reluctantly, but happily at the same time, I was one of them. Happy to be one of Boyington's boys, but also wondering why the hell I volunteered for this stupid mission as I sat in a clammy Corsair, waiting to taxi out.

The target was same as we had done several times before; a detachment of four of us would fly out; we'd split into pairs with two of us hitting Kahili, and the other two hitting Kara. This was supposed to be done right at dawn, as a little surprise for the Japanese, to show them that we hadn't forgotten where they lived (since yesterday). I almost never made it to our R&R in Sydney. But I think this time I'll show the combat reports first, and give you my version afterward. It's another good illustration that not absolutely everything gets into the combat reports...

Date unknown. Over enemy territory – the Japanese airstrip at Kara is seen in lower right. (McClurg collection)

WAR DIARY, VMF-214.

- -

C-O-N-F-I-D-E-N-T-I-A-L:

19 October, 1943.

At 0450, a strafing hop on Kara and Kahili airdromes. Boyington, McClurg, Ashmun and Magee took off. They ran into heavy weather over Vella Lavella, and captain Ashmun became separated. Ashmun flew on up over north Choiseul and circled for a time in instruments in order not to strike too soon. Coming down, intending to circle onto Kara (Ashmun and Magee were to strafe Kara, and Boyington and McClurg were to hit Kahili), Ashmun found he was over Fauro, too far off shore to get to Kara, so he made a strafing run at 40 feet, on the length of the Ballale strip at 0600, thoroughly spraying the revetment area south of the strip. He received no AA fire of any kind.

Too close to observe the results, he came down past the edge of the Shortlands and noticed an empty black rubber raft 20 miles from Baga Island on a bearing of 290 degrees, in midst of several oil slicks. Ashmun pancaked at 0630.

Boyington, McClurg and Magee continued up over the north tip of Choiseul, flying with their lights on unable to stay together in the heavy weather. Boyington nosed over, turned out his lights and disappeared from view.

Magee and McClurg continued north up the east coast of Bougainville and went down to 2,000 feet, then to 800 feet and circled inland around Luluai Point. There were a lot of clouds there, so they went up to 1,500 feet and circled around a Villa north of the Kara strip to be sure they located it. They went right down to 40 feet, into the clearing at the end of the strip and made a strafing run from west to east at 0605.

They observed the tower off to the right, about 75 yards down. It had a light in it. They held their fire until they saw something, opened up on 5 planes parked on the east end of the runway—spraying them thoroughly. Looking back, they saw the planes burning.

No AA fire was received. The two planes then went along the Shortlands looking for barges. They circled

to west and received heavy caliber fire of medium
intensity from AA and coastal guns. They pancaked at
0645.

Major Boyington went over Kahili strip, but didn't
see anything. He circled and made another run and
strafed 3 bombers on inland end of the strip—destroying
all. Returned here and pancaked safely.

Now, allow me to fill you in on what really happened... It
wasn't too much different from the war report; just a little extra.
For the record, my airplane ran just fine. As a matter of fact, it ran
like a bear. Originally, Pappy and I were supposed to hit Kahili,
while Ashmun and Magee hit Kara. We got good at improvising, as
Ashmun became separated and Pappy disappeared to do his own
thing; Magee and I wound up going after Kara. We had the benefit
of lousy weather, which was actually good in a way because it
helped to preserve the element of surprise: the Japanese were not
likely to expect us on such a rotten morning. As luck would have it
on this morning, the poor weather actually added to our precision, as
it forced us to go out a bit further and find a landmark, which we
didn't normally do. The result was that we came over the Kara
airstrip very well lined up, throttles to the firewall at about forty,
feet as the report says.

It was a terrific strafing run. I sighted in on some planes, and let
them have it. The run was perfect, and I was mesmerized by the
sparks and flames as my guns hit the bombers sitting idle on the
strip. I kept my focus on the targets, with my finger on the trigger,
sending burst after burst. That was my mistake... At the rate we
were travelling, we had at most a few seconds of good target
sighting. Among the concentration, a thought flashed through my
mind; TOWER!

I snapped my eyes upward, and sure enough, the lighted Kara
tower was just in front of me, to the right. Had I not rolled my
airplane, the tower would have taken off my right wing. With a
violent bank to the left, I went by the tower with what I would
estimate to be less than six feet to spare! In the instant before I
banked, I actually saw a fleeting glimpse of a figure in the tower,
who appeared to be diving for cover. I think I even closed my eyes
in the seconds after I passed by and leveled the plane back to
normal, thinking "OhmyGawd!"

That's pilot error for you. I almost killed myself because I became fixated on a target and stopped scanning my eyes. All said and done, that particular maneuver probably only helped to further impress our image on the Japanese, as the poor fella in the tower must have thought I was totally fearless, infinitely capable, or completely crazy. I'd bet the little guy had some wash of his own to do in the surf that morning.

Recovering just in time to avoid colliding with the Japanese tower wasn't the end of our action, either. McGee and I recovered together and headed back out over open water at the end of the airstrip. We roared out at minimum altitude, with our engines at full power. The Japanese shore batteries had awakened by then, and opened up on us. They would have liked to hit us directly, but their intent was more to shoot in front of us. Their hopes were that one of us would fly into the huge splashes of water caused by their large caliber projectiles. Neither of us succumbed to the shells or the water, but the splashes were immense - just like the explosions often seen as special effects in movies.

I had wanted to include some writing devoted more specifically to the Corsair early on, but it seemed more appropriate to cover some combat first. I have looked back at times and felt very grateful for the things that enabled me to make it home from the war. I thank God. I credit Pappy, without whom I surely think I would not be here. The Corsair is also on that list.

In many ways, the Corsair was just as much a Black Sheep as any of us were, albeit for different reasons. The reason the Marines got the Corsair was because the Navy didn't want it at first—it had some characteristics that made the Navy people nervous and they initially chose a more conventional aircraft (the Grumman Hellcat) for their carrier needs. The Corsair was also just as much a Black Sheep as any of us were in another sense of the term; she was a member of our squadron. We rode her into battle, and she got us home, time after time. Ground crews and grateful pilots were amazed on many occasions upon inspecting a battle damaged Corsair, and wondered how it managed to limp home.

Fortunately, my dilemma of writing about the Corsair need not be a terrible one because there is so much material already in print about the mighty F4U. The man who was test pilot for the F4U program wrote his own memoirs about what it was like. The book is entitled *Whistling Death - The Test Pilot's Story Of The F4U*

Corsair, authored by Boone Guyton. I never met Boone, but have read his book and recommend it highly to anyone interested in the F4U Corsair. The book is also an excellent personal story of how times were on the home front during World War Two; I think it would appeal even to those not interested specifically in the Corsair. Boone didn't have anybody shooting at him, but he had just as many near-death experiences as any of us did. At the time I write this text, Boone's book is back in print after many years—the ultimate compliment for a job well done. Another good book for the Corsair fan is *Corsair - The F4U in World War II and Korea* by Barrett Tillman. I believe this book is still in print also. Barrett's book is more a story of the Corsair's life, without specific dedication to any one man or fighting unit. There are many other books dedicated either partially or wholly to the Corsair. I don't mean to discredit any of them by not mentioning them here. I chose to name two books that I think will give the reader a good background on our bent-winged bird.

One thing I have learned for sure is that there always seem to be conflicting stories when the greatness of anything is recounted, whether it be a fighter plane or the action in a football game. There is always the story of "the fish that got away." With this in mind, I desire not to split hairs, but to give the story from a Black Sheep's point of view.

That said, I'll go into a little description of what the Corsair was, and what it meant to us. The Corsair represented a great feat of "thinking outside the box" in late 1930's engineering design. The people at Chance Vought Aircraft Corporation, (maker of the Corsair, long since sold and now part of the history within United Technologies/Sikorsky Aircraft Corporation) decided to take a fresh approach at creating a modern fighter airplane, and they did a great job at not simply offering their version of what others were already doing. Rather, the Corsair was to be something new. Chance Vought Corp. wanted to lead, and chose to begin their design with power: the engine.

Vought Corporation teamed up with engine manufacturer Pratt and Whitney (still in business today, a major supplier of jet engines), and began design of what would become the F4U Corsair around a new engine P&W was developing. The new engine was an air cooled radial type, with eighteen cylinders arranged in two rows of nine. It displaced 2,804 cubic inches (about 45.7 liters!), and eventually entered production developing just over two thousand horsepower. (For those not familiar with cubic inches and liters, the Corsair's engine size amounted to roughly eight of today's typical full-size pickup truck engines.) For a time, it was the most powerful engine available.

The rest of the airplane was essentially designed around the engine. First step was to mate the engine to a propeller. To harness the engine's high power, the prop ended up being a very large one (almost fourteen feet in diameter), and this created some other requirements which ended up being the Corsair's signature. In order to provide enough clearance so the large propeller could turn without hitting the ground (or the carrier deck), the landing gear would have needed to be very long. But long landing gear tends to be weak, or very heavy if designed with enough strength. To creatively solve this issue, the Chance Vought design team decided to lower the wings. For attachment to the fuselage, they bent the inner parts of the wings upward, to meet the fuselage at a right angle, and that was the origin of the Corsair's unmistakable inverted gull wing shape. This was an aerodynamically efficient solution as well, because it turns out that having the wing leave the fuselage at a right angle is "cleanest" for airflow reasons. From there, the fine engineering team at Vought put many other features into place "like dominoes," and provided for a clean and very sound overall package. Proceeding (and keeping with our idea of presenting the Corsair in short form here), they basically made the rest of the airplane as small and smooth as they could, without exaggerating anything, and the Corsair was born. She was at the same time beautiful, reliable, strong (both offensively and defensively), and fast. She carried three .50 caliber machine guns in each wing, and these were typically aimed so that they all hit the same point about 800 feet in front of the airplane. Having all six .50 caliber guns hit the same point provided a huge amount of firepower energy; with a good strafing run where the pilot knew just how to sweep that point across the target, you could cut a boxcar in half. On the topic of speed, the Corsair was, for a time, the world's fastest fighter; it was the first military fighter to be clocked at over 400 MPH in level flight. Remember; this was back in WWII before television! If you could go 400 MPH, you had either been shot out of a cannon, or you were in a Corsair. (Truth is that other aircraft broke the 400 MPH mark shortly after the F4U)

As a single seat fighter airplane, the Corsair was comparatively large. I think that, combined with its different shape, tended to give too many people the impression that the F4-U was an entirely different animal. I don't think the Corsair was so much of a completely different "species" of airplane; it flew smoothly and easily, much like many other single seaters of the era. In fact, you can read in many places that the Corsair is thought by some to perhaps have even flown a little easier and better than many of the others. Inside, the Corsair was actually fairly comfortable. The cockpit was meant for business, but well laid out, with sufficient room. However there were a couple things about the Corsair that were different (or more exaggerated) when compared to other planes, and I think these are where so much of the talk arises...

First, the Corsair was different in that its cockpit was placed a good deal farther back along the fuselage than was typical. Said differently, the Corsair had much more nose sticking out in front of the pilot than other airplanes. (There was more nose because there was more engine, and also a very large central fuel tank to feed that big engine.) In the air, that extra nose wasn't a bad thing at all. Some even thought it was a good thing, giving more ability for the pilot to look down the long nose and use the airplane itself as an orientation sight. Some also thought the long nose helped to give a feeling of security, in that the pilot didn't feel as if he was stuck so far out in front of everything (and hence distanced a bit, however meaningless it might have been, from oncoming fire or debris). Ah, but the long nose on the ground could be terrifying during takeoff or landing. The Corsair is a taildragger (as were most fighters of that era). That means the nose points upward when the aircraft is sitting (or moving) on the ground. It is true with many taildraggers that the pilot cannot see out the front of the aircraft very well when on the ground, and this was particularly so with the Corsair. When taxiing the aircraft on the ground, the pilot has no useful front vision, and it is really not practical to lean out the side of the cockpit far enough to see anything. To get a glance directly ahead while taxiing, you had to turn the plane partially to the right and look left, then turn it partially to the left and look right, etc. This was done back and forth, back and forth, referred to as taxiing with a series of "S" turns. Once in the air, this was no problem and hence presented no limitation at all in combat. But the first few hundred feet of a takeoff run could be intimidating, as you had to reach a speed of about 50 MPH before the tail would come up, and the nose would come down a little so the pilot could finally see out the front. Similarly, the last part of a landing roll could be hairy, as front vision is lost after the pilot slows below about 50MPH. In essence, we maneuvered the airplane to the runway, swung a bit sideways to get one last look down the strip, then straightened out. Next, we would rev the engine and do the appropriate checks, and hurtle down the strip for the first few hundred feet while looking out the sides of the airplane to center ourselves. Some guys had a real problem with that; others did not.

The second "different" thing about the Corsair was an inherent characteristic of its high power which I mentioned earlier, and was something that every Corsair pilot had to watch out for, no matter how confident or competent he was: it was torque. Time for a quick physics lesson here... The stuff that moves the Corsair (or any powered airplane, for that matter) through the air is thrust. The airplane takes air and blows this air toward its rear. That is the "action." Well, as some of us might recall, for every action there is an equal and opposite reaction; then for however hard the airplane is capturing air and blowing it backward, the airplane is getting pushed forward. This is true with a prop or a jet, just spoken about in slightly different terms. The Corsair was very fast because it had a very powerful engine which could turn its large propeller very forcefully and push large amounts of air backwards very fast. Keep that thought in mind as we focus on what the propeller really does... The propeller takes a turning motion from the engine and converts it to a thrust of air. The more thrust of air we want, the harder (and hence faster) we turn the propeller. As you're sitting in the cockpit of a Corsair watching the prop turn, the blades are coming up the left side, over the top, and down the right side (clockwise). Another way to say that is to say the engine is forcing the propeller to spin clockwise. Coming back to that thought of equal and opposite reaction, it is also true to say that the engine is also then trying to make the entire airplane spin (roll) counterclockwise. And here we have the second different thing, the "wicked witch" within the Corsair (or any high powered propeller airplane)... At high power settings, the engine's huge amount of torque trying to spin the propeller would also try to spin the entire airplane over in the opposite direction. The only thing to overcome this was if the plane's flying surfaces (wings) had enough air passing over them to allow them to sufficiently counteract that huge torque. Said differently, if the pilot applied full power at low flying speeds, the Corsair would start to roll left, and there was nothing he could do about it (except maybe reduce power!). This ruined many a landing, where a pilot would realize that he had come in short, or was going too slow, then ram the throttle full forward in an attempt to go around again, only to have the plane go out of control. Most often with that scenario, the pilot had much less than a hundred feet of altitude, and the plane would have about perfectly enough time to get onto its back before it hit the ground, so that the first thing to bear the impact was the cockpit... Hence the reason that mistake was committed only one time by most pilots. The takeoff roll wasn't much safer: the landing gear being in contact with the ground did help to keep the plane from twisting over (dipping the left wing), but the pilot who lifted too quickly and didn't hold his Corsair on the ground for a good takeoff roll to get some speed up was often in for a terrible surprise as he pulled back on the stick. It was a matter of knowing and respecting the airplane's characteristics, which were not unmanageable, but were horribly unforgiving in the case of an error. The torque effect also played a distracting role against making good gunnery runs in a high powered propeller airplane; it was just one more thing that made it difficult to hold a target in one's sights. As a little piece of trivia, jets operate on the same thrust principle I described above, but they do not have the torque effect, because the torque is all borne within the jet engine itself, and not by the airframe of the plane.

Let us not leave the impression that the Corsair is a defect-riddled war horse. It is a fine combat aircraft, was well ahead of its time, and recognized by some as possibly the best overall fighter of its era. Its huge power gave it not only speed, but also the ability to carry a huge bomb load. This helped the Corsair to be among the first to act as a fighter-bomber, a versatility which proved to be a great asset in WWII, and which was specifically focused on in future fighters. The Corsair was highly maneuverable for its size. We couldn't out-turn the Japanese, but we weren't that far off their performance, and we were much more heavily armored. We could take a hundred times more pounding than they could. And the Corsair was deceptively fast for its size. I can't say enough about what that speed meant. If we were in trouble, we could turn tail and run home, knowing we wouldn't be caught. But the converse was also to the Corsair's advantage; a Japanese plane could do many creative things in fighting a Corsair, but he could never choose to run away because the Corsair could simply "reel him in" and blast him out of the sky. I can't speak from the enemy's point of view, but I can imagine that the Corsair might have been a bit of an enigma. As I commented earlier, something coming at me with a propeller arc as huge as that of the Corsair must have been intimidating. To the technically knowledgeable opposing pilot, that was also a dead giveaway of very high horsepower contained inside its cowling. On the other hand, after first sight of the Corsair's size, I don't think I would have assumed the plane to be as fast or as maneuverable as it was. I'm sure this must have come as a horrifying surprise to many Japanese pilots.

The Corsair was a great combination of refinement, smoothness, high power, ruggedness, and sheer beauty. We were lucky to have it, we were happy to have it, and I don't think there is one of us today who doesn't wish that he could climb in and buzz the strip just once more in that beautiful bird. I still think Pappy said it best in his book; "She was a sweet flyin' baby if there ever was one."

Getting back to the war, and rounding out our first tour, we flew some bomber escorts on October 20, and then ferried our fighters to Vella Lavella on the twenty-first. We did not fly missions again until we left for R&R on November third and fourth.

First Rest Trip To Sydney

Our trip was almost over before it started; as we began to taxi out, a jeep was seen heading toward us in a hurry. Boyington had gotten himself on the wrong side of some higher up, who was coming in an attempt to stop us. Pappy quickly poked his head into the cockpit and gave some fervent advice, shortly after which the transport's engines revved up and our taxiing quickened. We made it to the runway, and soon were roaring along on a takeoff roll.

Whether it was pre-planned, or reaction to Pappy's input, the gents in the cockpit decided they would impress us with a very steep takeoff and hard, climbing turn. We all held hard to our seats for what seemed like an eternity, and when they finally leveled off and seemed to set a course, Pappy got up and again headed into the cockpit to have a talk with them. We had survived too many Japanese bullets to let something odd like a transport accident take us out.

Aside from that, the journey contained many of the same elements as the long trip to the South Pacific did: heavy fuel vapors and sick passengers. There was a crude restroom built into the rear of the transport plane. I think it was basically just a big container, enclosed in a little room, gross as that may sound. I don't remember who it was, but one of us succumbed to the noxious fuel vapors slightly before the rest. He headed into the toilet stall, shut the door, and stayed there. Of course, the poor guy in the stall was just the first and not the only one. After a short period of time, there were others of us who would rather use the rest room than leave a mess elsewhere in the cabin. We began to bang on the little door, half hoping it would rattle off its hinges. Our pleas went unanswered.

After a while, Pappy emerged from the cockpit again. They had finished their discussion, and I think the pilots may have had a little liquid refreshment up there as well. Upon discovering our dilemma (and probably suffering from it a bit, himself), Pappy came up with a quick solution. He unlatched a fire extinguisher from the wall, stuck its hose under the toilet door, and let loose. A few short seconds later, out came a dust covered, green looking Black Sheep, and the others got to use the toilet (also dust covered). It is funny, but I don't remember who it was that got "extinguished." I remember the figure of a man, covered in extinguisher dust.

At last, we were within sight of friendly land, ecstatic to be on leave, and eager to be on our way to see whatever was ahead of us. There would be nobody shooting at us, fine food, and ladies!

Now for a bit more about Australia... Its location was well within the intended sphere of dominance of the Japanese. Guadalcanal, where we had just fought our combat tour, wasn't just an outpost we traveled to and fought from; Guadalcanal had been taken from the Japanese in fierce fighting before we got there. The Australians felt a huge sense of relief at seeing the Japanese advances stemmed before their Aussie country was taken, and they credited Americans in part for this. So the country was very friendly to us. I think I have even seen Australian posters urging their people to show the Allied forces a good time, in thanks.

One of the first memories I have of Sydney was the cars. Because gasoline was being rationed at the time, it was popular to have some sort of coal conversion contraption on many cars. This appeared as a furnace or something, often mounted to a frame at the back of the vehicle. The furnace fed a tank at the top of the car, which is what they ran on.

We passed a sheep butchering and tanning factory, which had an awful stench. We remarked at the stink, going from nauseating gasoline fumes aboard the transport plane, to nauseating rotten fumes at the sheep farm. We joked that we would prefer to get right back on the transport and go back to square one, but we eventually arrived at a nice hotel. Once there, they grouped us with who we'd like to spend our eight days with, and assigned us quarters. I think it was me, Magee, Hill and Heier. We didn't actually stay in the hotel, but in the upstairs apartment of somebody's home. We had beds, a bathroom, a kitchen, and a living room. Having just spent many hours in a fume filled transport plane, one of the first experiences we had there was with the toilet... They had a toilet tank that was mounted high up on the wall, and it fed the toilet below. There was a chain that you pulled, and it emptied the tank and flushed the toilet. Well, one of us pulled the chain a little too hard, and it in turn pulled the tank partially off the wall. This, of course, occurred with much terrible noise and splashing water sounds, which immediately garnered us the attention of the landlord. Not wanting to get kicked out of the place, we managed to smooth things over and get the assembly patched together.

As fast as we could, we headed downtown. Our heads were filled with thoughts of all the things we could get there. Among the strongest thoughts was food. Think of all the foods we could get, and nothing was powdered from a box! We could have steaks, fresh vegetables, seafood, beer! Their beer was more potent than American beer, and they sold it in quarts. After a couple quarts of that stuff, we were pretty tipsy. That, combined with the fresh oysters we ate and the fact that we slobbered the ketchup sauce all over ourselves, made us look like walking wounded.

Full of confidence and relatively unaware of our condition, we headed out from the bar and down the street. Almost immediately, we spotted four Australian women. One was a gorgeous redhead, who I outlined as "mine" before we even approached them. Our service uniforms did the trick, stained as they were, and we opened some conversation. We told them we would gladly take them to dinner if they would show us what and where a good dinner was. Their recommendation was "stike and aigs," which, after several replays we learned was a nice cut of beef with a couple fried eggs atop it. This was one of their favorites, but very expensive and hence something the locals didn't get too much of. As this was the beginning of our R&R, we had plenty of money and bought the 4 ladies dinner. We made instant friends, and spent much time with them.

Money wasn't the only item of interest we brought along, for we had listened well to the wisdom of others back in the war; as items of barter, we knew to pack our parachute sacks full of cigarettes and toilet paper. Cigarettes were expensive in Australia. They had toilet paper, but theirs was akin to our gift wrapping paper. Even our military issue stuff was the greatest thing to those ladies. One rule of our living quarters was that we must have ladies out by midnight, and we respected that particular rule. One evening when it came time for the girls to go, we got up and offered to get their blazers for them, which had been piled on one of our beds. We became suspicious when they all declined our courtesy in perfect unison, offering to get their own jackets. Turns out they had been taking trips to the bathroom all night, and sneaking into the bedroom to stuff a roll of toilet paper into their jacket sleeves. Rather than become upset, we offered them a large sack of the coveted items, and all had a good laugh about it.

We concentrated largely on consuming vast amounts of fresh food, so happy to have access to real eggs and milk and steaks and vegetables. I can't say I saw it with my own eyes, but rumor has it that (I think it was Walton) began his each and every morning in Sydney by eating a dozen eggs and all the trimmings.

Our morning rendezvous point was a bar called the "Snake Pit," where we would all meet between 9 and 10 AM. Some of our boys would come from one part of town, others would come from another area, depending on where their quarters were. This was often a time to recount the events of the previous night, or to join heads on plans for the day. We could also be found at the Snake Pit on some evenings. The head barmaid there was a quick witted lady named "Frieda." She was a great entertainer, and she knew how to keep intoxicated servicemen from getting out of hand. I often wonder whatever became of Frieda. I wish I had a picture of her to place here.

Part of the group proceedings were invariably to review our partners and see who had the fairest company. Our executive officer, Stan Bailey, seemed to have some magic ability to attract goddesses. We heard rumor that he had paired up with an Australian beauty, and in fact she dropped him off one morning at the Snake Pit. She was a tall, slender blonde, as nice as anyone ever imagined. We all got a look at her, and there was a round of congratulatory jeers to Bailey after we thought she was out of ear shot. He aroused our curiosity by reacting sheepishly, rather than proudly. After some needling, he recounted the previous evening... They were to remain together for the entire evening (this occurred, even in the 1940's, but was much more scandalous and much less discussed than in the modern day), and time came to turn in for the night. As the story went, Stan got into bed first, and his companion finished her ritual of washing and preparing for slumber, as ladies often do. She placed a glass of water on the night stand, then got in bed and put her teeth in the glass. The water in Australia was not of good quality, and was rumored to cause tooth problems. Pappy made some comments that I chose not to include here, and we didn't inquire further about Stan's experiences.

Chris Magee and I stuck together quite a bit, and one of the things we did was to rent a car to do some sightseeing. We rented a very small car, which had the coal burner apparatus on it. Both of us wanted to go sightseeing, but neither wanted to drive. We both wanted to ride as passenger, partially because the car looked like some sort of cobbled up contraption with its apparatus on the roof and rear bumper, and partially because neither of us was sure we could negotiate Australia's motorways very well (they drive on the opposite side of the road.) Eventually, I found myself in the passenger seat, and Magee rounded our very first corner in the oncoming lane of traffic, at which time we met (but did not collide with) an oncoming Aussie native. We each waited at a standstill, hoping for the other to yield, but it did not happen. Magee, (who, I might add, was from the north side of Chicago), began to lose his cool and said to me, "I think I'm gonna get out and cold cock this guy." I responded, "Now wait a minute, Chris... We've only been here a short time and we don't want to get into trouble over this." Magee replied, "Yeah, but what the hell is his problem?" I explained, "We're driving on the wrong side of the road!" Magee said to me, "I am not!" At about that time, the oncoming Aussie pulled up next to us and inquired, in his down-under accent, "I say, old boy, what are your plans?" Well, that just broke us up. Magee and I laughed, then the Aussie laughed. The three of us went into a nearby watering hole and had some more of their 4.2 beer, and we became friends.

While in the watering hole, our newly found friend gave us some timely advice; he relayed to us a story, told to him by an old man who was a barfly. He asked where we rented our car, and we told him such and such place around the corner. Nodding, the Aussie told us that the rental car outfit was in the habit of conducting their business in a rather underhanded manner: they would rent a car to unsuspecting American military personnel. They would then return in the middle of the night to where the military personnel were staying (which we had to reveal in order to take the car), and they would steal the car. While the panicked American was frantically searching for the car, they would rent it again to a second party, thus doubling their revenues. We proceeded, forewarned with this knowledge. Sure enough, on the second night, our car disappeared.

On the next morning, we got someone else who had a car to deliver us back to the rental company; this was a more appropriate opportunity for Magee's north Chicago temperament.   He approached the clerk at the desk, identified us as patrons, informed him that we had seen the car taken, then promptly ordered the clerk to produce a car or else have himself and his entire establishment torn to pieces. Magee was not an overly imposing figure, but had a disconcerting air of seriousness and power about him.   The clerk indicated that there may have been a "little misunderstanding," and produced another car.

We spent the days sightseeing on nothing specific, really just whatever came into our minds.   We got around town a bit, and enjoyed the company of our lady friends according to their work schedules.

We left our critical bartering items in Sydney as intended, where several ladies were enjoying cigarettes and comfortable toilet paper, compliments of the Black Sheep. This left us with available cargo space for the return trip, which of course was to be occupied by as much good beer as we could get aboard the transport.   When we showed up and began loading our stuff onto the transport plane, we were met with a couple of smirking security officers who informed us that our cargo was too heavy and something would have to stay behind.   Of course, they quickly put forth the suggestion that our offending overweight cargo could be narrowed down to the beer. Some of you may have seen (I think it was Olander) explain in a recent narrative on television "History Channel" how we solved the problem: we drank the beer and left the bottles!   We endured the nauseating, numbing ride back to the war.   I suppose many of us didn't remember much of the ride, which might have actually helped.   In conscious moments, we recounted in our minds the experiences we had, the ladies we saw, and remembered our folks back home.

Second Combat Tour

Most of us came back from the Sydney trip more tired than when we left, but that was to be expected and was probably for the best. We were a bunch of Marines generally in our early to mid twenties, all in good physical shape, some in outstanding physical shape. (The pictures show you that I was one of the skinny ones. I think I weighed all of 120 pounds then.) I don't suppose anyone could have expected us to relax quietly. We didn't spend time in Sydney analyzing our plight or dreading the next tour; we just had fun, and our R&R was over before we knew it. As we made our way back to the combat area, I don't think there was much dread at all. If there was, nobody seemed to show it. The Sydney time did what it was supposed to, and I think we were all in a pretty solid state of mind. We had a pretty good fighting spirit among us, perhaps even eager to continue what we were doing. I remember my thoughts on the situation... I had started our previous combat tour as a bit of an outcast, someone nobody wanted to fly with because I had so little fighter time. By the end of the first tour, I had managed to shoot down 3 planes confirmed, and I had risen in our "gang" to the point where people weren't so reluctant to have me along on a flight any more. I had Pappy to thank for that, and the kindness of Chris Magee and Don Moore.

Upon returning, we didn't just hop into our F4-U's and fly missions; we still had to pass a test called a Snyder test in order to be deemed fit to fly fighters again. The test was a comprehensive physical and mental evaluation. Mentally, we all tested out well. But physically, not many of us passed when we got off the returning transport plane. It took about a week of rest and exercises before Doc Reames finally gave us the green light to fly again.

Our squadron roster was a bit different for the second combat tour. We received some new pilots to replace losses incurred on the first tour, and one or two of the first tour veterans (for whom our first tour as VMF-214 might have actually been their third tour, etc.) took the opportunity to go stateside. Again, a squadron is made up of people. For this, our second tour, I just happened to find Frank Walton's listing of second tour personnel while thumbing through the original combat log :

S E C R E T:

```
ROSTER OF FLIGHT ECHELON
MARINE FIGHTING SQUADRON TWO FOURTEEN


        Major Gregory BOYINGTON,   Commanding Officer.
        Major Pierre M. CARNAGEY, Executive Officer.
        Major Stanley R. BAILEY
        Major Henry S. MILLER
        Capt. George M. ASHMUN
        Capt. Fred V. AVEY
        Capt  Gelon H. DOSWELL
        Capt  Cameron "J" DUSTIN
        Capt  Marion J. MARCH
        1stLt John F. BEGERT
        1stLt John F. BOLT
        1stLt Henry M. BOURGEOIS
        1stLt Glenn L. BOWERS
        1stLt Robert M. BRAGDON
        1stLt John S. BROWN
        1stLt James E. BRUBAKER
        1stLt William N. CASE
        1stLt Rufus M. CHATHAM, JR.
        1stLt Ned J. CORMAN
        1stLt William L. CROCKER, JR.
        1stLt Warren T. EMRICH
        1stLt Bruce FFOULKES
        1stLt Don H. FISHER
        1stLt Denmark GROOVER, JR.
        1stLt Edwin A. HARPER
        1stLt William D. HEIER
        1stLt James J. HILL
        1stLt William H. HOBBS
        1stLt Herbert HOLDEN, JR.
        1stLt Alfred L. JOHNSON
        1stLt Harry C. JOHNSON
        1stLt Perry T. LANE
        1stLt Fred S. LOSCH
        1stLt Christopher L. MAGEE
        1stLt Alan D. MARKER
        1stLt Bruce J. MATHESON
        1stLt Henry A. McCARTNEY
        1stLt Robert W. McCLURG
        1stLt Donald J. MOORE
```

```
1stLt  Paul A. MULLEN
1stLt  Edwin L. OLANDER
1stLt  Roland N. RINABARGER
1stLt  Sanders S. SIMS
1stLt  Burney L. TUCKER
1stLt  Frank E. WALTON, JR., Intelligence  Officer
Lt(MC) James M. REAMES, USN, Flight Surgeon
2dLt   Harry R. BARTL
```

Some of the names above appeared also in the first combat tour of VMF-214; those are Black Sheep who served both tours. Some Black Sheep, like Bourgeois, served first tour only. Others, like Al Johnson, served second tour only. This is all spelled out neatly in appendix "A" of Walton's book, *Once They Were Eagles*.

Sheep in a Jeep: Tucker, Chatham, Avey, Harper, Bolt, Reames, Doswell, Groover, Fisher (Driver, date, location unknown) (McClurg collection)

Our second combat tour officially began on November 27, 1943. We flew orientation and training flights until about December first, then began patrol and combat again. We made use of escort missions and strafing to brush up on our knowledge of enemy territory for the first few days. I flew a mission with Boyington on December 4 in which my plane sustained some damage from Japanese anti-aircraft fire, but I made it home without incident; the Corsair was hearty. We continued our escort and strafing runs through December 16, really raising hell with the enemy by destroying supply dumps, barges, trucks, huts, etc. I'm not sure exactly why, but we didn't see much air to air combat in the first half of December. Maybe the Japanese were avoiding us, or maybe we were intentionally concentrating on the strafing.

I scored my fourth victory on a morning mission, December 17, 1943. We were flying fairly high over Rabaul harbor, and we were itching for some combat. I spotted a "Rufe" float plane far below us, and I decided to go after it. The "Rufe" was a Japanese float plane version of the vaunted "Zeke." As such, a "Rufe" was highly maneuverable as float planes went, but still a float plane burdened by the large float device hanging underneath it, and hence very vulnerable to something like an F4U. Boyington comments on this score on pg. 219 of his book, "Baa Baa Black Sheep." Following is Walton's combat report from that mission :

```
WAR DIARY, VMF-214
- - - - - - - - - - - - - - - - - - - - - - - - - - - - - - - -


                         COMBAT REPORT

DATE:    17 December, 1943

TIME: Take-off from Vella Lavella 0515; Pancake
      Torokina at 0600.  Take-off Torokina 0900; 1020
      due over Rabaul.

MISSION:    Fighter Sweep over Rabaul.

RENDEZVOUS:
      None.

FORCES ENGAGED:
      OWN                              ENEMY
      8 F4U's - VMF-214       15 Tony's, Rufes.
      8 F4U's -     222
      8 F4U's -     223
      8 F4U's -     216
      8 F6F's - VF- 40
     16 F6F's - VF- 33
     24 P-40's N.Z.

CONTACT :
      Altitude : 10,000 feet.
```

```
Location : Over Simpson Harbor, Rabaul
Time     : 11:00
```

RESULTS:
    ENEMY LOSSES: 1 Rufe destroyed - McClurg.
                2 Zekes destroyed - Moore.
    OUR LOSSES : None.

NARRATIVE ACCOUNT:

At 0515, Boyington, McClurg, Magee, Moore, Sims, Brown, Heier, Ffoulkes took off for Torokina to participate in Rabaul fighter sweep.   All planes pancaked at Torokina at 0600 for topping off tanks.
Ffoulkes nosed up on landing damaging his plane slightly.

At 0900 Boyington, McClurg, Magee, Moore, Sims, Brown, Heier, Ffoulkes (in borrowed plane), Bragdon, took off from Torokina to participate in fighter sweep over Rabaul.

There were so many planes that it was apparently impossible to get joined up so that the New Zealand P-40's proceeded on course without waiting for the join up.
Plan was for the F4U's to fly 20-26,000; the F6F's 15-20,000 and the P-40's 10-15,000.

The formation proceeded to the Northwest up the West coast of Bougainville, circling to the west to avoid a heavy front.
As they approached Rabaul all planes began to climb and Sims plane was unable to keep up so he and his wingman return to base pancaking at 1125.
Apparently the P-40's arrived over the target ahead of the rest of the flight and were engaged by a flight of Tony's.
Boyington's flight arrived over the target area at 28,000' at 1045.   30-40 fighter planes were lined up on the Lakunai strip.   Boyington fired a few rounds from 10,000 feet in an effort to get the japs to take off.
At 1100 McClurg observed a Rufe at 10,000 feet over the Harbor and went down on it in a high stern run, opening fire at 400 yards.   A huge cloud of smoke burst from the cockpit and pieces fell off it.   Then the Rufe crashed burning, into the harbor.
After patrolling for 35 minutes with no other activity Boyington's flight left the area at 1120.

A few rounds of heavy calibre AA was seen, inaccurate.

Approximately 30 ships were seen in the harbor including DD's and several large merchant ships.

The airfields in the Rabaul area seemed to be a rust color or a dark brown.

Ffoulkes and Heier were over the area at 30,000' at 1040 and patrolled for 25 minutes; returning without contact.

Bragdon off late joined up, finally with another plane and was over Rabaul at 1100.

He went down in a strafing run on Rabaul continuing alone when the other plane left him.

He leveled out at 5,000' and headed out the harbor mouth when he saw tracers going over his wings and turned around to find he'd been jumped by 6 Tonys.

He dived into a cloud, got his bearings, opened full throttle and headed for home with a setting of 2700 r.p.m. and pulling 50 inches.

The Tony's took up the chase.

They were a vivid California blue, shiny with white tails.

They had white diagonals on the wings and white diagonals, longitudinal stripes on the fuselage extending from the rear of the cockpit to the tail assembly.

The meatballs were indistinct; it was difficult to make them out against their blue background.

Roundels were definitely on the fuselage and possibly also on the upper wing surfaces.

Bragdon's plane was indicating 280 at 5000 feet and he was opening very slowly.

The Tony's pursued him for 65 miles.

Weather was good over the target.

Boyington, McClurg, Heier, Ffoulkes, Bragdon, pancaked at Cherry Blossom between 1205 - 1225. Took off from there at 1540 and pancaked here at 1630.

Moore - on way back to base made an emergency landing at Treasury - details are unknown except that he is due to return on the 19th.

Major Boyington is of the opinion that far too many fighter planes were sent on the sweep. He thinks 24 sufficient. He is also strongly of the opinion that all planes should be the same type - thus eliminating the necessity for continually checking on other planes in the sky.

All in all the sweep was not too successful since the Japs failed to accept the challenge - perhaps this was partially due to the landing which had been made at Arawe.

The period of time in early to mid-December, 1943, was actually a pretty rough one for the Black Sheep. Boyington was enduring social and political hardships, having upset one particular superior ranking officer with his nonchalance about regulations. On top of the military hassles, Pappy had begun to attract some unwanted press attention with his large number of victories. (At this point, he had six victories from his A.V.G. days, and fourteen victories from our "first" combat tour, but had yet to knock one down in the second combat tour, which we were roughly three weeks into at the time.

Date and location unknown, and the photo has seen better days. The reader will have to take our word for it, but this is Pappy, airborne somewhere over the South Pacific. (Bourgeois collection)

The pressure was really on to beat so and so's record, or to just get more. To most of the pressmen, it was a game. They had very little idea what actual combat was like, and they didn't seem to care much. To them, it was whether or not the subject was newsworthy, whether they could create headlines and feed the folks back home what they wanted; and this didn't sit well with any of us. Pappy's misfortune was to find himself in the center of it all. Things weren't going well for the Japanese by this point, and they seemed to know about us. Maybe they didn't know specifically about the Black

Sheep, (Maybe, indeed, they did, because they had spies who monitored our news, too.) but they did know Boyington. This was the time period Pappy mentions in his book *Baa Baa Black Sheep*, where he would actually call insults to them over the radio when we got over their fields, trying to get them to come up. That statement might sound hard to believe to you, figuring that nobody in a military situation would be enticed off the ground by verbal taunting if they had decided they were not going to fly. But it was true; Japanese culture was very different from ours, and honor was something hugely important to them. To remain in the presence of their peers while being ridiculed by enemy fighters for being too cowardly to come up and fight was often more than they could stand. They would send their planes up, and of course we would send them back down. But even that didn't last too long before Pappy's taunting wouldn't even bring them up. They apparently preferred to lose planes on the ground, rather than lose planes and pilots (which were becoming a precious commodity to the Japanese – remember all those extra lunch trays I speculated about) in the air. For completeness, here is the action report from December 17, 1943:

(AIRCRAFT ACTION REPORT)

(ALL TIMES- GCT)

At 1815/16 Boyington, McClurg, Magee, Moore, Sims, Brown, Heier, Ffoulkes took off for Torokina to participate in Rabaul fighter sweep. All planes pancaked at Torokina at 1900/16 for topping-off tanks. Ffoulkes nosed-up on landing, damaging his plane slightly.

At 2200/16 Boyington, McClurg, Magee, Moore, Sims, Brown, Heier, Ffoulkes (in borrowed plane) and Bragdon took off from Torokina to participate in fighter sweep over Rabaul.

There were so many planes that it was apparently impossible to get joined up so that the New Zealand P-40's proceeded on course without waiting for the join up.

Plan was for the F4U's to fly 20 - 26000', the F6F's 15 - 20,000', and the P-40's 10 - 15,000'.

The formation proceeded to the N.W., up the coast of Bougainville circling to the W., to avoid a heavy front. As they approached Rabaul all planes began to climb and Sims plane was unable to keep up so he and his wingman returned to base, pancaking at Vella Lavella at 0625/17.

Apparently the P-40s arrived over the target ahead of the rest of the flight and were engaged by a flight of Tonys, Boyington's flight arrived over the target area at 28000 at 2345/16. 30 - 40 fighter planes were lined up on the Lakunai strip. Boyington fired a few rounds from 10,000 ft. in an effort to get the Japs to take off. At 0000/17 McClurg observed a Rufe at 10,000 ft. over the harbor and went down on it in a high stern run, opening fire at 400 yards. A huge cloud of smoke burst from the cockpit and pieces fell off it. The Rufe crashed burning into the Harbor.

Moore observed 7 Zekes well below - waggled his wings and peeled over in an overhead run.

Boyington did not see the signal and continued on course.

Moore went down in an overhead pass on the last of the 7 Zekes which were flying in a column. However, his guns failed to fire so he pulled off, circled, charged his guns and came in on a level stern run on another Zeke. Again his guns failed to fire. He pulled up alongside of the Zero and could look into his cockpit. Chandelled up, recharged his gun once more and came down in an overhead pass on another straggler - firing until a wing came off the Zeke. Moore climbed and circled out over the southern part of the harbor. He saw P-40's fighting with enemy planes and saw 1 enemy plane crash in the water.

About this time the P-40's headed for home and a lone Zeke at 10000' passed over them, headed for Rabaul.

Moore went down on the Zeke in a high stern run, leveling out and opening fire at 300 yards getting a long burst into him - following him through a slow roll. The Zeke fell off on one wing and crashed into the water off Vunakanau airdrome.

He then headed for home but his compass was evidently off as he by - passed Torokina in the weather and was getting low on gas when he sighted Treasury.

He zoomed the field once and circled, firing his guns to warn them he was coming in. Setting his plane down nicely, he had almost stopped when he struck a boulder in the runway, throwing his plane over on its back and knocking him unconscious. He sustained a laceration of the left arm and a severe blow on top of the head.

While he was unconscious, the workmen on the strip (possibly members of an acorn outfit) took his goggles and helmet, removed the clock and other parts of the plane.

Moore was finally returned to Vella on 20 December via Dumbo. The 214 Flight surgeon has grounded him for a few days. Boyington and Magee patrolled for 35 [minutes] with no activity and left the area at 0020/17.

A few rounds of heavy caliber AA were seen, inaccurate. Approximately 30 ships were seen in the harbor including 4 DD's and several large merchant ships.

The air fields in the Rabaul area seemed to be a rust color or dark brown.

Ffoulkes and Heier were over the area at 30,000' at 2340/16 and patrolled for 25 minutes – retiring without contact.

Bragdon, off late, joined up, finally, with another plane and was over Rabaul at 0000/17.

He went down on a strafing run on Rabaul, continuing alone when the other plane left him.

He leveled out at 5000 feet and headed out the harbor mouth when he saw tracers going over his wings and found he'd been jumped by 6 Tonys. He dived into a cloud, got his bearings, opened full throttle and headed for home with a setting of 2700 rpm and pulling 50 inches. The Tonys took up the chase. They were painted a vivid California blue, shiny, with white tails. They had white diagonals on the wings and white diagonal,longitudinal stripes on the fuselage, extending from the cockpit to the tail assembly. The meatballs were indistinct, it was difficult to make them out against their blue background.

Roundels were definitely on the fuselage – and possibly also on the upper wing surface.

Bragdon's plane was indicating 280 at 5000 feet and he was opening very slowly. The Tonys pursued him for 35 miles.

Weather was good over the target.

Boyington, McClurg, Heier, Ffoulkes, Brown and Bragdon pancaked at Cherryblossom between 0105 – 0125. Took off from there at 0440/17 and pancaked here at 0530/17.

Major Boyington is of the opinion that far too many fighter planes were sent on the sweep. He thinks 24 sufficient. He is also strongly of the opinion that all planes, should be the same type – thus eliminating the necessity for continually checking on other planes in the sky.

All in all the sweep was not too successful since the Japs failed to accept the challenge. Perhaps this was partially due to the landing which had been made at Arawe.

Lt. Bragdon's guns failed to fire in his strafing run apparently due to inferior ammunition.

Lt. Moore's guns also failed to fire in 2 attacks on Zeros. Both Zeros would have been destroyed had his guns been functioning properly.

Once more, we have an illustration of how a second telling doesn't necessarily change the story, but may bring out some new or different items. From the action report, we can touch on a number of topics. For one, there was a new Japanese airplane being seen more often; the "Tony," as we called it. They were apparently faster than the Zero, but, fortunately for Moore, not quite as fast as the Corsair. Moore had a bad day; he had a landing accident (which was just plain bad luck) prior to the mission. Not only did he get hurt, but they stripped his plane while he was hanging unconscious in the seatbelts! Then he lost two opportunities which we believe would surely have added two definite scores to his tally, both because his guns wouldn't fire when he pressed the trigger button. But if the Corsair hadn't been as powerful and fast as it was, the Tonys would have gotten him. I'll bet they were disappointed, and possibly a bit surprised at having the opportunity to chase down a Corsair and not being able to do it. I'm sure that Moore was sweating bullets (pun intended) as he slowly pulled away from the pursuing Tonys, but I'd also bet it was regarded as a bit of a dishonor to the Japanese that they couldn't catch him. The fact that Moore's plane performed as it should have when he needed the extra "punch" was very fortunate for him; I have already covered instances of engines not performing when we needed them most, including one of my own. Again, it wasn't the fault of the engines or the maintenance crews. We were in a terrible humid environment, with a minimum of spare parts. What about our mechanics? As far as I'm concerned, they were wizards and miracle workers. They did so much with so little, and have received so little recognition for it.

Date and location unknown. Mechanics working on some of the VMF-214
Corsairs. (McClurg collection)

Overall, I think the above combat report is an excellent example
of how life was during that time period on the second combat tour.
We were flying worn-out machines, incurring functional problems
like guns that wouldn't fire and bad ammunition, and fighting over
enemy territory all the while. I simply cannot find the words to
express the frustration felt after you've worked long and hard to get
an enemy in your sights, then you pull the trigger and the guns
won't fire; at the same time, you must watch a score slip through
your fingers, and also realize that you are unable to defend yourself
if challenged. Just a bit more on the subject of guns... Quite often,
the cause of gun failure at high altitude was the extreme cold
temperatures up there making the guns freeze. In fact, part of the
airplane's equipment includes gun heaters which are intended to
eliminate this. It was also discovered through trial (I think Pappy
and John Bolt were the major contributors on this one) that we
seemed to encounter guns that wouldn't fire quite often when we
were pulling negative G's in dogfights. To alleviate this, they found

through experiment that the manner in which we loaded the ammunition could correct the problem; they loaded the ribbons of bullets so they fed from the top, rather than the bottom. This corrected the problem; it was the weight of the bullet strips themselves which was keeping our guns from firing under high negative G's. Our experience also suggested to us that we need not use so much armor-piercing ammunition, as the enemies we were fighting had very little armor. Instead, we used more incendiary rounds (fire starters) and tracers. This allowed us to more easily see our own gunfire so we could "steer" it, and worked to bring the enemy planes to flames even faster.

Pressure was increasing for Pappy to keep scoring. For the record, my own log book shows that I actually had three flights in aircraft #17938 on Friday, December 17, 1943; a fighter sweep between two ferry flights. Total time for the three flights that day was six hours.

I didn't fly again until next Tuesday, December 21, and my records indicate that this was Pappy's next flight, also. A bunch of us ferried our planes to Cherry Blossom in anticipation of a mission covering bombers at Rabaul. The strike didn't materialize, and we returned later that afternoon. I didn't fly on December 22, and I don't think Pappy did, either. December 23 turned out to be a very important day for me, as you will see...

[Author's note: left hand side of original combat report was not reproducible, so some text is omitted, indicated by ???]

```
War Diary, VMF-214
- - - - - - - - - - - - - - - - - - - - - - - - - - - - -

23 December, 1943
???   Avey, Lane, Fisher, Chatham, On station 1555 over
???   - "Camel Base" - 10,000'
???   Left station 1800 - 4DD's; 3 Cruisers; 35 miles
Southwest
???   treasury - left him 35 miles West of Treasury on
course
???   Pancaked 1800.
0715 Bolt and Miller to Torokina Via TBF to return 2 of
???   (our) planes.
???   0800 Dustin, Matheson, Olander, Bartl, Carnagey,
March,
???   (Brubaker), Hobbs,  Off for Cherry Blossom to
```

participate in
??? Strike. Pancaked 0900.
??? 0830 Boyington, McClurg, Magee, Harper, Sims,
Brown, Ffoulkes. Off for Cherry Blossom to participate
in Fighter Sweep. Pancaked 0900.

War Diary, VMF-214

- -

COMBAT REPORT

DATE:' 23 December, 1943

TIME:	TAKE-OFF	RENDEZVOUS	STRIKE
STRIKE:	1130	1200	1330
SWEEP:	1230	1245	1350

MISSION: Rabaul Strike and Fighter Sweep.
RENDEZVOUS: 1200 Over Cherry Blossom
FORCES ENGAGED:
      OWN: STRIKE
         24 B-24's - Bomb Rabaul
         8 F4U's VMF-216 - High Cover
         8 F6F's VF-40 - Medium High
         16 F6F's VF-33 - Medium
         8 F4U's VMF-214 - Low
         8 F4U's " -222 - Close

            SWEEP
         8 P-38's - High
         8 P-38's - Medium Cover High
         12 P-38's - Medium
         8 F4U's VMF-214 - Low
         12 F4U's " -223 - Close

STRIKE:

Carnagey(Missing)plane395	Dustin Pancaked 1540
March(pancaked 1400	Matheson " 1540
Brubaker(missing) 451	Olander " 1515
Hobbs(pancaked 1400)	Bartl" 1540

SWEEP:

Boyington Pancaked 1630	Sims Pancaked 1540
McClurg " 1600	Brown CherryBlossom1600
Magee " 1520	T.O. 1620 Pancaked 1700
Harper " 1600	Heier CherryBlossom1600
Bolt " 1445	T.O. 1620 Pancaked 1710
	Ffoulkes (missing-443)
	Miller Pancaked 1530

ENEMY : 40 Tony's and Zekes

War Diary, VMF-214

- -

RESULTS : ENEMY LOSSES:
Zeke-6000' St.Geo.Channel-hi 6o'clock-burned,Pilot
  bailed-Boyington-1350.
Zeke-8000'-St.Geo.Channel-level 6o'clock-burned-
  pilot bailed- Boyington- 1355.
Zeke-500'-St.Geo.Channel-hi 6'o'clock-burned-
  Boyington-1355
Zeke-10,000'-Simpson Harbor-hi 6o'clock-burned-
  Boyington- 1410.
Zeke-10,000'-St.Geo.Channel-level 6-crashed-Bolt-1350
Zeke-4000'-St.Geo.Channel-level 6-burned-Bolt -1355
Zeke-4000'_St.Geor.Channel-level 12-pilot bailed-
  Miller – 1350.
Zeke-200'-St.Geo.Channel-hi 5- hit water-McClurg-1350
Zeke-8000'-St.Geo.Channel-hi 5-blew up-McClurg-1355
Zeke-2000'-Cape.St. George-level 9-crashed in water
  Heier-1350
Tony-4000'-S.E. New Ireland-hi 4-exploded-Heier-1355
Zeke-18000'-St. George Channel-level 6-burned-Magee
  1355
2 Tony's-10,000'-S.E. New Ireland-hi 5-probables-
  Heier – 1400.

OUR LOSSES:
Carnagey, Brubaker and Ffoulkes – Missing.

NARRATIVE ACCOUNT:

Rendezvous of bombers and fighters was made 15
minutes late (1200) over Cherry Blossom and the strike
proceeded on course, crossing New Britain and circling
to the East, coming across the target from West to East
at 21,000' at 1330.
As the bombers got into their runs, a flight of 15-20
Zekes came down on them from above. At this time only
4 or 5 of the scheduled 24 plane F6F medium cover were
in position over the bombers. These remained above as
the Zeros went on down in overhead runs on the forward
bombers.
After their drops the bombers proceeded out St.
George channel in two groups of 9 each, with 10-15
Zeros continuing to attack the last group.
About 12 of the scheduled 24 plane F6F medium cover
scissored 1500 feet over the forward group of bombers,

where no fighting was going on, while the remaining 6 F4U's fought the 10-15 Zeros off the second group of bombers.

One bomber was hit in one motor which began to smoke but the pilot feathered his prop and was staying in formation.

AA over the target was both medium and heavy in calibre and intense. It was accurate as to level but off to the left.

A number (25-30) of aerial bombs were observed, exploding into huge white phosphorous balls which looked like huge silver cream puffs some 50' in diameter – with 15 foot silver streamers.

These seemed to have been fired rather than dropped since several near misses were observed at varying altitudes.

Also a Zeke apparently fired one at an F4U as the Corsair was making a stern run on the Zero. It exploded just over the Corsair wing, rocking his plane but doing no damage.

The bombing left the town of Rabaul smiling and set several fires in the harbor. Nine ships were observed in Keravia bay with one sunk, one smoking badly and its stern at water level, and another burning badly.

In Simpson harbor a large transport was broken in two – the stern and bow were showing – middle under water – smoking.

The fighter sweep, scheduled to sweep the area an hour and 15 minutes behind the bombers, arrived over the area just 15 minutes behind because the bombers were half an hour behind schedule and the fighters slightly early.

This time was ideal since it permitted the fighters to engage a great many Zeros as the bombers were leaving the area – and thus, divert their attention from the heavies.

One sighting was made of the new type of weapon mentioned in COMAIRSOLS bulletin of 16 December. It was described as resembling a man in an unopened chute which was streaming out above him. It was oscillating in a pendulum-like manner and struck the water of Simpson Harbor with a splash but no explosion.

VMF-214 pilots shot down a total of 12 enemy planes; Major Boyington, Commanding Officer, getting 4 to bring his total to 24. Lt. Magee's one brought his total to 8 while Lt. McClurg dropped 2 Zekes to raise his total score to six.

Most of the action involving planes on the fighter sweep took place over St. George Channel and at altitudes far below that of the bombers.

As the bombers circled to initiate their run, a submarine on course 260, was sighted 2 miles southwest of Watom Island.

The planes on the fighter sweep arrived over St. George Channel at exactly the right time to engage and destroy the enemy planes which came down to lower levels in broken and straggling formations after attacking the bombers.

Most of the Zeros shot down were destroyed in individual dog fights and as the result of individual runs.

Major Carnagey and Lts. Brubaker and Ffoulkes are missing. The last seen of the first two was shortly after the bombing run when they were defending the heavies.

Ffoulkes was last seen over St. George Channel as he initiated an attack on a lone Zero. Late in the fight he called Lt. Heier and asked for his position.

The fighter sweep came into the New Britain-New Ireland area on a number of scattered Zeros and split up and ran them down individually.

Most of the enemy planes were Zekes, although some Tony's were seen.

On his way home alone, Major Boyington spotted a submarine 2 miles East of Sperber Pt., headed South. He went down on it in a strafing run and managed to get in 2 or 3 bursts before it submerged.

*   *   *

The day before Christmas eve, 1943 was a big one for me; I got scores number five and six. For the rest of my life (however short I feared it might be), I would be able to say that I was a fighter Ace. But there was little to rejoice about in the squadron at the time. Fact is, all these many years later, what I remember more about that time is not my becoming an Ace, but rather that three more of our Sheep were missing. That was a big loss for us.

There is one other thing I remember about that mission, and this is the stuff that doesn't appear anywhere in the records. I couldn't get the engine started in the first airplane I boarded that day, so I got out and climbed into a second. After many tries in the second plane, I wasn't able to get its engine going, either. It wasn't unusual to require a few tries in order to get an engine started. To have to try a second airplane wasn't common, but wasn't totally out of the question, either. It was uncommon, however, to have attempted to start the engine in two different airplanes, and failed both times. The third time was a charm, as the engine in the next Corsair fired promptly, and I proceeded to garner scores number five and six.

Date unknown. F4-U #833, frequent mount of McClurg, in a revetment on Vella Lavella (McClurg collection)

[Author's note: McClurg also flew an F4-U #883, depicted in aviation art.]

I suppose I had pretty well made my mark; I was an Ace, and I was often flying wing on Pappy. That description sounds more glamorous than it really is; most often, complete chaos breaks out in a dogfight and you don't always stick with your wingman. Everybody gets busy taking care of themselves, and looking for others in trouble whether they are wingmen or not. Next is a bit more; the action report from December 23, 1943...

AIRCRAFT ACTION REPORT

Rendezvous of bombers and fighters was made 15 min. late (1200), over Cherry Blossom, and the strike proceeded on course, crossing New Britain and circling to the E., coming across the target from W. to E. at 21,000 feet at 1330.

As the bombers got into their runs, a flight of 15-20 Zekes came down on them from above. At this time only 4 or 5 of the scheduled 24 plane F6F medium cover were in position over the bombers. These remained above as the Zekes went down in overhead runs on the forward bombers. A.A. was intense, medium and heavy caliber up to the proper altitudes but off to the side.

Bombing was good, leaving the entire town smoking from scattered fires - and several fires were seen in the harbor. Nine ships were observed in Keravia Bay with 1 sunk, 1 smoking badly - its stern at water level, and another burning badly. In Simpson Harbor - a large transport was broken in two; the stern and bow were showing, the middle under water, smoking.

The fighter sweep, scheduled to sweep the area an hour and fifteen minutes after the strike, arrived over the area just fifteen minutes behind the bombers, because the heavies were half an hour behind schedule and the fighters slightly early.

This timing was ideal because it permitted the fighters to engage a great many Zero's as the bombers were leaving the area, and thus divert their attention from the heavies.

VMF 214 pilots shot down 12 Zero's sure and 2 probables, Tonys, with Major Boyington getting 4 to raise his total to 24. Boyington was at 18,000 ft. over St. George Channel when he saw the flight over to his right. Heading that way he saw a Zero below him - heading toward Rabaul. Swinging in behind him in a level 6 O'clock run, he held his fire until he was within 50 ft. range. Then he gave the Zeke one short burst and it flamed immediately and crashed into the waters of St. Georges Channel with the pilot's chute stretched out along side.

Climbing back up to 11,000 feet over St. Georges Channel, he spotted 2 Zekes at 10,000 feet, one flying straight and level, the other maneuvering about him.

Boyington went down, made a level 6 o'clock run on the lower plane - opening fire at 100 feet. The Zeke burst into flame as the pilot bailed out. The plane crashed into the water in the middle of the Channel.

Boyington climbed back up into the sun and watched the other Zero as it circled about the crashed plane at 300 ft. Boyington slid down out of the sun in a level 6 O'clock run - opening fire at 100 ft. The Zeke began to burn, rolled slowly onto its back and went into the water in a flat glide. Climbing back up to 18,000 ft., Boyington circled Rabaul harbor for 20 minutes before he spotted any more Zeros.

This was a 9 plane formation at 10,000 feet. coming

out of the sun in a shallow throttle-back glide in a high 6 o'clock pass, he opened fire at 100 yards, closing fast and firing continuously until he passed under and out to the side.   Pieces flew off the Zekes cowling and then it burst into flame and went down burning.   Boyington nosed down and headed W. with the remainder of the flight chasing him for 10 minutes.

They were closing on him although he had on full throttle.   However, when they leveled off, Boyington began to climb at 180 knots and climbed away.

Lt. Bolt peeled off from 20,000 ft. into a formation of Zekes at 13,000, opened fire at long range, scored hits on the L. wing of a Zeke and continued on through the formation.   Climbing up to 15 - 16,000' he spotted a single Zero below at 8,000' on his right, Bolt went down on him in an overhead and made 2 or 3 passes as the Zeke kept scissoring with him, trying to get away.   Getting directly behind the Zeke at last, Bolt was making a level 6 o'clock run about 400 yards out when an aerial bomb exploded directly between them. He thinks it was a phosphorous bomb exploded by a light explosive in it.   As the phosphorous particles burn, they leave a cloud which resembles a white cumulous cloud.   Bolt continued his run at 8,000', opening fire at 200 yards as the Zeke went into a right turn, Bolt saw his bullets striking the engine and cowling.   The Zeke went into a gentle glide and crashed about 100 yards inland from the mouth of the Warangoi river.   Circling over toward New Ireland at 8,000' he observed another Zeke coming 2,000' under him at 2 0'clock.   As Bolt dove in on him, the Zeke turned up on one wing.   Thinking this might be an allied plane because of the apparent recognition gesture, because the position of the sun prevented his seeing the meatballs, Bolt momentarily pulled over to the left.

The Zeke leveled off and at this time Bolt could see the meatball on the fuselage.   Reinitiating the attack Bolt sparred with the Zeke for a while in diving turns, pulling streamers until finally the Zeke straightened out and began heading toward the New Britain Coast.

Bolt opened up to 2600 and 45 inches at 4,000' and then to 2700 closing slowly.   Since the Zeke was attempting no evasive action at all, Bolt held his fire until he closed to 200 yards.   As he opened up, the Zeke started into a split S (at 4,000', 230 knots). As he got about ½ way over he burst into flames.   The mass of wreckage struck the water of St. George Channel about 2 miles [?] of Put Put.   Lt. McClurg got into the fight at 19,000' over St. George Channel when he heard Maj. Boyington say "This is it, fellows" and then began

to let down. He and the Major made individual runs on
2 Zekes. McClurg's Zeke was already being followed by
a Corsair which lost its opportunity then the Zeke
turned sharply to the right and sharply skidded
out. McClurg came down in a high 5 o'clock run and
circled wide and partially opened his cowl flaps to
keep from overrunning. Mushing in on him, McClurg
opened fire at 100 yards range. The Zeke leveled off,
dropped his nose, skipped twice on the water and
went in sinking immediately; only the tail visible.

McClurg chandelled up to the left, climbing to 4,000'
when he looked behind and to his right and saw 2 Zekes
coming in on him in a high 5 o'clock run. McClurg gave
his plane 2750 rpm full throttle, full rich mixture,
closed his cowl flaps and headed for a light, fleecy
cloud. The Zekes were gaining when he entered the
cloud. Making a sharp flipper turn to the right,
almost blacking out, he came out of the cloud heading
directly for the 2 Zekes. Immediately, they both
banked sharply up, then down to their right. McClurg
tried to bring his guns to bear on the first one but
could not hold the rudder down with his foot, and
therefore could not get him in his sights. Hitting the
rudder trim tab and getting complete control of his
plane, McClurg lined up the second plane which started
to turn more to the right. McClurg gave him two short
bursts from 150 yards and both wings of the Zeke
folded, (the right one first) and he exploded, leaving
only a big cloud of black smoke and little pieces
falling.

Lt. Heier was at 18,000 feet with Lt. Ffoulkes when
he saw 15 scattered Zekes over St. George Channel at
19,000 feet. He pulled up and began climbing, going up
to 20,000 feet. Spotting a Zeke off to his left, he
swung to the left in a 3 O'clock pass opening fire at
200 yards, closing to 100 yards. A flash of fire came
out of the Zeke's engine, then it split S'd downward
and Heier followed him in the maneuver. The Zeke
rolled 360 to the right as he went straight down; Heier
following him through the roll, still firing. Pulling
out at 13,000 feet, Heier watched the Zeke continue to
8,000 feet leveled off and head for a cloud. Heier
followed him into the cloud, 4,000 feet above him in a
gentle turn to the left, retaining his altitude as the
2 planes came out of the cloud with the Zeke about
2,000 yards ahead of him. Cutting his gun, Heier
swooped down and then under the Zekes tail in a low 6
O'clock run. Only one gun was firing, but it was
enough to finish off the crippled plane. It glided
down to the water, bounced once and then skidded to a

stop, partially afloat. Heier headed for the clouds and the Tony blocking his way also turned and headed for the cover. The two planes entered the clouds about 50 yards apart with Heier firing at the Tony, swinging from 5 to 7 o'clock. He could see his bullets striking the engine, fuselage and tail. This Tony is considered a probable.

At this time the cloud closed in so Heier climbed to 8,000 feet on instruments, poked his head out of the cloud and saw 4 Tonys in a column flying along the side of it at 4,000 feet. About this time Ffoulkes called Heier asking for his position; Heier answered him and told Ffoulkes to head for home. Heier then pushed over in a 4 O'clock high side run on tail end Charlie of the formation of 4 Tonys, opening fire at 100 yards and closing right in. The Tony exploded - the left wing came off and he spun in. At this time he saw a lone Tony at 7,000 feet. [??] Heier climbed up on his right quarter, closing slowly. Inching [??], He opened fire at 300 yards at which the Tony turned sharply to the right. Heier being slow in his climb, was able to turn inside of him and continued firing as the Tony turned.

The two planes scissored once and then the Tony headed for a cloud and Heier tried to close. Just before the Tony reached the cloud it turned to the left and Heier gave him a long burst from 150 yards. At this time they were at 2,000 feet. The Tony slid off on his left wing as Heier's speed carried him into the cloud. Coming back out Heier could not locate the Tony. This is considered a probable.

Looking about for a plane to join on, Heier spotted a lone Corsair but it refused to let him join with it. This other Corsair was Lt. Magee who had been fighting at 22,000 feet without oxygen and was too ill to recognize him.

Diving down to intercept 2 Zekes apparently headed for Rabaul, Magee spotted a Zeke 300 feet below him and 300 yards in front of him on an opposite course and at 18,000 feet. Too low to make an overhead and to high to make a headon, Magee pushed his nose over until his sights showed a 300 mil lead, opened fire and let the Zeke run through it. Another Zeke coming in from the front on Magee's left prevented his observing the results of this burst as he lifted his nose and opened fire on the second Zeke from a range of 400 yards. This Zeke split s'd out and down. Magee then saw another Zeke off to the left and about 300 feet below him. Swinging to his left onto his tail in a level 6 O'clock pass, he closed the range to 300 yards and then opened fire. The Zeke immediately split Sd downward,

Magee followed him through the maneuver. Then the Zeke rolled to the right and pulled out with Magee following him.

At this time Magee's oxygen went completely off; They were at 18,000 feet. Still astern of the Zeke as it pulled up, Magee fired again. The Zeke again started to split S but **Magee** dove beneath him and pulled his nose into firing position just as the Zeke went over on his back in the beginning of the split S. Magee opened fire at 150 yards and gave him a steady burst as he went past. The Zero continued on straight down and splashed into the water in St. Georges channel. Climbing back up to 20,000 feet, still with little or no oxygen, (he was down below 500 pounds and every time he pulled any G's, his oxygen would go completely off) he headed along the coast of New Ireland to the Duke of York Islands. He saw no other planes around, a number of Jap crash boats were scurrying about in the harbor trying to pick up their downed pilots. Magee then headed over by Cape St. George by this time getting sick from the lack of oxygen and from fumes in the cockpit.

At this time Heier tried to join with him but Magee turned on his emergency oxygen and dived to 10,000 feet, looked around Cape St. George and came home.

Major Miller nailed his Zeke at 9,000 feet from above. He was letting down in a huge spiral when he spotted the Zeke 1,000 feet below him on a parallel course chasing a Corsair. Miller headed toward him at which time the Zeke saw him and climbed off to the right as Miller closed. Miller opened fire at 250 yards right in the Zeke's belly. The Zeke rolled to its right and then on to its back as the pilot bailed out. Major Boyington, on his way home alone, spotted a submarine headed S. 2 miles E. of Sperber point. He went down on it in a strafing run and managed to get in two or three bursts before it submerged.

Major Carnagey and Lts. Brubaker and Ffoulkes failed to return from the flight. The last seen of Major Carnagey, and Lt. Brubaker, who was flying his wing, was shortly after the bombing run when they were defending the heavies. Ffoulkes was last seen over St. Georges channel as he initiated an attack on a lone Zeke. Late in the flight he was heard to call Heier asking for Heier's position.

Major Boyington is strongly of the opinion that the fighter sweep should be within 10 or 15 minutes of the strike. This permits it to have its best effect. End

Major Boyington observed the new type weapon mentioned in the ComAirSols bulletin of Dec. '16. He described it as resembling a man in an unopened chute which was streaming out above him. It was oscillating back and forth in a pendulum – like manner and struck the water of Simpson Harbor with a splash but no explosion.

25 – 30 Aerial bombs were observed, exploded into huge white balls which looked like cream puffs some 50' in diameter with 15 foot silver streamers. Some of them seemed to have been fired rather than dropped as several near misses were observed at varying levels. Also, a Zeke apparently fired one at a Corsair as the F4U was working a stern run at a Zero. It exploded just over the Corsair's wing, rocking it but doing no damage.

Left: Frank "Flatfoot" Walton, our intelligence officer (L) and Jim "Doc" Reames (R) our squadron doctor. Location and date unknown.
Right: The eccentric Chris Magee in a hula skirt. Location and date unknown.
(McClurg collection)

Date unknown. The chow line on Green Island. L-R Emrich, Tucker, Losch, Heier, Magee, Hill (McClurg collection)

Date and location unknown. Humor during the off hours, enacting a battle. L-R front row Al Johnson, Harry Johnson, Moore (prone) L-R back row Heier, Ashmun, McClurg (with Bible) (McClurg collection)

Movie theatre on Espiritu Santos (McClurg collection)

We celebrated Christmas 1943. Flights continued through those days. I didn't score again until the December 28, but Pappy got one on December 27.

WAR DIARY, VMF-214.

- -

27 December, 1943.

1410 Dumbo Spotter Escort - Emrich, Losch, Groover. Rendezvoused at 1420 with 2 Dumbos - up the slot- 15-20 miles off Kiete ran into 2 Cruisers and 4 DD in a line abreast.
Relieved by RNZAF-17 at 1600 - Weather bogey below 6,000 2-3 miles visibility; 6 layer down to 2500. 8,000 - 11,000. Pancaked 1640.

0615 Boyington, Harper, Tucker, Corman, Mullen, Fisher, Avey, Crocker, Miller, Holden, Doswell, Bowers. Off to Torokina to participate in fighter sweep. Pancaked 0715.

COMBAT REPORT

DATE: 27 December, 1943.

TIME: TAKE-OFF   RENDEZVOUS   STRIKE
          1000   1030   1130

MISSION: Rabaul Fighter Sweep.

FORCES ENGAGED:
    OWN:
        12 F4U's - VMF-214
        12 F4U's -   " -216
        12 F4U's -   " -223
        8 F4U's - " -321
        12 F6F's - VF -33 Ondonga
        8 F6F's - VF -40

    Boyington 1310-C.E.; T.O.1515; 1615 -here
    Harper 1310 - 1410 - 1510.
    Tucker 1345
    Corman 1310 - 1410 - 1510.

    Mullen 1325   Miller 1615-C.B.; 1722-V.L.
    Fisher 1325   Holden 1320
    Avey   1325   Doswell 1310
    Crocker1325   Bowers 1330

    ENEMY: 60 Zekes, Hamps and Tonys.
CONTACT:
    Altitude: 14,000 - 20,000 feet.
    Location: Simpson Harbor.
    Time   : 1130

RESULTS: ENEMY LOSSES:
    Zeke(black)-12000-Praed Pt.-Hi 8 then 7-burned-
        Mullen 1145
    Zeke(black)-10000-Praed Pt.-Hi 7 burned-Avey 1200.
    Zeke(Mot. Brown)-9000-South Simpson Harbor-
    several-burned-Harper - 1145.
    Zeke(dirty brown)-14000-West of Praed Pt.-Hi 6-
    burned Boyington - 1140.
    Zeke(Mot brown)-20,000-Kerovia Bay-Head on-blew
    up-burned-Fisher - 1140.
    Zeke(Mot brown)-18,000-Kerovia Bay- Hi 6- burned -
    Fisher - 1145.
    Zeke(Mot brown)-12,000-Kerovia Bay-level 6-smoked-
    Fisher - 1150.
    Hamp(muddy, greenish, red)-16,000-Kerovia Bay-Hi
    side-clipped tail, damaged- Holden - 1140.

OUR LOSSES: None.

NARRATIVE ACCOUNT:

At 1030 the formation with Major Boyington in tactical command, headed on course toward Rabaul, climbing gradually.

They went up St. George Channel stacked from 18 to 30,000 feet.

Then Major Boyington led the formation into a huge tilted Lufberry circle with its high side at 20,000 and its low side at 14,000. They were over Simpson Harbor at 1130.

The circle was 5-6 miles in diameter with 30-40 Zeros in the center of it.

Then Major Boyington began to let down on them; Corsairs would make passes, climb and re-enter the traffic circle.

AA of medium intensity, heavy calibre was thrown up from vicinity of Praed Pt.

VMF-214 pilots knocked down six Zeros sure, one probable with another damaged.

AIRCRAFT ACTION REPORT

At 1030, the formation with Major Boyington as tactical commander, proceeded up the west coast of Bougainville climbing gradually. They went up St. George Channel, stacked from 18 to 30,000 feet. Then Major Boyington led the formation into a huge tilted Lufberry circle with its high side at 20,000 feet and its low side at 14,000 feet. They were circling Simpson Harbor at 1130.

The center was 5 - 6 miles across with 30 - 40 Zero's in the center of it.

Then Major Boyington began to let down on the Zero's - with Corsairs making passes, climbing up and rejoining the traffic circle.

A.A. was of medium intensity, heavy caliber from vicinity of Praed Point.

Boyington did a masterful tactical job of leading the formation - retaining his altitude advantage and completely bottling up the Zero's. Major Boyington went down on his Zeke, a mottled brown Zeke at 14,000 feet, in an overhead, swinging in on his tail as the Zeke split S'd out and then pulled out in a high 6 O'clock run, opening fire at 150 yards. The Zeke went down burning.

Fisher spotted a Zeke off to his left at 20,000 feet break away from a run on a Corsair. As the Zeke turned to the right, Fisher came in on him in almost a head-on run - opening fire at 350 yards - blowing off the canopy of the Zeke before it flamed.
Climbing back into the traffic circle Fisher saw a single Zeke out in the center of the circle, at 18,000 feet out, a thousand feet below him, climbing away from him. Fisher went down on him in a throttle-back glide, opening fire at 100 yards and closing, firing continuously. The Zeke smoked, pieces came off him, and then he went down, burning.
Coming in on a third Zero from level 3 O'clock, Fisher opened fire at 200 feet, closing fast. The Zeke went down smoking. This is considered a probable for Fisher.
Mullen letting down from 26,000 feet to 14,000 feet, spotted a single Zeke at 12,000 feet, heading away. Coming down behind him, closing fast, Mullen opened fire at 300 yards. The Zeke turned on his back trying to split S out. However Mullen closed in, firing and passed over the Zeke as it burst into flame.
Cutting across to rejoin the circle he saw four Zekes at 10,000 feet out coming up on a F4U just off his left wing. Swinging to his left, Avey came in at 7[?] O'clock on the tail end one of the four, opening fire at 200 yards. His bullets appeared to be hitting the Zeke's motor. The plane, a black Zeke, fell away to the right, smoking badly from the engine, and then burst into flame from the motor. The flame covered the entire fuselage as the Zeke went straight down.
Lt. Harper came out of the clouds at 10,000' from the N. side of Simpson Harbor. He saw a number of Zero's scattered below him at 9,000 feet. Harper went down in a high stern run on the last one in a string of three. as he closed the Zeke pulled up in a wingover, slowing up as Harper closed right in fast. Harper opened fire at 200 yards, striking the Zeke in the left wing tip, as it dropped through the wing over and came diving out. Harper followed him through the rest of the wing over passing below and along side the other Zekes with him.
    Evidently the first Zeke had led Harper past them so they could protect [?] tail. Knowing that the other Zekes would jump him if he continued the run, Harper nevertheless pressed home his attack. His quarry apparently expected him to pull off because it took no evasive action as Harper closed in. Harper held his fire until he was within 200 yards and then got in a medium burst before the Zeke pulled up on one wing,

rolled and split S'd downward; as he did so smoke began
to come out of the Zeke. Hesitating momentarily   in
order to let him straighten out, Harper split S'd after
him. The Zeke went down vertically with Harper diving
vertically after him.   Closing to 100 yards, Harper
again opened fire, at which time the Zeke did a 360d
aileron roll, going straight down.   The Zeke then
started to pull out burning, but never made it as
Harper gave him another burst from 50 yards.   Harper
pulled out, gave his motor   full throttle, and climbed
away from the Zeke trailing him.
Lt. Holden went over in a high side run on a muddy,
greenish red Hamp at 16,000 feet and saw his bullets
chopping through its tail.
The Hamp split Sd down and out. This is considered a
damaged plane for Lt. Holden.
Phosphorous Aerial bombs were again observed, but no
damage was seen.

1745 Boyington, McClurg, Magee, Moore, Sims, Heier,
March, Brown, Dustin, Matheson, Olander, Bartl. Off to
Torokina to participate in early strike tomorrow.
Pancaked 1845.

I think a couple comments are in order on the action of
December 27. First, the summary lists something about Holden
clipping the tail of a Hamp, but the report doesn't elaborate on it. I
really wish I could remember more about that story, but I simply
can't. I do remember a story (or two) about guys chopping tails of
other planes with their props; maybe this was one where Holden did
so. I really wish I could remember more, because prop–chopping
always seems to be a favorite among listeners. Anyway, there are a
couple other things about the action of the December 27 that I'd like
to emphasize. First, this sweep was one where Boyington was
allowed to organize it his way. We had fighters organized to make a
muscular, aggressive attack.   Boyington's arrangement in the
Lufberry circle worked extremely well; it was like an assembly line
for shooting the enemy. (The idea in a Lufberry circle is that no
enemy can enter the circle because the next "friendly" to the rear in
the circle will blast him apart.) Boyington's implementation of a
tilted Lufberry circle allowed us the protection of a circle, with an
added dimension of ability to dive out from the high point, make a
run, then climb back and re-enter at the low point. The constant up
and down while in the circle wasn't as easy as flying a circle at a
constant altitude; in order to maintain power as you got higher in the

sky, the Corsair's supercharger had two stages that could be engaged separately. We would start out in "low" blower, and the engine manifold pressure would fall as we climbed (due to the thinner air). When the boost fell to a certain level, we would throttle back a bit and engage "high" blower, which would bring the boost back up. We would then throttle up again, bringing the boost to some upper limit. That was what maintained performance at high altitudes. Conversely, when coming down in altitude, we had to watch the boost gauge to make sure it didn't get too high. As we descended, the boost would increase. At a certain upper limit, we would have to shift to "low" blower and add throttle. Failing to do that would let the boost get too high and cause the engine to fail. (We could also disengage the supercharger completely by shifting it to "neutral," done mostly at landing.) In a tilted Lufberry circle where we were constantly going up and down, there was lots of hand movement in the cockpit to keep the engine settings where they needed to be. Same thing held true in a dogfight, with the addition of gun charging and sighting. But by that time we were well-seasoned pilots, and used to the task.

Another aspect of the December 27 raid was the continuation of Boyington's aggressiveness. The Sheep were out there, seeking the enemy. We didn't fight merely if our paths crossed; we made sure our paths crossed, and blasted away. I think Harper's exploits on that day are an excellent example of this. He knew very well that if he continued with his attack, following the Zeke he had started to pursue past some of the Zeke's own mates, that he could count on having one or more Zekes on his own tail—and he did it anyway. As is sometimes said in the modern lingo, "that takes balls." Actions like that helped to make sure the Japanese pilots understood that we were out there actively seeking combat. In Harper's case on December 27, I think it is evident that the Japanese pilot he pursued might have been either a little naïve or a little green; the Japanese pilot seemed to assume that Harper would not continue the attack once in the company of more Japanese pilots, and did not offer himself the safety of continued vigilance. (Among the ranks of fighter pilots, that is also referred to as "just plain dumb.") That Japanese pilot also did something which, by then, should have been known to the Japanese as futile; he tried to out-dive a Corsair with a Zero. That sealed his fate. Remember, the Corsair is much heavier and will out-dive a Zero with ease.

Date and location unknown. McClurg posing with an F4-U that had been marked up for Boyington press photos. (McClurg collection)

In fact, that is how we used to get Zekes off our own tails; just push the nose over and add power, and they couldn't stay with us for anything. In Harper's instance, he had a great advantage at following the Zeke down, closing in behind him, all the while knowing that he was also pulling away from any other Zekes that might be following. As the final notes indicate, I found myself in Torokina on the morning of December 28, ready to hit Rabaul again. I didn't know it then, but this was to be one of my last flights with Pappy...

WAR DIARY, VMF-214.
- -

28 December, 1943.

    0600 Boyington, McClurg, Magee, Moore, Sims, Heier, March, Brown, Dustin, Matheson, Olander, Bartl. Took off on fighter sweep over Rabaul.

                        COMBAT REPORT

DATE: 28 December, 1943.

TIME: TAKE-OFF   RENDEZVOUS   STRIKE
         0600   0630   0730

MISSION: Rabaul Fighter Sweep.

FORCES ENGAGED:
    OWN:
            12 F4U's - VMF-214
            19 F4U's - " -216
            9 F4U's - " -223
            6 F4U's - " -321

    Boyington   Sims 0840;1000 C.B. 1120 Here
    McClurg 1015   Heier0840;1215   1315
    Magee 0840; 1000 C.B   March 1005   1120 Here
    Brown 0920
    Moore (910) Missing

                 Dustin (908) missing
                 Matheson 0950
                 Olander 0945
                 Bartl (831) Missing
    ENEMY: 50-60 Zekes, Hamps and Tonys.

RESULTS: ENEMY LOSSES:
          Hamp(light tan; brown top)-11000-Gredner I.-Hi 6 -
            crashed water- McClurg - 0800.
          Tony(brown)-12000-Rabaul-low 6- crashed in water-
            Magee - 0750
          Zeke(light brown)-10000-South New Ireland-Hi 6 -
            burned- Matheson - 0810

Zeke(brown)-15000-Simpson Harbor-Hi 6-crashed in water-Olander - 0800
Tojo(black)-13000-Simpson   Harbor-Hi   6-smoked-Boyington - 0745
Zeke(brown)-14000-Praed Pt.-low 6-smoked-McClurg - 0810

OUR LOSSES: Capt. Dustin, Lt. Moore and Lt. Bartl missing in action.

NARRATIVE ACCOUNT:

At 0630, the formation led by Major Morrell of VMF-216 headed on course up the West coast of Bougainville.

Morrell led the formation in a huge circle to the left at 19,000' at 0730, around the outside of the North end of New Britain - a long way Southwest and then out over St. George channel, making such a slow long circle that it gave the enemy planes time to climb to altitude over Rabaul.

Another formation of enemy planes circled to the rear of the flight of Corsairs and climbed into the sun above and behind them.

When the Corsairs engaged the Zeros over Rabaul, those above and behind came down on them.

There were 50-60 Zekes, Hamps and Tonys in the sky.

At least 20 large ships were observed in the Harbor; one of them probably an aircraft carrier, 2 Cruisers, 8 Destroyers, 6 large, 2 medium and 1 small ship (Transport or Cargo) were observed in Keravia Bay.

A number of aerial bombs were observed over the West coast of New Ireland opposite Rabaul at 20000'.

Morrell did a poor job of leading the division, putting them in the disadvantageous position where they were completely outnumbered and below the enemy planes.

The enemy planes flew in sectional and divisional formation better than they have in any previous engagements.

A number of divisional and sectional runs were made by the Japs; they also seem much more aggressive than previously.

Boyington spotted a Tojo; a black, stubby, square, wingtipped, fighter with an amazing rate of climb.

Three of our pilots - Capt. Dustin, Lt. Bartl and Lt. Moore are missing. They were not in trouble when last seen.

One Corsair was seen to hit the water just north of Cape Gazelle.

AIRCRAFT ACTION REPORT

At 0600 the planes took off for Torokina, heading on course at 0630. The formation, led by Major Morrell of VMF 216 headed up the W. coast of Bougainville. Taking the formation up St. George Channel, Morrell started a huge circle at 22,000' circling N. of Rabaul at 0730, a long way South West into New Britain and then out over St. George Channel again, losing altitude and making such a wide sweep that enemy planes taking off from Lakunai airdrome had plenty of time to climb to altitude before the formation had completed its first circle.

Also, during this time, another formation of enemy planes climbed up in the back of the formation into the sun. When the Corsairs engaged the enemy planes over Rabaul, those above and behind came down on them. At least 50-60 Zekes, Hamps, Tonys and Tojos were in the sky. At least 20 large ships were spotted in the harbor, one of them probably an aircraft carrier, 2 cruisers and 8 destroyers, 6 barges, 2 medium and 1 small ship transport or cargo ship, were observed in Keravia Bay.

The enemy planes flew in excellent sectional and divisional formation making a number of passes in formation.

They also seemed more aggressive and experienced than usual, possibly they were off the aircraft carrier.

VMF 214 pilots shot down 4 enemy planes and probably destroyed 2 more.

Capt. Dustin was leading a division at 21,000', made up of Matheson, Olander, and Bartl. Spotting 8 to 10 Zeros above at 22,000' feet, Dustin led his division in a climb toward them, getting slow in the climb, down to 160 knots. The Zeros slid down on them and the division split up. Olander rolled on a Zeke as it went by and went down with him. He gave it a long burst from 250 yards, rolled off to the left as he saw tracers go past his wings, and saw his Zeke crash into the water almost vertical. Attacked by half a dozen Zeros, he turned and dived for some 5 to 10 minutes trying to get out from under the roof of enemy planes, sustaining 3-20 mm., 2-7.7, and 2-51 cal. hits in his right wing, left wing and right elevators.

Matheson went down with a Zero on his tail but shook it in about a thousand feet. Trying to climb, he found the sky roofed in with enemy planes. He nosed over again and moved over to New Ireland, and tried to climb again but found his path upward again blacked by enemy planes.

Spotting a thick layer of clouds over S. New Ireland, he headed into it, climbed out on top of it and then flew along the edge.

He heard that Zeros usually waited around there, looking for cripples, strays, and stragglers on the way back to Bougainville. Sure enough he found them; he was at 16,000 feet and saw three Zekes in formation at 12,000 feet. Getting into the sun, he waited until one lagged behind, and then pushed over onto his tail in a high 6 o'clock run, closing fast, he opened fire at 150 yards. He continued firing as he closed to 50 yards, seeing his tracers hitting the Zekes tail. A huge flash flared from the cockpit and then went out. The plane a light tan Zeke with dark brown roundels on its wings, began to smoke and went gliding down, crashed into the mountains and exploded.

Dustin and Bartl were not observed again after the initial Breakup.

Boyington, McClurg, Magee and Moore were flying in formation with Moore lagging, Moore was not observed after the initial breakup. Boyington and McClurg initiated runs on enemy planes at 15,000 feet, 3000 feet below them. McClurg came in on his, a brown Zeke, in a low 6 O'clock pass, swooping down and then up under his tail. He opened fire at 300 yards giving the Zeke 2 bursts, after which the enemy plane began to smoke, turned slightly to the right and then nosed down. At this time tracers passed in front of him, so he pulled off to the left and pushed over. The last he saw of the crippled Zeke, it was headed downward smoking. This is considered a probable.

McClurg dived, gathered speed and climbed again into the sun. Spotting a Hamp about 800 yards in front of him crossing downward from right to left, McClurg dropped his nose and closed in on him at 11,000 feet. Coming in, in a high 6 O'clock run, he gave the Hamp a short Burst with no apparent effect. Then the enemy plane turned slightly to the right and then pulled tighter to the right. McClurg turned with him, at this time within 150 yards range. He gave the enemy a long burst, holding slight left rudder to make his shots go home. Pieces flew off the Hamp and smoke came from its cowl. Then it slid over, went down trailing smoke and crashed in the water off Gredner I.

Lt. Magee at 21,000 ft. spotted a Tony at 14,000 ft. flying level away from him. Doing a wingover, Magee swooped down to a point about 200 ft. under and ½ mile back of the Tony, and closed in fast.

Coming in at low six O'clock, he opened fire at 60 yards, striking the engine and forward part of the

wings, running in so close that he had to jerk on the
stick to miss the enemy plane. Magee watched the Tony
split "S" downward and then hit the water in a semi-
crash landing.

Boyington, at 17,000 ft., dived down on an enemy
plane 4000 ft. below him, coming in on a high six
o'clock run. The enemy plane pulled up into a climbing
loop and Boyington, thinking his superior altitude
would have given him sufficient speed to stay with him,
tried to stay on his tail. However, the enemy plane
climbed straight up and over away from him, leaving a
black trail of smoke. Boyington was unable to see the
enemy plane crash so this is considered a probable.

Boyington thinks this plane may have been a Tojo. It
was black with larger than usual roundels. It had
stubby wings with square tips.

Boyington remained all night at Torokina.

29 December, 1943 Bad weather all day.

1710 - 1800; Boyington returned to Vella from Torokina.

The Hamp and pair of Zekes I dispatched on December 28, 1943
would mark my last combat victories as a fighter pilot. By late
December, I had become comfortable with the Corsair, comfortable
with my marksmanship. I had pretty well managed to shed the
status of the inexperienced flyer. Hell, I was even flying some
missions as wingman to the skipper.

Shortly after our mission on December 28, I fell victim to one of
those stupid things we fought in the jungle... I had to arise in the
middle of the night to answer the call of nature. Not the typical call
of nature, mind you; this was dysentery. Like diarrhea, but maybe 5
times as bad. I awoke in the wee hours, with the knowledge that I
would soon soil myself. It was raining like mad as I headed toward
the latrine at full speed. Distracted and in the dark, one of my feet
found a tent wire, and down I went, spraining my right wrist in the
process. Because it was so close to New Year's, I'd like to tell you
that I got drunk and did this at our New Year's Eve party on
December 31, but the truth is that I didn't drink. I believe my wrist
injury happened just before, probably on the December 30.

Date unknown. McClurg in posed photos on Vella Lavella. Bandage is
visible protruding from glove on right hand. (McClurg collection)

Doc Reames looked at the swelling, put my hand in a simple
bandage for a few days, and grounded me. The Black Sheep flew
a mission on January 2, 1944, in which Groover and Losch scored
victories. In a scene from what could have been a typical John
Wayne movie, I tried to sneak onto that mission. I managed to get
myself into a Corsair and get the engine fired up, but Doc Reames
was just a bit too quick and realized that I wasn't accounted for on
the sidelines. Before I could taxi out, he had his jeep in front of my
right wing, pointing at me and dragging his index finger across his
throat. I was frustrated, but he was right; as a pilot, I needed to be
in top notch shape so I could protect whomever I was teamed up
with, let alone so I could prevail against the enemy myself. As it
happened, I would sit out a couple more days while someone else
flew wing on Pappy, and I'll remain wondering "what if" for as long
as I will live...

WAR DIARY, VMF-214

- -

COMBAT REPORT

DATE: 3 January, 1944.

TIME: TAKE-OFF   OVER TARGET
         0640   0800

MISSION: Rabaul Fighter Sweep.

FORCES ENGAGED:
    OWN:
           8 F4U's VMF-214
          20 F4U's
          20 F6F's

        Boyington (missing)   Olander (oxygen 0815)
        Ashmun (missing)   Lane (hydraulic-Torokina
        Hill (electrical 0855) 0835; 1410-1510)
        Johnson,A.L. (0855)   Matheson (Torokina 0945
                   1045-1135)   Chatham (electrical - 0920
                                   1410-1510)

    ENEMY: 10-12 Zekes.

CONTACT:
        Altitude: 19,000'
        Location: Off Ropopo.
        Time   : 0815.

RESULTS: ENEMY LOSSES

        Zeke (light brown)-19000-off Rapopo-Hi head on-
           burned Matheson -0815
        Zeke (light brown)-19000-off Rapopo-Hi 6- Burned
           Boyington - 0815

             OUR LOSSES: Boyington and Ashmun - missing
        in action.

NARRATIVE ACCOUNT:
    The formation with Major Boyington as tactical
commander, headed up the west coast of Bougainville,
arriving over Cape St. George stacked at 20, 22 and
24,000'.

Boyington led the formation in a huge right turn around Rabaul at 0800.

After a 180° turn, contact was made by Major Boyington's division at 0815 off Rapopo at 19,000.

At this time Major Boyington was leading a division made up of Ashmun on his wing, Matheson heading up a second section, with Chatham on his wing.

All of the other 4 planes of the original 8 of VMF-214 had returned to base with various mechanical difficulties.

The 2 sections split up on sighting a formation of 12 Zekes with Boyington going down from 22,000 on the formation which was at 19,000.

Coming in in a high 6 o'clock run with Ashmun on his tail, Boyington shot down 1 Zeke in flames. "223" pilots confirm this plane for Boyington which is his 26th.

Matheson selected a straggler and went down on him in a high head on run, opening fire at 200 yards and knocking pieces off his motor and cowl. He then pulled up hard to the right at which time he saw his Zeke going down burning.

Matheson circled for some 20 minutes looking for another Corsair on which to join but was unable to locate one on account of the haze which made visibility poor. His wingman had returned to Torokina after the first pass when his electrical system failed.

Neither Boyington or Ashmun were contacted by sight or by radio after the initial pass.

On the return trip, someone was heard to call Dane Base reporting that he was going to have to make a water landing.

Ten large and 1 especially large ship were observed in Simpson Harbor. The large one threw up quite a bit of AA.

Weather was clear but visibility was poor due to the haze. There was a solid overcast at 28,000 feet.

1425 Miller, Tucker, Bolt, Harper, Mullen, Crocker, Bragdon, Groover. Off to Torokina to go on search for Boyington and Ashmun. Pancaked 1515.

4 January, 1944.

0550 Mullen, Crocker, Bragdon, Miller, Tucker, Bolt, Harper. Off on search for Major Boyington and Capt. Ashmun, missing in yesterday's action.

Went up to Cape St. George - then up St. George Channel along the west coast of New Ireland and circled Duke of York Island and Credner Island.

Three Miles off Rapopo they spotted a barge underway to the west and strafed it, leaving it smoking.

Continuing on down the coast of New Britain they strafed 2 Jap bivouac areas, starting fires at Kabanga plantation.

The flight strafed 3 more barges off Bilung Plantation; one of the barges exploded. Search was negative. Pancaked 0820.

AIRCRAFT ACTION REPORT

The formation of approximately 50 fighter planes with Major Boyington of VMF 214 as tactical commander, headed up the W. coast of Bougainville, arriving over Cape St. George stacked at 20, 22, and 24 thousand feet. Boyington led the formation in a huge right turn around Rabaul at 0800. After a 180° turn, contact was made by Boyington's division with a formation of 12 Zekes.

At this time Major Boyington was leading a division made up of Capt. Ashmun his wing man; Lt. Matheson leading his second section, with Lt. Chatham as Matheson's wingman. These 4 had joined when 2 men out of each of the original 2 divisions had been forced to return to base with various types of motor trouble.

The 2 sections of Boyington's division split up as they initiated their runs on the formation of 12 Zekes climbing toward them. Boyington went down in a high six o'clock run with Ashmun protecting his tail, while Matheson and Chatham went on a pair of stragglers.

Chatham's guns failed to fire as he settled into position so he climbed up and away and saw both Boyington's and Matheson's Zekes go down burning.

Matheson nabbed his in a high headon run, opening fire at 200 yards and knocking pieces off the cowl and motor of the enemy plane. Matheson then pulled up hard to the right and watched his Zero go down burning, At the same time he saw Boyington's Zeke going in. VMF 223 pilots confirm both planes.

Matheson circled for some 20 minutes looking for a Corsair which to join but was unable to locate one because of the haze which had made visibility poor. His wingman had returned to base after the first pass when his guns failed to work due to an electrical failure. No further sight or radio contact was made with either Boyington or Ashmun after this initial pass - although someone called Dane base and reported that he was going to have to make a water landing.

This was Major Boyington's 26th enemy plane - every one a fighter plane - and every one destroyed over enemy territory. It ties the record established in the last war by Capt. Eddie Rickenbacker and tied at Guadalcanal by Marine Corps Major Joe Foss.

10 large and especially large ship transports or Cargo ships were observed in Simpson Harbor. The largest one threw up a great deal of A.A.

A.A. otherwise was intense, heavy caliber and quite accurate.

The new loading developed by VMF-214 after a number of tests - is proving extremely satisfactory.

This is:

2 incendiary, 1 AP, 2 incendiary 1 tracer,
2 incendiary, 1 AP, 2 incendiary 1 tracer, etc.

This is particularly effective against Japanese planes because of their tendency to burn.

The following is a supplemental report found in the war diary. It details the January 03, 1944 mission. Signed by Pappy on October 4, 1945, it was added to the files after speaking with him in a debriefing session when he was recovered at war's end...

SUPPLEMENTAL REPORT

Most of details covered in original. This supplemental report deals only with activities of Boyington & Ashmun.

Boyington & Ashmun went down on 2 Zekes at tail end of a formation of 6 at 15,000 feet.

Boyington opened fire at 400 yards, closing fast and the Zeke flamed and spun down. The pilot bailed out.

"You got a flower, Skipper." Called Ashmun over the radio. This was #26 for Boyington.

The two went down to 12,000 feet & found themselves surrounded by enemy planes.

They immediately began to scissors. They scissored only 3 or 4 times during which both Ashmun & Boyington shot down flamers, each picking one off the others tail. It was Ashmun's first enemy plane and Boyington's 27th.

At this time Ashmun's plane began to glide downward at a 45 degree angle, smoking.

Boyington called to him to dive out. But Ashmun was apparently hit because he continued downward in a throttle-back 45° glide.

At this time the Zekes swarmed on his tail and raked him from prop to tail.

Boyington pulled in behind them & kicked his rudder, skidding from one side to the other, spraying the Zekes to get them off Ashmun's tail.

Other Zekes swarmed over Boyington, raking him. Holes began to tear in his wings and fuselage. Boyington stayed in behind Ashmun spraying the Zekes on his tail and during this period he got another flamer. This was number 28.

He followed Ashmun on down and saw his plane begin to burn & then crash in the Water in St. George Channel. Boyington thinks Ashmun was killed although there's a thousand to one chance that he might have bailed out before his plane started its downward glide.

Boyington then leveled out & headed for home. He had only gone half a mile when his main gas tank went up in flames, filling the cockpit with smoke & fire.

Unable to see, Boyington took his safety belt with one hand, his rip cord with the other & pulled both & kicked forward on the stick with his foot at the same time. He was thrown clear by the negative G's--either going through the canopy or pulling it off as he went out.

He was 100-200 feet off the water at the time.

He felt a tug on his shoulders as the chute caught & then crashed into the water on his left side with sufficient force to crush his canteen & to smash his wrist watch.

He attempted to inflate his Mae West but it was full of holes from shell fragments. After 2 hours he inflated his rubber raft and climbed aboard. Getting out his first aid equipment, he patched himself up.

He floated all day in his rubber boat, seeing no planes but hearing an occasional one above the overcast.

Just before dusk he was picked up by a Nip submarine, taken to Rabaul and held there for 6 weeks.

He was then flown to Truk by Betty bomber—held there 16 days, flown to Saipan via a Nip Admiral's DC, remained 1 night at Saipan, 1 Night at Iwo Jima & then landed at a Yokohama airport & taken to a secret Navy Intimidation camp at Ofuna. He was held at Ofuna for 13 months, then moved to Omori, a prison camp at a tiny island in the Tokyo harbor between Tokyo & Yokohama. He was released on 24 August by a detachment of Marines

under command of Commodore Simpson and Commander
Stassen.

He was flown to Ewa where he remained a week for
Medical checkup & then flown to San Francisco—arriving
12 September.

Thus, January 03, 1944 was the day that emptied Pappy's bunk.
Henry Miller, a highly capable individual with experience, became
C.O. We were in a state of shock. The invincible lion had
disappeared. The mission had gone horribly wrong, with half of the
intended planes turning back for various reasons. Perry Lane
returned with problems in his hydraulic system. Jim Hill's electrical
system failed almost completely, forcing him to turn back, and
Chatham would drop out later in the mission, also with an electrical
problem. Jim Hill didn't know it then, but his electrical failure
wouldn't be the first surprise for him on January third. Following is
a letter Jim wrote to me on October 30, 1999, recounting that day...

I'm sure all of the Black Sheep had exciting
experiences. One mission that is still very clear in
my mind was the one when we lost Pappy Boyington and
George Ashmun. We had taken off when I discovered my
radio was not working. This wasn't unusual and when it
happened we used hand signals to communicate. This
mission was a fighter sweep to Rabaul, a Japanese
stronghold.

As we approached the combat area we tested our guns.
Mine wouldn't fire, - I tried every trick I knew, but
they just would not fire. Rather than be a sitting
duck, I decided to return to base 300 miles away. I
signaled to my wingman that I was having trouble with
my plane and turned the lead over to him. In trying to
return to base, I discovered my compass wasn't working
either. By checking the position of the sun and
gauging the wind and water, I flew a course that I
thought would take me back to base. It didn't work out
that way - I was lost and very low on fuel and nobody
knew my position, so there wouldn't be a search for me.
Not an island in sight, nothing but the blue Pacific.
I thought "This is it! Shall I bail out or land in the
water." Either way I wouldn't last long in a rubber
raft. I got the feeling of a man ready to be executed.
But--at this moment a Corsair flashed in front of me
and gave me the join up signal. It was my wingman who
had been following above and behind me. Realizing I
was lost, he led me back to base with an almost empty

```
fuel  tank.    If  he  had  stayed  with  the  formation  I
wouldn't be here to write about it.
```

```
                    Jim Hill
                    VMF-214
                    BLACK SHEEP SQUADRON
```

Jim Hill's wingman was Al Johnson, the fourth plane of the group to turn back. Of course I wasn't there, but heard all about it over the next few days. From the description and our subsequent conversations, we were almost certain that Ashmun was dead when he hit the water. The description of Ashmun's final glide was much like that of one of my first victories. An airplane that remains on a steady, unresponsive course is almost always an indication of no pilot input. I sat alone for long periods of time in the days immediately after that mission, looking at the bandage on my right hand, and thinking. I will forever wonder how the chips would have fallen had I been there. Maybe I would have chanced to fly in a way that allowed Pappy to score and return home. On the other hand, maybe I would have played the same part Ashmun did, and never been heard from again.

For the purposes of this book, I chose to include the actual combat reports whenever Pappy or I had a score. My last combat victory occurred on December 28, 1943 and of course Pappy's was January 3' 1944. Scanning the war diary beyond that point, I can offer some further information.

In the days immediately after January 3, the Black Sheep, who were previously known as aggressive, antagonistic fighters— became demons. There was a fighter sweep to Rabaul on January 4 (in which I did not participate). I believe three definite and two probable scores were logged then. There were stories of strafing runs, the aggressiveness of which was even beyond our previous exploits. Interestingly, the combat logs for January 4 also contain complaints about too many pilots from other squadrons aborting for either contrived reasons or no reason at all. The report suggests that pilots fabricated problems in order to turn back. There is also a statement made about radio calls in which pilots indicate turning back for no specific reason. Perhaps those comments shouldn't speak as much about the other squadrons as they do about the mental state of our own.

Date and location unknown. Six Black Sheep Aces
Back row L-R: "Moon" Mullen, John Bolt, Bob McClurg
Front row L-R: Ed Olander, Chris Magee, Don Fisher
(McClurg collection)

I did fly again on January 5; an escort and strafing run to Rabaul.
Our thoughts were still with Pappy and George. We typically did a
pretty good job of tearing things up on strafing runs, but that
mission illustrated for me how much more we could turn up the
wick. If it moved, it got shot. Second strafing passes, which were
normally taboo (because the plane was much more likely to get hit
on a second run after he had gotten everyone's attention), were more
common. We strafed a light tower, which was a strategic item to
put out of commission (they could be used as landmarks for
outbound enemy bombers on early dawn missions). We strafed
barges, houses, troop transports.   Levels of destruction that
previously left us satisfied that we had disabled something, now
were not enough. I don't think it was so much increased effort on
our parts as it was decreased concern for ourselves. We were out to
make payment in full for the disappearance of Pappy. We flew
another similar mission on January 6, again with terribly heavy

concentration on strafing. On that mission, Harry Johnson had the presence to remember something Boyington taught him; as Johnson was following a Zeke in a shallow turn, he remembered Pappy saying "If it seems too easy, look for the catch." Johnson twisted his neck, and sure enough found two other Zeros coming in behind him. He was able to get away, while still adding the first Zeke to his list of accomplishments. As if to symbolize our mood, the weather on these days had been gloomy and generally unpleasant.

January 7 had us all resting, and the second combat tour ended officially on January 8. Between January 8 and 20, we cleaned up, had malaria tests, official paperwork and citations were made. I received the Distinguished Flying Cross on January 18. On January 21, we all began that long, cold, nauseating trip to Sydney for some R&R.

Second Rest Trip To Sydney

The second trip to Sydney was mechanically the same as the first; long hours in a strong stench of gasoline. We seemed to tolerate the journey better than the first time. Perhaps it was because we had made the Sydney excursion once before, but I think it was more than that. Our entire mood was different. The absence of Pappy, who had entertained us with his escape antics, cockpit conversations and fire extinguisher toilet evacuation on the first trip, was still the subject of our thoughts, but now in a vacant sort of way.

As home away from home, we were happy to find Frieda still at the Snake Pit. Some of us stuck together for a time, others were more independent. We all had our initial dose of good cooked food and hot showers. But this time, I chose to spend my liberty just a bit differently... Our second R&R tour had us checking into a hotel. During the check-in process, I noticed a receptionist at a separate desk. She took reservations and also worked as a representative of the Australian red cross. She had a wholesome, intrinsic beauty that captivated me. There was a time when I wouldn't have known what to say, but I had the benefit of experience, and also membership in a fighter squadron that had gained some notoriety. For me, there were also no romantic attachments back home, or anywhere else at that point. I noticed from afar that she was wearing a ring in a place which might indicate that she was "taken." That notwithstanding, I waited until we had all been checked in, then I approached her desk and introduced myself. I offered dinner, but not in the same context as we had done on our first tour. On this second tour, I knew a little more about where to go for food, and thus didn't need to ask so earnestly. I think the events of earlier that month had also affected our mood; we didn't seem so fixated on high energy ramblings. Many of us really wanted to get away and relax. My offer for dinner came from within, along with a sincere interest in conversation and maybe a little companionship. She thanked me, then politely informed me that she could not accept my offer. I managed to learn that she would be working at the hotel regularly during my stay, and closed our conversation at that point.

On the next day, I made an interesting observation... Where there was a ring yesterday, there was no longer a ring. I wondered "what does that tell me?" and found myself taking dinner with her that evening. We went to a nice place, with good food, and we did a lot of talking. We talked about her family, and we talked about my family. Her husband (of course, an Australian man) was a member of the Australian Army, and had been killed in action. They had been married 6 weeks when he perished. She turned out to be seeking the same type of conversation I was, and we hit it off very well. I learned even more about her when I received an invitation to spend a couple days at the home of her mother and father, where she lived. We approached a magnificent sheep ranch. I think the number of sheep they kept was something like eight thousand. The home itself was splendid. I will never forget the opening of the front door, and my journey across the living room to shake hands with her parents; the floor was covered with sheep pelts, all finely tailored and sewn together. It looked like fine wool wall-to-wall carpeting, but the pile was so deep that my shoes disappeared into it with every step. It was really something. They also had a swimming pool, which was a rare luxury in those times. The young lady's parents informed me that the two of them would be there for another day, after which they had to travel. They extended permission for me to stay at the house, along with the resident cook, who I assumed would act as enough of a chaperone to make the offer possible. Indeed, we did enjoy two or three days of relaxation in a resort-like atmosphere. I couldn't have asked for anything more. Many of our boys in the service came home with wives, and I might have been one of them. The timing was really too soon for her, and the concept of leaving Australia was not appropriate, either. Likewise, I couldn't imagine not returning home to mom if I survived the war. We parted company on pleasant terms.

Third Combat Tour

We made the return hops once again, droning along in a freezing, smelly "gooney bird." Sydney to Brisbane. Brisbane to Tontua. Tontua to Espirito. By January 31, 1944, I was back in the combat area for commencement of my third tour. We rested and took the usual tests until about February 5, then began flying again. We did the typical tactical formations and gunnery practice until mid-March. Although still VMF-214, the squadron was different. Pappy's absence made it a different world to begin with, and we were now under the command of Henry Miller, with Stan Bailey as executive officer.

Known among the Black Sheep as the "Bailey patch", this felt insignia was updated shortly after Pappy was lost, during the time when Henry Miller was in command and Stan Bailey was executive offer. The main difference was the addition of "214" in the lower right. (Bourgeois collection)

Henry was a fully competent leader, but completely different from Pappy in composure. Henry was thorough, mechanical, highly organized and "by the books." That meant we didn't adopt such an aggressive stance, which translated to less aerial contact with an enemy who was getting scarce by that time, anyway. Oddly, I learned later that the Japanese didn't do so much patching up of their aircraft, for whatever reasons. An American aircraft could expect to be patched up many times, as many of our own were even regularly by stopping off at an interim airfield on the way home from a mission. But the Japanese were different... I have learned that one of their aircraft in need of repair would often sit for an extended period of time. Perhaps their availability of spare parts was worse than our own. By this time, they didn't exactly have an excess of pilots, either.

McClurg taxiing aircraft #154 on Espiritu Santos Feb 24, 1944
(McClurg collection)

Black Sheep Corsairs taxiing out for a scramble 2-24-1944 Bougainville
(McClurg collection)

Two of the more interesting flights I had were photo missions in
which I took a couple photojournalists up in an SNJ on March 12.
They weren't religious experiences, but were at least a break from
the ordinary. They wanted to fly over leper colonies, so we did.
They were interested in jungle shots and wreckages, which were
plentiful. Our third tour began officially on March 16, 1944, with
each of us still wondering every day about Pappy.

The Black Sheep got some new members to replace others who
had been wounded or completed their third tour, etc. I made a new
friend by the name of Czarnecki. We were doing more sharing of
aircraft and sticking to a limited number of airframes than in the
past. Like me, Czarnecki was also mostly a non-drinker, and we
pooled our resources to get in the good graces of our ground crew
by giving them our liquor. In return for this, we got a multitude of
small favors which totaled together in the form of convenience for
us. The planes we flew were then a little cleaner and a little more
polished. They would simonize (wax) the leading edge of the wings
for us, which added three or four knots to the top speed. We made

patrols, strafed, escorted bombers. We also seemed to spend more time than in the past escorting "dumbos." These were the flying boats often used to pick up downed pilots. Unfortunately on March 29, I flew a mission searching for two of our Black Sheep who failed to return; they were Daly and Czarnecki, who happened to be flying one of our highly polished "pets" when he disappeared. We don't think they disappeared at the hands of the enemy. Rather, we think it was weather which got them lost in the water. I almost think a pilot had better chances getting shot down by the enemy, even in enemy territory; most often if that happened, it was witnessed by squadron mates. The location would be noted and a rescue would be mounted. The pilot then had to avoid capture, avoid sharks, and tend to his wounds for a while, but had the solace of knowing that his buddies saw where he was. A lost pilot who ditched at sea often had the same issues to worry about, but often would have no search for himself because nobody really knew where to look. Pilots who got lost, then found... had gotten very lucky indeed.

My writing for our third tour is admittedly short, because there wasn't much aerial action for us, compared to the first and second tours. However, it is important to me that this not be viewed as a weakness on the part of our new C.O. in comparison to Pappy. The truth is that by early 1944, the Allies had the Japanese fighting forces pretty well confined to their own mainland and a few of the nearby surrounding islands. We either had them bottled up, or bypassed and isolated, left to fend for themselves; there simply weren't as many opportunities for us to engage the enemy in aerial battles. The Allies had achieved a pretty fair air superiority by then; the Japanese were pretty much in the situation that if they sent anything up with a propeller on it, odds were very high that they'd never see that particular aircraft again. The Japanese were mainly in a defensive mode. They knew this, they were becoming desperate, and that is the primary reason why the kamikaze attacks on our Navy became a real issue around this point in time. I don't think we'd have had much more aerial contact with the enemy (if any), had Pappy still been skipper.

The tour continued into April, with more "typical" missions and lots of strafing. I didn't shoot down any opposing aircraft, but our mission on April 8, 1944 is worth a short story. The flight began with myself and Chris Magee as a bomber escort out of Green

Island to hit Rabaul. Heavy weather caused the bombers to scrub their mission shortly after takeoff, and the tower gave us permission to either return to base or make a fighter sweep. Magee and I had flown as a team many times; we chose to keep going and rose above the clouds. We set a heading, and timed it blindly - I think it was 220 miles to Rabaul. I can't take any credit for the navigation, and I think if Magee were alive today, he wouldn't, either. We just flew for a certain amount of time. Of course, we were in radio silence, but our plan without saying it was to drop down through the clouds and choose whatever targets of opportunity we might find, with the knowledge that we might see nothing and head home without firing a shot. When the clocks said so, we dropped our noses and descended through the clouds. The cloud ceiling turned out to be at 800 to 1000 feet, and luck smiled on a couple of the Black Sheep once more; we were exactly over Rabaul harbor. Situated in perfect position for us to line up on were 3 barges full of troops, a few hundred feet off the shore. Boy, did we let them have it. After a few passes, the water around the barges was bright red. Any return fire we received was ineffective, and must have been limited to small arms. I don't recall any damage to our planes after that mission. I think of those Japanese warriors on the transports, bobbing along through the mist, slowly heading toward shore... It must have been a terrifying thing to discover the engine sound they heard approaching was, of all things, a couple of Corsairs come to visit them. Most of the troop movements were done at night to avoid just such situations. But this was a day of terrible weather, and nobody thought the enemy would come calling.

We went barge hunting in the Duke of York area on April 10, and strafed New Ireland and Kavieng areas on the April 12. It was about all we had to do.

The end of April was the end of our third tour. For the record, my last combat flight occurred on April 28. It was actually a ferry flight, moving our Corsairs. I hadn't seen a Japanese airplane in the air, and so hadn't shot at one. There were some more long transport flights, but this time we were heading Northeast to a staging area, toward home, instead of South to Sydney.

After The War

After a few ferry flights, it was on to an ocean liner for the long journey back. I don't remember feeling any elation at the prospect of going home. I do remember noting again how vast the ocean was, but not being so affected because it was the second time for me. The entire trip was speckled with concerns about being torpedoed, but we were spared. After what seemed like far too long, I arrived at San Diego.

From there, it was on to Cherry Point, North Carolina where I finally had a few days to get accustomed to our homeland again. My last flight in the combat zone had been April 28, when I ferried a Corsair to Buttons. The next time I flew was almost 3 months later (!), in a B-25 on July 20. I remained in Cherry Point until the end of July, at which time I moved to Kinston, North Carolina to continue my military career as a fighter pilot instructor with VMF-911. I spent a couple weeks there, then moved to Greenville, North Carolina, and resumed instruction for roughly the month of September, 1944. Greenville was particularly fun for a couple reasons. I think it took me two or three months to readjust and really accept the fact that I was back in the U.S.A. There were lots of girl's schools in Greenville, and we weren't living under impending threat of enemy attack. The Black Sheep had become pretty well known back in the states, and the girls went for this in a big way. I spent my nights enjoying the local community, and my days sharing my experiences with our new fighter pilot recruits. One of the pilot candidates assigned to my class was named Luke Tallman. I always remembered him because he was great overall at everything - the flying, the navigating, the gunnery. He was the only one I taught who eventually went overseas and bagged a Zeke. So many of the young recruits I taught who had worked just as hard as I did never got to shoot at anything in combat; targets had become scarce by the time they made it to the combat theater.

The month of October '44 had me back to Cherry Point. I remember one of my neighbors there was the actor Tyrone Power - we even shared bathroom facilities. He was a real character, as social as could be. He occupied every free minute with something social. I wouldn't go so far as to insinuate that he was up to anything terrible, but the guy never wanted his wife to know where he was. That in itself was a great source of entertainment for the rest of us there. We took turns answering the telephone for him, explaining not where he was, but rather why he wasn't in the barracks at the time.

I continued as a fighter pilot trainer in Cherry Point through December '44, basically enjoying life. I was also getting access to some other aircraft for checkout and familiarization. I spent some time with the B-25 bomber, this time as co-pilot. I also got into a solo stint with a hairy bird called the F7-F. This was a twin engined light bomber, designed to be fast. It was powered by twin Pratt & Whitney R-2800 engines (the same engine used in the Corsair). That plane had power on top of its power. It was November 18; on my first foray with the mighty F7-F, I made another classic error that could have taken my life so easily; I got the thing all set to go, followed all the check lists, and prepared for takeoff. Extremely powerful, I don't think I can adequately describe to you how muscular the airplane was when it came to rolling down the runway under power. Even though it was my first time flying the airplane solo, I knew something wasn't right because the nose tried to come up way too soon in the takeoff roll. I had studied the flight handbook for the plane enough to know that my airspeed wasn't nearly enough to lift off the runway, but the nose was quite obviously trying to come up. With some quick sweating and much rapid fiddling of my hands, I held the stick forward (to keep the nose down) and fumbled with the nose trim to get the plane adjusted so it wasn't trying to lift off too soon. (The flight surfaces on airplanes all have trim adjustments on them, so you can adjust their positions such that the pilot doesn't have to hold the stick at all. This is normal for airplanes, because the ideal control surface position varies with things like altitude, weight and speed.) Still not sure what exactly had gone wrong, I held the thing on the ground until the air speed came up enough, then lifted off as normal. Once airborne, I was able to adjust the various flight controls and get the plane trimmed up so everything was reasonable. After some in-air studying, I discovered what I had done wrong: the text book elevator trim for the F7-F was something like 2 degrees "up." To explain a little about where this comes from, the developers of the airplane would have done tests and learned that when you set the elevator trim at about 2 degrees "up," then the airplane would tend to lift itself off the runway gently and at about the correct speed. That is the reason (and the origin) of where they come up with all those specific settings. Anyhow, my mistake was simple... I had misread the marks on the dial for the elevator trim, and set it at 20 degrees "up," not 2 degrees. If I had let the nose come up when it first wanted, the airplane most likely wouldn't have flown. It probably would have risen a few feet, stalled, and crashed back onto the runway. (Stalled, in airplane jargon, doesn't mean that the engines would have quit. It means the wing would have stopped flying, and I would have fallen back onto the ground.) God had forgiven me one more time, but I continued to push my luck... Impressed (and perhaps a bit intoxicated) by the F7-F's brute power, I did some aerobatic maneuvers. (The F7-F had tremendous performance, but never actually made it to combat because the war would end before the mighty plane could be deployed.) I finished with a power dive, in which I came hurtling toward earth at some horrendous speed, yanking back on the stick with both hands at the end to recover to a level flight path. During the dive, I felt a shudder, then noticed that the airplane felt somehow different on the controls, but I couldn't pinpoint just exactly what the difference was. All the engine gauges and flight instruments continued to work, and all gave normal readings. My first confirmation that something was indeed amiss was during my final taxi back to the hangar where the flight mechanic awaited. As I approached, the odd movements of his neck and head told me that it was something visible. Turns out it was an external boarding ladder. I think it was a retractable device I had, uh, forgotten to retract. I forget what we did, but they extracted me from the airplane via some other means. From previous knowledge, I was told that the ladder would bend along the fuselage as it had—at approximately 575 miles per hour! During that period in my life, being a Black Sheep pilot got me many free cups of coffee and other little preferences. That, combined with the fact that I apparently wasn't the first one to make such an error with the F7-F, bought me absolutely nothing with this particular flight mechanic.

In mid-December '44, I reported to Quantico, Virginia, to attend Marine Air Infantry School. This was essentially what we know in the modern day as "war games" for fighter pilots. It consisted of all sorts of different tactics, aerobatic maneuvering, scrambles, etc. All were aimed at impressing and honing the tactics and efficiency for fighter pilots. There was a shortage of available aircraft to fly, and many of us ended up taking rides with others in order to meet the required number of logged hours for flight pay. I'm not even sure whether I was able to make it home for Christmas 1944. I do have record that I graduated from Marine Air Infantry School on March 3, 1945. Also, I was promoted to the rank of Captain while there, on February 2.

I spent a couple weeks back at Quantico, then received sealed orders to report to some place in New York City. My journey came without much notice, and without much information. "Just go, and they'll fill you in when you get there..." For a while, I wondered whether I might find myself heading across the Atlantic, say to London. I couldn't imagine why it would be so, and something like that just didn't make sense in the whole context of things. When I arrived, I learned that I would be staying at the Waldorf Astoria, and that the main purpose of my trip was five days R&R, during which time I would appear on a radio show called "Let Yourself Go." Also on the show at the time I appeared were Milton Berle and Errol Flynn. I got to go because I was one of the Black Sheep (good for publicity and motivation at the time), and I was relatively close and able to make the trip. There were swank parties that defy description. There were beautiful girls at every turn. I felt largely outclassed in many instances, but enjoyed it nonetheless. I wasn't the life of the party by any means, but managed to get in the good graces of someone there, who made a phone call or two, and got my stay extended another three days. In all, it was eight days of lavish life, top-shelf parties, and the most beautiful ladies anyone could dream of. About the radio show... I managed to find an old script for it, which appears in the appendices.

Back to Quantico once more, then off to Memphis, Tennessee, to the Naval Air Technical Training Center, where I attended Engineering Officer's school through April, May and June of 1945. That was like an engineering and mechanic's school for aircraft.

We learned more in-depth technical items about all the different systems used on aircraft; engines, hydraulics, electrical systems, etc. We worked in teams (I think our team had eight to ten people). We studied the aircraft systems, and spent some time "hands on," working with a specific aircraft. Ours happened to be a Corsair. At the end of the course, they would test a group's troubleshooting abilities by intentionally putting a defect of some sort into the aircraft, then having the group find it. We had to tear a good part of the plane apart to find the defects they introduced. Fortunately one of the guys on our team was a real technical whiz. He found an electrical problem they had introduced, and we managed to get our bird back together with no extra pieces left over at the end. We did all the ground checks, and everything seemed fine. We drew straws to see who might pilot the test flight. (It was a requirement to obtain the Engineering School certificate that the aircraft had to pass all checks and be demonstrated flyable.) I got the short straw, and proceeded to make several touch and go passes (that's where you come in for a landing but don't stop - just touch the runway, then add power and take off again) to demonstrate that all was well. I think ours was the only group to successfully fly the aircraft we worked on. We graduated on July 7, 1945.

From there it was once again back to Cherry Point, where I went through August and September working with Corsairs. There were newly installed racks that fired rockets from the wings. We worked with high altitude gunnery, glide bombing, and new strafing techniques. The new strafing techniques were aimed at optimizing close air support (no pun intended); it had been discovered that Army or Marine troops having difficulty on the ground could call for a strike, use a special method of telling the pilots where to hit, and then often watch the enemy disappear before their eyes. In the latter part of this stint, I got some flight time as co-pilot of a couple different aircraft, including the PBJ and R4D-5.

October, 1945 had me traveling once more toward the west coast, via Fort Worth, Texas, to Kearney Mesa, San Diego. The main purpose of this trip was to determine the next direction for my military career. In November, after some settling in and the usual orientations, I learned what lay in store for me; if I stayed in the service, my future would still involve flying Corsairs, and I liked that just fine. However, I would be flying Corsairs from aircraft carriers, and I knew what the level of difficulty was there. I figured I had pushed my luck far enough; the good Lord had spared me many times. To let an experienced pilot out like that wasn't what they had in mind either, and my arms were twisted every which way in efforts to get me to reconsider. But I simply felt that it was time for me to cash in my winnings without further play. In early December 1945, without a specific plan for what else I might do, I finished my time in the service. I took advantage of my location, and headed from San Diego up to Seattle to visit my brother, Justus, who was a hydraulic systems mechanic at Boeing. After catching up with my brother, the military had provided for my travel back east, and this becomes a story in itself. I was basically given a "green light" to have transport back east, but exactly how that transport would occur was left to the people at NAS Seattle to arrange for me. I might have had a seat on a standard transport, or as luck would have it, I might end up with a very different mode of transportation.

I poked around the air station at Seattle, and got my name on the list for transportation back east. The NAS was a busy place, with people and aircraft scurrying all over. There were pilots who ferried aircraft back and forth across the country, taking whatever passengers or cargo they could fit on the way. This is why one never knew what aircraft one might get, or what might be the accompanying cargo. I got connected with a Navy pilot, who was preparing to ferry a Grumman Widgeon back east, but there was a problem: there was a Navy captain who had also been waiting a couple days for transportation East. The Navy captain outranked me significantly, but he had a drawback. To the Navy pilot flying the plane, the captain was too much of a "stuffed shirt," and the pilot didn't relish the thought of flying cross-country with him. (Remember, in those days, cross-country was not a one-day affair.) In talking with the pilot, I learned of his sentiments. He wanted to stop and do some duck hunting along the way. He asked me, "Do you hunt?" "Oh yeah, I hunt," was my reply. He then asked, "How much luggage do you have?" I had only one duffel. And so the Navy pilot gave me these instructions: be here in the morning, before opening time. Don't wait in the ready room, where everyone else will be waiting; wait just outside, around the corner where you can watch the airplane. When you see the ground crew pull the chocks away from the wheels, you run like hell to the airplane, and be ready to roll.

Next morning, I watched from my vantage point as I was told to do. All of a sudden, I saw two army girls—WAVEs—run toward the airplane. Not sure what was going on, I ran like hell after them. As we approached the plane, the Navy pilot motioned and urged us aboard in a big hurry. He revved the engines, and we taxied away. The Navy captain had been watching, as well. He was a little slower than we were, and remained on the ground. The Navy pilot had known about the Army girls all the while; the four of us were off for a few days of fun, with our Eastern destination being almost a secondary item on the agenda. The widgeon is a slow flying airplane, and that left much time to get to know each other. It turned out that the Navy pilot was well acquainted with this routine, and it ended up being a great vacation for me. We had time with the ladies, and we stopped at Navy air stations along the way. The procedure involved landing and turning the girls loose for a few hours to shop and explore (which they enjoyed), while we went duck hunting at locations known by the pilot. Our first night's foray is worth mentioning a bit further...

We got a hotel room and brought in our luggage. Luggage for the two men consisted of my duffel, and two identical suitcases for the pilot; one contained his clothes, and the other contained several dead ducks. He went into the bathroom, and commenced to cleaning the ducks in the tub, using the commode to dispose of the unwanted internals. As you might imagine, things became a bit messy. Meanwhile, he had me order a round of cocktails for us all. I answered a knock at the door, at which time the room servant handed me a tray of drinks, and remarked something like "holy mackerel there, man!" after looking over my shoulder and seeing the mess in the bathroom. After I shut the door, the pilot realized that we might soon be in trouble. He instructed me to take one of the pillows and put a knife in it. I made a mess of feathers while he frantically cleaned the bathroom and stuffed our hidden cargo back into the suitcase. Sure enough, there came another knock at the door about ten minutes later; it was the manager wanting to know if everything was OK. We told him that we'd just had a little pillow fight, and agreed to clean up the feathers and pay for the pillow. That satisfied the manager, and we finished cleaning the ducks after he left.

We brought the ducks to a local restaurant, and supplied our own main course. The pilot had gotten to know some of the chefs; he would bring them several ducks, and they would cook two or three for us. The restaurant would provide all the rest of the trimmings; we got a nice meal, and the restaurant got some fresh duck to sell to other customers. Imagine what the local health regulations would have to say about that nowadays! With food and fine companionship, we eventually made it to Wildwood, New Jersey. From there, I took a train back to New Castle, Pa. and spent a terrific Christmas with my mom and sister, Dorothy, who was serving in the Navy as a Lieutenant in the supply corps. Then I began to re-enter civilian life.

While in college, one of my part time jobs had been with Universal-Rundle Corporation, a plumbing ware manufacturer in New Castle. Fortune had it that I would return to that same company as a full time employee in the human resources department. I also attended night classes at the university of Pittsburgh to pursue my Masters degree.

I began to enjoy our local community in New Castle and was happy to call it "home". I attended the church where I grew up. I liked the preacher because he was a great fisherman and we began to fish a lot together with his two sons, Dave and Don. One Sunday, I noticed a fine young lady and expressed my interest in her to Don. I was met with a sneer. "She's way too young for you, Bob. That's my little sister, Julia!" However, I persisted and we began to date when she was home on breaks as a junior at Muskingum College. To make a long story short, we married in 1948. I was then assistant personnel manager at Universal Rundle Corporation. Our first son, Scott, was born in 1949. In 1950 I was one of the first two salesmen hired for Universal Rundle, and we moved to Syracuse, New York. Syracuse is where our second son, Mark, and daughter, Mary Beth, were born.

In 1961, I made a change and opened my own business, acting as a manufacturer's representative for various plumbing supply companies. Collectively, we Black Sheep were pursuing life and raising our families.

The Seventies And Beyond

By the early 1970's, most of us were in our early 50's and going through life. I don't know if any of us were still in military service; several of the Sheep had pursued careers in military service, but may have been retired by then. WWII had been in the past long enough to be forgotten, but not long enough to have become such a topic of nostalgia as it is these days. We had been into and out of Korea militarily, and the Vietnam action was just coming to a close. Many of us had adolescent children - the babyboomers - who were driving us nuts with all the flower power and free love, long hair and "I don't care." I had a business of my own started as a manufacturer's representative in the plumbing field, and I was doing OK. Other Sheep had done all sorts of things; a couple of them had become career airline pilots. Others entered the legal and political arena. Successful business men, law enforcement officers, college professors; we had them all. We had our first reunion in Hawaii in 1976—roughly our thirtieth service anniversary, and the bicentennial of our country.

I still wonder sometimes what possessed them to do it, but somehow somebody got the idea that a Black Sheep TV show would be a good thing, and apparently the whole gamut of approval was negotiated successfully, and it got to production. Our real wartime experiences were interesting, to say the least, but there was a problem: first, it would have been socially unacceptable to recreate enough of the specific stuff that defined "interesting" in our context. Second, our "interesting" wasn't quite "interesting" enough to appeal to the general masses (which a TV show had to do), so they took some "artistic license." To represent us as a bunch of young men, eager and willing, but without specific assignment for any of multiple reasons, wasn't catchy enough for them. What came out on film was a bunch of cutups, always scheming. They sometimes made it look like we treated our combat with the Japanese almost as a distraction to our other unsavory conduct. That treatment infuriated Frank Walton, our intelligence officer, and was what prompted him to write his own book, *Once They Were Eagles*. The book chronicles our combat life in a real fashion, and Frank was in about the best position to recount such things (as it was part of his job during the service!). The title he chose for his work runs deeper than most people realize; it was partially intended as a confrontation to the TV show, in the context "Once they were eagles, but look how you've represented them now…" Frank never accepted the way that was done, referring to it as "that turkey of a TV show." I don't think Pappy subscribed to the exact representation of us either, but he was more willing to accept the idea of pleasing the masses. Pappy appears in some of the TV show credits as a technical consultant; this wasn't to imply that Pappy himself had reconstructed all the scenes with impeccable accuracy. Pappy knew it was a business of entertainment; his flair for this is also a good bit of the reason he survived his time in Japanese prison camp, when so many others died. The show's existence accomplished two main things; first, it sent the squadron into a turmoil, the likes of which our enemy never cast upon us back in the combat days. Second, although our wartime exploits had already gained us notoriety among historians, I think the TV show did a great deal to establish us firmly in the minds of the masses, even those who didn't necessarily have a firm knowledge or interest in WWII history. Sometimes, it just isn't as attractive to know things as they were. And sometimes, things get taken a bit too far in that way when they are recounted. The TV show had a tabloid aspect to it. Sensationalism sells, and also causes turmoil. The Black Sheep continue to experience this.

Good and bad, often inaccurate, the Black Sheep memory seems to live on. We continue to receive mail from all over the world, and the amount doesn't seem to wane as the years go by.

Pappy continued to attend air shows and sell his book(s), and the rest of us continued our own pursuits. The dawning of the 1980s saw some of the Sheep retiring, while others were in the home stretches of our careers. I retired from my business in 1981.

I don't think it is well understood that the squadron's image as it has been re-created over the years, and how we really were, are so different.

On the subject of books, I'd like to mention one or two others. Those who have studied the Black Sheep and read most of what they could find about Pappy may recall seeing a book whose author represents himself as the one who shot down Pappy. The book was written many years ago. Not to be elusive, but I'll avoid mentioning the author's name or book title here, because we have strong indications that it's a work of fiction. I'll refer you to another book by a credible author, Henry Sakaida. The book's title is *Pacific Air Combat - WWII*, and it gives a good perspective from the Japanese point of view, to which the author (who lives in the U.S.A.) has good connections. A chapter in Sakaida's book is devoted to the author I decline to mention above; the chapter is titled "The Man Who Didn't Shoot Down Pappy Boyington." Sakaida's research indicates that if you study the man's own log books, they will show that he didn't even fly on the day Boyington and Ashmun went down.

Henry Sakaida's research, as well as that of others, strongly indicates that an accomplished Japanese pilot named Takeo Tanimizu was really the one who brought Pappy down. As we understand it through a mutual acquaintance, Tanimizu is still living in Japan as of this writing, having lived a quiet, industrious life. My personal message to Tanimizu would be one of respect and good will; he was doing his job, just as we were doing ours.

The "mutual acquaintance," himself, has sometimes gotten incorrect attention. Bob Strickland is an American businessman who made his living operating a very successful restaurant in Japan.

Bob got to know Pappy very well in the years after the war, and Pappy considered him a friend. Although not a Black Sheep in the sense that he did not fly with us in WWII, Strickland represented the Black Sheep through Pappy in Japan in the years that followed. He also experienced the wrath of many people who didn't understand his role, and thought he was trying to pass himself off as a Black Sheep pilot. It is little known, but the Japanese fighter pilots association has, through Strickland, sent gestures of respect and good will to Pappy and the Black Sheep. The feeling is mutual.

At the Hawaii reunion in 1976 – roughly the thirtieth anniversary of Black Sheep service. L-R Pappy Boyington, Julia McClurg, Robert McClurg, Jo Boyington (McClurg collection)

At the Hawaii reunion in 1976
L-R Fred Losch, Pappy Boyington, Ned Corman
(McClurg collection)

Date unknown. Est. late 1970's, Pappy visiting Syracuse, NY
L-R Robert McClurg, Pappy Boyington, Al Johnson
(McClurg collection)

Robert McClurg with hands on shoulders of Chris Magee, 1996 reunion
Ed Olander is in background at right (McClurg collection)

Robert McClurg with Michael and Denise Wagner, relatives of Henry
Bourgeois. Photo at the Bourgeois family compound, 1996 reunion.
(McClurg collection)

Robert McClurg (R) with son, Scott, posing by a Corsair decorated as
Pappy Boyington's mount. Naval Air Museum, Pensacola, FL, 2000
(Marketos collection)

Date and location unknown. Pappy posing with an F4-U decorated with his credentials (Strickland collection)

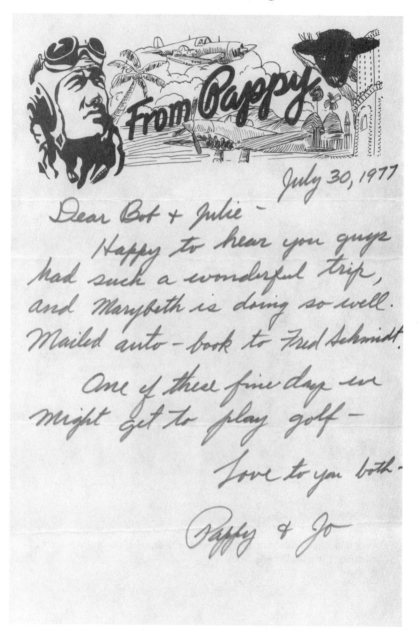

July 30, 1977

Dear Bob + Julie –

Happy to hear you guys had such a wonderful trip, and Marybeth is doing so well. Mailed auto - book to Fred Schmidt.

One of these fine days we might get to play golf –

Love to you both –

Pappy + Jo

Late July, 1977 A note from Pappy to Bob McClurg and his wife, in Pappy's handwriting and on his own notepaper, which was actually medium green color. (McClurg collection)

Takeo Tanimizu, squadron leader, 253rd Imperial Air Wing, 37 victories. On Rabaul, 1943; the Japanese pilot believed to have downed Pappy Boyington. (Strickland collection)

Takeo Tanimizu (L) and Bob Strickland in Japan 1981
(Strickland collection)

Pappy passed away in January of 1988, and along with all the other Sheep who have died, he is now flying high cover for those of us who remain here, earthbound for just a while longer. Pappy was buried in Arlington National Cemetery, with full military honors. (He was, of course, a Medal of Honor recipient.) It was a very serious, solemn occasion, with the riderless horse and reversed boots. They closed the Washington airport to allow for a flyover in his honor; something rarely done. Following is the eulogy, delivered by Pappy's friend, and former prison camp comrade, Ray "Hap" Halloran:

Today, Colonel Gregory Boyington, U.S. Marine Corps, joins others in this hallowed ground at Arlington National Cemetery.
He will be with those who, like "Pappy," contributed so much to the good of our country.
I know that Pappy would like us to recognize his wife of 13 years - Jo - and members of her family.
Also, his son, Gregory Boyington Jr. and his family.
They are gathered here today with a deep sense of pride.
I'm sure that Pappy would want to express a special thanks to the Corps for their all out efforts to recognize one of their own.
My feeling after discussions with many Marines is that they consider Pappy as one of their very best - the original top gun - a hero - a legend in his own time - an inspiration.
I first met Pappy in a prisoner of war camp in early 1945 at Omori on the southern edge of Tokyo. He was already a hero to me with is 28 aerial victories long before our B-29 was shot down over Tokyo.
He obviously had lost much weight, like the rest of us on our meager rice diet.
However, he maintained the sparkle in his eyes - the built in look and mannerisms of a natural leader.
He instilled confidence in us in a quiet way. I know I felt I would be OK as long as Pappy was there.
He took things in stride and did not complain.
He set the pace.
He was extremely solicitous for fellow P.O.W.s in our special barrack at Omori - especially the very young fellows. He spent many evening hours tending to them - talking to them and exhorting them to hang in there and to perpetuate their desire to survive.

I sensed that when U.S. carrier planes and B-29s strafed and bombed our immediate area, that he craved to be free of his confinement and to join them in their exciting missions on the road to victory.

He always wanted to be in the thick of the action - a fearless warrior - and yet a gentle, caring and considerate person.

He inspired us not only by reputation, but also by actual performance.

His exploits with the Black Sheep squadron are legendary. These were professional, skilled flyers - a tough fighting group that, under Pappy's leadership and training, scourged the enemy in combat. Two of the original Black Sheep visited Pappy at the hospital in Fresno shortly before his death. Their clear message was: Pappy led us - taught us and always took care of all of his boys.

After the war years, and a variety of ventures, he eventually settled into the more stereotyped role of family man and home body. He loved his grandchildren, and was hooked on late night movies.

He loved golf - lived alongside the course in Fresno. He attacked the game with the same intense vigor of his days of aerial combat.

I can recall vividly caddying for Pappy when he played in the Bing Crosby Pebble Beach Pro-Am eight or nine years ago. After four days of pressure-packed golf, his group was on the sixteenth green at Pebble Beach. A massive crowd surrounded the green - Pappy had a forty foot, downhill, sharply breaking putt. He coolly knocked it in for a crucial birdie. He enjoyed it - he smiled - another victory. He always performed well under maximum pressure.

His days at the air shows were special, happy days over the years - at places like Reno and Chino and Phoenix and Oshkosh and Yakima - Jo worked these shows with him.

He loved to meet his friends and admirers - to pose for photos with the kids and grownups of all ages - to autograph his books and color prints - sheer joy - "fulfilling days" is how he described them.

On Tuesday and Wednesday of this week, there was a constant line of people all day long at the mortuary in Fresno to pay their final respects to Pappy Boyington. Some had driven hundreds of miles for a final good-bye to him.

I talked with some of these people.
Some of their comments were :

"Never met him - but I admired him and just wanted to
say thanks to him for all that he did for my country
and for me" (anonymous).

"He was always so nice to our children at air shows
over the years. We just had to stop by and say thanks
and good bye" (A husband and wife)

"Pappy always was and always will be a hero to me.
I'll miss him - the country will miss him." (an elderly
gentleman)

And later-
The Marine Corps Honor Guard at the mortuary and the
Marine fly-by pilots of the present day Black Sheep
squadron from Yuma, Arizona, commented almost in
unison:
"We are proud to have been selected to participate in
these ceremonies. Pappy Boyington is a great Marine -
a true hero and inspiration to us. A great Marine!

Pappy, we all share the hope and conviction that our
memories of you and your spirit and inspiration will
remain with us over future years.
We need people like Marine Corps Colonel Pappy
Boyington to keep our country strong.
We'll miss you, Pappy.

(Delivered in the chapel at Arlington National Cemetery
by Ray "Hap" Halloran 1-15-88)

Funeral procession for Pappy Boyington – riderless horse in foreground. Arlington National Cemetery, January 1988 (USMC Photo)

Pappy Boyington's casket in foreground. Background shows Robert McClurg offering condolences to Pappy's widow, Jo Boyington. (USMC Photo)

The only thing they didn't do was play TAPS; this was because the weather was so awfully cold that the young man's lips would have stuck to the mouthpiece of his instrument. A bunch of us Sheep met in D.C. for the occasion. Henry Bourgeois rented a van to cart us around in, and we got lost trying to exit Arlington Cemetery. About the only joke for the time was that we were going to run out of gas looking for the exit, at which time we'd all immediately freeze to death, and they'd have to bury the rest of the Black Sheep right there and then. I think any of us Sheep would credit Pappy for making us what we were, and in fact influencing part of our adult lives well beyond our combat tours. With Pappy's passing, a part of each one of us was gone, as well. Among my things, I found a form letter, mailed from Henry Bourgeois to the rest of us Sheep. It is dated 9 February, 1988, and contains Boo's thoughts just after Pappy's funeral. As the reader will see, it also contains Boo's thoughts about our beloved F4U's;

```
Dear Fellow Blacksheep:
     It was great seeing you again in spite of the
occasion of the loss of our leader again.  I thought
the Marine Corps did a fine job of honoring Pappy.
     I remember the first time I met him.  He was the
senior officer in charge of a group of replacement
pilots going to the Pacific.  I believe it was just
before Christmas, 1942.  We traveled on the converted
luxury liner, LURLINE.  Took about 21 days to reach the
islands.  I sat in awe listening to this experienced
combat pilot tell of his exploits in China.  He was
taking a case of scotch to a General.  About the third
night out he began to tap it.  By the time we reached
New Caledonia I don't believe there was much left.
     The Blacksheep tour with Pappy was an experience you
can't forget.  He always conned me into flying his wing
because I had a gift of seeing airplanes at a very long
distance.  These so called patrol missions turned out
to be two hours of loops, rolls and every other
maneuver you could think of.  I quickly learned to ask
for the dawn patrol, for which he was never available,
and dodged his request.  I'll never forget his disgust
at my breaking off a combat before he was ready.  His
praise at a mission done well.
     Couldn't believe he was down and lost when I heard
the rumors.  The joy of his return and reunion.  The
disappointment in his life after retiring.  The elation
of meeting him again at the Corsair rollout in
```

Maryland.   His thoughtfulness in returning my son's
telephone calls at air shows, and saying nice things
about me.
    Meeting Jo with him in Texas and spending two hours
talking.   The longest I had ever talked to him.   We
agreed on the past being gone and we should think about
now and the future.   I was so happy to find he had
finally found his way.
    They say the streets of Heaven are guarded by United
States Marines, I believe that.   I believe Pappy is now
up there flying high cover leading the lost Blacksheep.
I pray when my turn comes to join them, there will be a
brand new Corsair for me to fly and join the squadron.

                         Happy Landings

                              Boo

    Truth is that most often, we cannot anticipate what life will send
our way. Our son, Mark, was taken from us by melanoma in 1996
and that was an awful blow.   Morbid as it may sound, you're
supposed to eventually bury your parents—that is how life was
designed. But you're not supposed to bury your children, and the
pain endured in doing so is indescribable.
    Today, my wife, Julia and I are proud grandparents of three
handsome grandsons and five beautiful granddaughters. We are
further fortunate that all live reasonably close to our home, and we
visit often. The remaining Black Sheep also still stay in touch, and
we try to have a gathering roughly every two years. Our next one is
slated for October 2003, roughly the sixtieth anniversary of our
service. It may be the last of our reunions, as time is taking its toll;
of the fifty-one original pilots, I think about fifteen remain.
    When I began work on this book, I never thought it would take
us seven years to complete the writing. I also never dreamed that
during this time, there would be at least three other books published
by other people, dealing with either the Black Sheep or Pappy
himself. Reruns of the Black Sheep TV show appear on television,
sometimes twice a day or all weekend long. Memorabilia sells for
unbelievable prices, and so much of it is fake. Fred Losch called me
a couple years ago to tell of an ad he saw in his local newspaper;
someone was selling what they advertised as my original combat
flight jacket for an unbelievable sum of money. Without identifying

himself, Ropetrick contacted the seller and asked to see the jacket. It was in mint condition, size 44. I never wore anything close to a 44 in the service, and my jacket was gone decades ago, after succumbing to many years of wear, including construction work around the house. It was in tatters when I got rid of it. We continue to have people write us to sign things for "collectors," only to have those items appear for public sale shortly afterwards. Many of the people who contact us are genuinely interested in our history. Some others are not.

When we read something in print, or see a documentary on television, we tend to assign an unquestioned authenticity to it; we assume that if someone went to all the work of assembling it, then the content must be accurate and definitive. What we don't always realize is that every account begins as a picture with some parts missing, and the researchers often paint in the missing parts to complete the picture. Even when done with no bias, the possibility exists to end up with a re-created picture that is different from what actually happened. Part of my purpose in undertaking this work was to paint one more "picture" from the perspective of one of us who was actually there. As another piece of the picture, here is a toast given by Black Sheep John Bolt (the double Ace - once in WWII and again in Korea). John delivered this on May 10, 1993 at our Black Sheep reunion in New Orleans...

To our fallen companions whose bones rest on the bottom of the sea in the Solomon Islands, cut down in the bloom of youth, denied the pleasures of life, which by chance, the rest of us have enjoyed.

To Gregory Boyington, the courageous, charismatic leader of our days of glory.

To Frank Walton who from our early days has not only been our Boswell, our biographer, in creating the Blacksheep legend, but by his own life has been a friend, inspiration and role model to all.

To Jim Reames our compassionate squadron doctor, whose medical treatment, Lejon brandy, and cheerful good humor helped each of us to bear the stress of combat when death was a frequent visitor to our squadron.

To our wives and ladies without whom life would have been a fruitless, cheerless existence without meaning.

200 of us, once a proud, brave brotherhood in arms, today we are bound by our own actions in the Blacksheep legend, as friends forever.

Please rise and join me in a toast to all of these.
SEMPER FIDELIS

Last to our beloved Marine Corps. We all knew when we put on the forest green uniform that it would ask us to put our lives at risk, which it did, and it would give us only pride and self respect, which it has.
Please join me
TO THE CORPS

200 On Boyington's Wing

To each of us, once a proud, brave brotherhood in arms, today we are bound by our own actions in the Blacksheep legend, as friends forever.

Please rise and join me in a toast to all of these.
SEMPER FIDELIS

Last to our beloved Marine Corps. We all knew when we put on the forest green uniform that it would ask us to put our lives at risk, which it did, and it would give us only pride and self respect, which it has.
Please join me
TO THE CORPS

Closing Words On Pappy

Now we bring this work to a close. To me, perhaps the most profound thing of all is how the interest in the Black Sheep has remained. It has also been intriguing to see what parts of the story have been most interesting, and how that interest has changed over the decades. Focus seems to have shifted from the technical, through the dramatic, and into the tabloid. One might comment that the interest has had to progress to other aspects as the first ones were fully explored and exhausted, but I wonder about that. Overall, it seems that the attention is greater now than ever.

Southern CT, 1996 L-R Hill, McClurg, Bourgeois stand in front of a restored Corsair at an air show. (Marketos collection)

Southern CT, 1996 L-R Hill, McClurg, Bourgeois stand in front of a sign
greeting the Black Sheep in a hotel lobby. (Marketos collection)

I have mixed feelings when I see attentions given to Pappy's
family history and upbringing.   I wonder if this research is
constructive, or if the resulting picture has had too many of its
missing parts painted in again. It is important to keep our focus on
who Pappy was as it applies to his accomplishments.

For the record, we never flew while intoxicated. It is true that I
was one of the lesser drinkers in the squadron, but the reality
remains that our squadron doctor wouldn't have allowed us to
jeopardize ourselves or our mates (or our precious aircraft, no
matter how war-torn) by flying drunk.   There may have been
hangovers on occasion, but not drunkenness.

I can't describe Pappy with any one single word.   His value
stems from the fact that he was good at so many things.   In the
technical areas, he was a born aviator—a natural at the controls of
an airplane. He was also an excellent marksman, able to put bullets
on the bullseye. Navigation was a forte of his, also; I don't think
you'll find Boyington getting lost in any of the combat logs. He

returned late a few times from having to stop for fuel, or to have battle damage looked at, but I don't think he ever got lost.

Pappy was also highly unconventional; I think that is the perception that came across strongly to the public. He marched to his own drum, but maybe that wasn't such a bad thing. Although he didn't use the typical avenues, Pappy was a better leader than many of his superiors. I think it was his abilities that got him into trouble, just as much as his unconventional ways. Pappy could organize a group and inspire its members, just with who he was. That is leadership. He was big on teamwork, and would grow large fangs at the first hint of any cliques or division within the group. He didn't put forth a proposal for what we were going to "try" to do; rather, he laid out what was going to happen. We didn't spend much time worrying about how to respond with contingency plans; we concentrated on living in the offensive mode, and letting our opponents react to our initiatives.

I don't think we idolized Pappy in the sense that we wanted to imitate him. Rather, we had complete confidence in his abilities, and we knew he wouldn't ask any of us to do something he wouldn't do himself. I am sure his influence stayed with us through our lives. We were a unified group, and we had complete respect for our leader.

To this day, the remaining Black Sheep still keep tabs on each other. We still manage to gather for a reunion now and then, and the camaraderie is as strong as ever. Ed Olander serves as one of our internal "checkpoints." Although we have had several updates since then, I think the reader might enjoy the following communique Olander sent out near the holiday season in late 1996 :

Dear Fellow Black Sheep:
Your collective response to my July letter was somewhat less than overwhelming, but my intention here is to pass on what news I can.
The remains of Chris MAGEE where buried in Arlington National Cemetery on May 8th. So in death, as in life, he and Greg are not far apart.
Jack BOLT has retired from the law and when he's not terrorizing the Florida fish population he and Dottie are traveling a good bit.
The squadron's other two legal eagles (Denny GROOVER and Hank MILLER) continue to practice law. Denny, I am told, is no longer in the Georgia legislature-but he

has regained his seat before and may try again. Hank
wrote of WAYLAND BENNETT who disappeared during a
training flight from Espiritu Santo in the fall of 1943
and whose remains were discovered and recovered only
two years ago. Some of you will remember him.
Although Glenn BOWERS suffers from severe arthritis and
a pair of bum knees he refuses to cease hunting big
game. He and wife Betty raise tall bearded iris, have
in excess of 600 named iris and are engaged in a
breeding program to develop one they can name and
claim.
Ned CORMAN and Ruthie have abandoned the heights of
Lake Tahoe for the sea-level ambiance of Maui.
Tom EMRICH is relatively incommunicado in Phoenix, but
if you direct a message to his FAX telling him a party
is brewing he'll come a-running.
Hank BOURGEOIS must have little spare time on his
hands.   He writes of white-water rafting, mountain
climbing, fishing, building and flying model airplanes
and this "thinking of" building an ultralite, now that
he has stopped pursuing a flying license (can't find an
instructor).
Now here's a twist: Jim HILL reports his son Jeff has
started a new business and named it Black Sheep
Interactive. Jim works summer and winter on improving
his golf and tennis games.
Ed and Jane HARPER continue to "hang loose" in Lake St.
Louis, Mo., although neither of them is still employed
by McDonnell Douglas.
Bill HEIER penned a note while airborne enroute with
Carolyn to the Bahamas for a couple weeks of sailing.
Whimsical as ever, he signed the note "just plane
bill."
I have not heard from Herb HOLDEN, Al JOHNSON or Harry
JOHNSON but I suspect I'll not be far afield if I
report Herb is spending beaucoup time on North Carolina
golf courses.
Perry and Carmen LANE live on a Florida lake from which
an alligator emerged recently and attacked a man mowing
his neighbor's lawn. Needless to say, after nearly
mowing off his own toe, then hearing this alligator
story, Perry hired a lawn service to do his yard work.
In October snow and cold persuaded Jean and Fred LOSCH
to close up their Idaho Slash/E ranch and repair to
their Fallbrook, Ca. digs for the winter. Fred reports
that radiation treatment in the throat area had yielded
successful results.
Rusty MARCH failed to check in.   Redeem yourself,
Rusty. Send us news.

Al and Nancy MARKER continue to live the lives of country gentry in Sonoma. In your next note, please send hard news.

Jo and Bruce MATHESON are still active in the business world in Kailua (she in real estate, he with H. & R. Block). But they get off the rock once in a while; they joined the Bolts in September at the MCAA convention in San Diego.

Allan (Hank) McCARTNEY has been spreading the Black Sheep story in speeches to service clubs, church groups, etc. He and Evelyn live in Vero Beach but escape Florida's summer heat in Black Mountain, N.C.

Julie and Bob McCLURG lost their son Mark a few months back and that has been a blow. They ran into Denny and Carol Groover in St. Simons Island last winter and briefly relived old times.

Many of you are already aware that Doc REAMES is not at all well and has been confined to a longterm care facility.

Gregg and Sandy SIMS divide their time between their home in Cambridge, New York, and Normandy. Sandy still paints and admits "there are a few good Sims' paintings out there". I must find out where and try to acquire one.

On New Years day Flo and Ed OLANDER take off for Oahu and will be there January-February-March.

HAPPY HOLIDAYS! SEMPER FI! STAY HEALTHY! KEEP IN TOUCH!

The combat experiences remain in our minds. Following is a brief excerpt from a letter sent to me by Glenn Bowers in early 1998:

"I know what Rabaul looked like because the first time there, Bragdon took us on a sightseeing tour; we flew down the main street on the rooftops and never fired our guns! We were so low I could see the seams in the paving of the street!"

Robert McClurg standing on the wing of a Corsair decorated as Boyington's at the Naval Air Museum in Pensacola, FL 2000 (Marketos collection)

The Black Sheep continue to keep tabs on one another. We went through hell together, but I wouldn't trade a million dollars for the experience of having been... On Boyington's Wing.

Appendix 1
Songs of the Black Sheep

I happened to find some tattered old papers, heavily yellowed with age. On them were the words to some of the songs we used to chant in the evening hours. I didn't think I'd find this material, and am happy to include it here. The most significant ones are first. Be forewarned - some of the lyrics aren't exactly church material...

Perhaps those of you who have seen the opening of the Black Sheep TV show did not realize that there really was a black sheep song. The Black Sheep song was developed from the Yale "Whiffenpoof Song", which had its own origins from Rudyard Kipling's "Gentlemen-Rankers". The Black Sheep TV show opened with a chorus of some lines from the song pertaining to "Black Sheep", but those lines were actually written decades before!

```
THE BLACK SHEEP SONG :

To the tables down at Morie's,
To the place where Pappy dwells,
To the dear old temple bar we loved so well--
Sing the Whiffenpoofs assembled
With their glasses raised on high,
And the magic of their singing casts a spell.
Yes, the magic of their singing of the songs we loved
so well.
"Shall awasting" and "Mavourneen" and the rest.
We will serenade our Pappy while life and breath shall
last--
Then we'll pass and be forgotten like the rest.
```

```
CHOROUS :
We are poor little lambs who have lost our way,
Baa, Baa, Baa.
We are little black sheep who have gone astray,
Baa, Baa, Baa.
Gentlemen songsters off on a spree
Damned from here to eternity.
God have mercy on such as we--
Baa, Baa, Baa.


If the home we never write to, and the vows we never
keep,
And all we know most distant and most dear
Across the snoring barrack-room return to break our
sleep,
Can you blame us if we soak ourselves in beer ?
When the drunken comrade mutters and the great guard-
lantern gutters
And the horror of our fall is written plain,
very secret, self-revealing on the aching whitewashed
ceiling,
```

This next one was also one of our (short) favorites :

```
IN A ROWBOAT AT RABAUL :

If you lose your airspeed now
You'll come down from forty thou
And you'll wind up in a rowboat at Rabaul

In a rowboat at Rabaul, we'll be throwing in the towel,
Cause they'll never send a Dumbo over here.
We'll be prisoners of war, with a nifty Nippo whore,
Getting drunk on saki and New Britain beer.


AFTER RABAUL IS OVER :

After Rabaul is over,
After the close of day,
Count up the Japs and Zeros
But just let me get away.
Take all your Navy Crosses,
Medals and Ribbons too,
Along with my orders and stuff them
Right up your avenue.
```

After Rabaul is over,
After Bull Halsey's day.
MacArthur can have the credit,
Just send me home to stay.
I don't want to be a hero,
So take your wings of gold,
To hell with the Southwest Pacific.
I just want to grow old.

Now that Rabaul is over,
None of them got away.
Fifty-four Japs is the record
Shot down in a single day.
Give Douglas our Air Group's story,
To claim in his Army bunk.
Just give me a bottle of whiskey,
I just want to get drunk.

Now that Rabaul is over,
I want to spend my days,
Back with the wine and women,
Reading Army communiques.
I'll take the stateside duty,
A desk job and what is more,
Take all the Admirals and Generals.
To hell with the God-damn war.

DOODLIE DOO :

Sweet Sally Jones went out with a show,
Called Doodlie-Doo, Doodlie-Doo.
She made a hit by doing her bit,
Called Doodlie-Doo, Doodlie-Doo.
Made twenty a week, there wasn't much to it,
All she had to do was Doodlie-Doo it.
Drives a Rolls-Royce but not by her voice,
But by Doodlie-Doo-Doo-Doo.

Please play for me that sweet melody
Called Doodlie-Doo, Doodlie-Doo.
I like the rest, but the one I like best
Is Doodlie-Doo, Doodlie-Doo.
The simplest thing, there isn't much to it.
You don't have to sing, just Doodlie-Doo it.
I love it so, wherever I go,
I just Doodlie-Doo-Doo-Doo.

(UN NAMED) :

Oh he floats through the air,
With the greatest of ease.
The daring young man in his blue SBD.
He scatters his bombs all over the sea.
O' the ocean ain't safe any more.

T'was in a battered fighter plane
Away up Rabaul way
T'was in a shot up Corsair plane
A young Marine lad lay.
His wingman spinning down in flames.
Was shot completely dead.
Now listen to these very last words,
This fighter pilot said.
"I'm going to a happy land
Where everything is bright
Where whiskey comes from bootleg
And it's wrought out every night
You do not have to fly at all
You just have one big fling
There are beaucoup of women
O Sydney is the thing.
The beds are soft and downy,
a clam in every one,
The girls down there are nice girls,
They even aim your gun."
His comrades circled round him,
As he spun down in the rain,
Then pushed it to the firewall,
To catch that Sydney plane.

Appendix 2
Excerpts from Tribute to Robert Alexander

Excerpts from a tribute to Robert Alexander by Deane Doolen :

In the chapter covering our first combat tour, September 30, 1943 represents a terribly unfortunate day in which one of our Black Sheep met his end in an incident involving one of our Navy's PT boats. The PT boat also encountered casualties. All those lost were bright young men with dreams in their heads and all kinds of ideas about the future. However, a war intervened and left instead a group of families and friends who would be deprived of everything but the memories of their lost loved ones. The tribute covered here is evidence of how long lasting the losses can be; Deane Doolen's relation to Bob Alexander is that Alex's mother and Deane's mother were close friends back in the 1940's. Deane was about 9 years younger than Bob, and admired him as he went off to serve his country in a far away place. The memories of Bob Alexander's loss endured through many decades; Deane Doolen researched Bob Alexander's past (and also that of the men on the PT boat), and wrote his tribute in July, 1995; Almost 52 years after Alex's loss. Deane's work serves as a vivid reminder that each and every one of those lost in combat (American or other) was a member of a family - someone's child, brother, sister, sweetheart.

Doolen's original work is on 8.5 x 11 paper, with photographs manually adhered onto the text pages. The original work was never intended for mass publication. To my knowledge, less than 50 copies were originally made and distributed to close family and friends. I got to know Deane when he contacted me and requested information and photos from my own personal collection.

Following are excerpts from Deane's work:

"Let us look back over those 'undone years' of Bob Alexander, another soldier who wrote poetry. As we reflect on his life, we will also in this story remember John Daley, Bertis Paul and Tom Ross."

[Daley, Paul and Ross were three PT boat crewmen who lost their life in the incident with Alexander.]

"Bob Alexander was born January 24, 1921 in Davenport, Iowa, the only child of Robert and Joanna Lamp Alexander." ... "Robert Austin Alexander, nicknamed both 'Bob' and also 'Alex', was a member of the Davenport High School class of 1939. The 1939 Yearbook, Blackhawk, notes next to his photograph; 'Alex, Track, Hi-Y, Student Council, wrestling co-captain, Gold D for wrestling, 1938 Student Leaders conference, gym circus committee, football, Boys State candidate and senior class vice president.' He would also be named salutatorian of his graduating class... ...he was awarded a 'Gold D', the high school's top athletic award, won by just six boys at Davenport High in 1939.

In 1938, the American Legion of Iowa started their Hawkeye Boys State program aimed at developing civic leadership in high school students. The second session was held in 1939 when 600 boys were elected from Iowa's ninety-nine counties to spend a week in camp at Des Moines learning how democracy works. PArt of the learning process was a campaign and election among the delegates for state offices. Bob Alexander, representing Scott county, was elected Governor ! The American Legion June 1939 publication ran a story noting that:

Victory for the eastern Iowa youth came after a tremendous campaign in which his supporters marched miles upon miles behind a group of musicians playing 'Alexander's Ragtime Band'... The new chief executive... has blue eyes, blond hair and a most pleasing smile, speaks snappily but easily, loves to paddle a canoe, says he dances fairly well, likes girls but is not 'crazy' over any of them, and wants to be a physician or engineer, although he is keenly interested in the aviation branch of the Naval service.

[Deane goes on to report that the war broke out while Alex was in his junior year at Iowa State College (now Iowa State University). As he had done in high school, Bob wrestled on what became the championship winning team. The war broke out while he was a junior in college, and Alex enlisted in the U.S. Naval reserve at Kansas City, Missouri. Alex went through the rigors of training, and something else as well...]

"In spring 1943, Alex became engaged to Dorothea (Dot) Dunagan, an Ames, Iowa native and a senior at Iowa State College. Alex penned these thoughts after his engagement while stationed at the Jacksonville Air Station :

Marriage
At darning socks, I'm not so hot,
So I just wear them 'till they rot.
My worn-out shirts cause me to feel
That their construction should be steel.
The only remedy for this
Is life in peaceful wedded bliss.

A wife can make one's life complete
In many ways one can't repeat:
Towards having kids you soon make tracks,
For each one lowers income tax.
If you could have them two by two,
You'd find the country paying you.

But wives can fuss and fume and fret;
They'd know what salary you get:
They'd take your checks, then drive your cars,
Then ration you upon cigars.
A small price, that, to pay for this-
Oh, here's to peaceful married bliss !

Robert A. Alexander

[Bob proceeded through the training steps as was typical, and Deane's work continues tracing his progress...]

"On 30 April 1943, Alex arrived at Kearney Mesa, San Diego, California for service with Marine Fleet Air Wing, Pacific. He began to keep a notebook which would eventually contain 32 neatly printed pages of his activities and thoughts. The last entry was dated Sunday, 26 September, 1943, four days before his death. Kearney Mesa was a pool of officers and men awaiting overseas assignments. There was little to do while waiting in limbo. A few classes, hikes in the hills, trips to the beach and one to Tijuana, Mexico were highlights Alex recorded. in mid May he was sent to the nearby desert to act as an instructor for aerial gunners. He described an incident there in his notebook:

'On my first familiarity hop, I went hedge-hopping up and down canyons, flying through trees, etc. I was caught, grounded, and sent back to Kearney Mesa with an unsatisfactory report. At Kearney Mesa, I was given a hearing. The charges against me included, "Flying in canyons and gullies below ground level and zooming out dangerously close to the rims, performing dangerous and violent maneuvers at low altitude, flying between two trees spaced twenty feet apart (my wing span was thirty-five feet) in such a manner as to remove foliage from both trees with the wing-tips, etc." Although it was necessary to tip the plane up on one wing to get through, my wing tips touched no branches-any leaves floating around were caused by the rush of air when I passed through. I was eventually dismissed with a warning, and told the evidence would not be entered into my fitness report. As a result of the episode, I am no longer an instructor, and have been stationed at Kearney Mesa again waiting for sailing orders. Naturally, the boys have been kidding me a good bit about the affair.'

In a 1994 interview his high school best friend, Robert Kem, would say: 'Alex was a wonderful young man and a very close friend. He would do things to get attention. As a wrestler he used to challenge carnival wrestlers for the $50 prize and win, but we made him quit so he could keep his amateur status.' In 1995 college fraternity brother Edgar Peara would say: 'He was just about the finest person I've ever known. he was bright, handsome, fun-loving, concerned about others, and somewhat of a daredevil and a little reckless.'

Fellow Black Sheep Ed Harper says: 'I remember a really good looking, well built and aggressive young man. He could not wait to get into combat and was determined to make his mark on the war.' In an August entry in his notebook, Alex wrote 'The boys say I'm a typical hot pilot, and are betting that I won't live long because I've always got my neck stuck out looking for trouble.'

Bob Alexander eventually did make it to the South Pacific, aboard a ship as most did, and sharing a state room with two others who would also become Black Sheep; Chris Magee and Don Moore. During training in the South Pacific, a friend of Bob's was killed in a flying accident. As many were prone to do in their free time, Bob wrote a poem about his fallen buddy. Deane Doolen's work picks up the subject…

"Alex's epitaph for Andy was to be chillingly prophetic. Now, fifty years later, Alex's friends remember him with such comments as: 'He was a very special kind of guy' (Cousin Mary Gray); 'He was a wonderful young man' (Black Sheep Sandy Sims); 'I admired him. He was very courageous, top of the line' (Black Sheep Jim Hill); 'He was tall, robust, handsome, and friendly' (Black Sheep Ed Olander); and, 'Bob was an All American boy, naïve in the sense that he would never suspect anyone of wrongdoing (Black Sheep Chris Magee).
Alex would write this poem shortly after his friend's death:

W.T. Anderson

A dozen fighter pilots
Standing at salute,
In honor to their comrade,
who's lying cold and mute.

The flag drapes o'er his coffin,
Beside the pile of earth
Which soon shall claim his body,
But give his soul new birth.

A dozen jungle flowers,
A bit worse for wear;

The chaplain stands beside him,
And slowly says a prayer.

This man has met his maker,
By falling from the skies;
The escort fires a volley
O'er where the dead man lies.

A dozen negro workmen
Step up with spade in hand,
And cover up his body,
In this far distant land.

Robert A. Alexander (1943)

[As I covered earlier in this book during our first combat tour, Bob
Alexander went on to find himself in a terrible situation on
September 30, 1943. As we return to Deane Doolen's work, a U.S.
Navy action report will help add some detail to the occurrence. It
also adds names to those unfortunate men on the PT boat;]

At 0735, three planes were sighted approaching the boats from the
northeast tip of Kolombangara approximately 300 feet off the water.
The planes were immediately identified as F4-U's by all the boats
and the gunners were so informed. The planes turned to a right
echelon and headed down sun towards the PT-126 which had just
completed its strafing run on the barge. When the planes headed for
the PT-126, immediate orders were given for full speed ahead, hard
right rudder, and the American flag was waved. Both actions in
accordance with standard recognition procedure. The two outboard
planes appeared to recognize the PT's but the inboard plane
continued its run and opened fire on the PT-126. Due to the
movement of the PT 126, only its stern was under fire. Ensign John
F. Daley, USNR, who was at the after gun station was hit as well as
Bertis I. Paul, MoMM2c, who was in the engine room of the PT-
126. Thomas M. Ross, GM1c, who was manning the after gun was
probably knocked overboard by the impact of the bullets which
riddled his gun station.

After the plane opened fire, the starboard turret of the PT 126
opened fire. The attacking F4-U was hit with one short burst. It

turned and crashed about 200 yards inland from Ropa Point, Kolombangara, exploding as it hit the ground. It was found that a small fire had been started in the engine room of the PT 126 and Paul, machinist on watch, apparently was killed instantly and that the starboard engine of the PT 126 had been hit and was out of commission. The other two planes violently wagged their wings to establish identification and circled the area. Ensign Daley was transferred to the PT 124 as he was still thought to be alive. The PT 124 departed for base at 0755 arriving at 0850. The PT 116 was ordered to search the area for the missing gunner. Only his watch cap was found. The PT 126 and 189 arrived at base at 0910; the PT 116 arrived at base at 0940.

A portion of Deane Doolen's closure says it best;

In one of the horrors of war, four young men died on a mild September day in 1943 in a remote part of the Pacific Ocean. The irony of death by friendly fire continues to haunt their friends and families fifty years later. Millions died in the conflict of World War II. Yet the deaths of John Daley, Bertis Paul, Tommy Ross and Robert Alexander seem particularly poignant. They gave their youthful lives in the cause of freedom. We honor their sacrifice by remembering their bravery and courage.

Appendix 3
Boyington's Tactics

Part of our second combat tour involved extensive effort to itemize and record all the things Boyington felt were contributors to victory in air combat. From the war diary, here they are:

HEADQUARTERS, MARINE AIRCRAFT GROUP ELEVEN,
FIRST MARINE AIRCRAFT WING, NAVY NO. 140 (ONE FOUR ZERO),
   c/o FLEET POST OFFICE, SAN FRANCISCO, CALIFORNIA.

12 January, 1944.

MAJOR BOYINGTON'S TACTICS

   GENERAL OBSERVATIONS APPLYING TO ALL MISSIONS

   1.   Tactics in the air should be studied and developed in comparison with time-tried tactics on the land and on the sea.
The principles of scouting, out-flanking, ambushing, etc., etc., all provide a basis for the development of air tactics.   Of course allowances and modifications must be made for our speed, for the additional dimension in which we operate, etc.   But land and sea experience provide a starting-point.

   2.   Fighter aircraft are designed, and fighter pilots are trained, to fight.   If there are enemy aircraft in the air, and contact is not made, something is wrong. The only exception to this are those situations where we must stay close to something we are expected to protect; where to attack means that we have been lured away.

3. All missions must be preceded by thorough planning and briefing, with respect to the purpose of the mission and the purpose of any alternate missions, with respect to the rendezvous point and any alternate rendezvous points, etc. All possible contingencies must be considered in advance, particularly because all of our present operations are over enemy territory far from our bases. Success in the air is a lot of little things. Most of them can be taken care of before takeoff.

4. All missions must be flown as planned and briefed unless there is real justification to the contrary – there must be discipline. Along with realizing the purpose of the mission, each pilot must realize fully his responsibility for its successful execution.

5. With proper planning and briefing, no use of the radio should be necessary except in emergencies and except in situations where tactical considerations require otherwise.

6. Every effort must be made to obtain relevant weather information and to make intelligent use of such information.

7. All fighters must realize the critical importance of recognition, in order to distinguish our planes from those of the enemy, in order to identify the enemy's different types so that his particular points of weakness can be exploited and his particular points of strength respected, etc.

8. Fighters must not go into combat feeling that the division leader or at most the section leader will answer for problems of tactics, navigation, communications, etc. In these regards leaders and wingmen are the same – at any moment the customary leader may go down or may be required to return to base, or may become lost, or may be without a radio, and every one of the others must be ready to take over. And in particular. all pilots are equally responsible for spotting the enemy and for initiating immediate action either through their leader or by taking over the lead themselves.

9. Pilots must make steady careful observation a habit. They must have a system and a routine for scanning the air both above and below, behind, on the flanks and ahead. The vigil must be unceasing.

10. When bogies are called the call must be so worded that everyone will know the location of the division from which the call has come, and the location of the bogies either with respect to a geographical landmark or with respect to the line of flight of the friendly force.

11. Surface bogies should not be called unless it is practically certain that they are enemy bogies. The comparative slowness of movement of friendly forces on the water makes any revelation of their presence and position undesirable.

12. In the execution of all missions, all advantages of sun, weather, terrain, etc., must be exploited.

13. In danger areas high speed must be maintained. In the less dangerous areas, such a speed must be carried that all formations can stay together comfortably.

14. We must not climb into bogies. We must gain our altitude away in a position from which the action can be observed, and our climb must be made with a high forward air speed.

15. We must not pull up when closely and dangerously attacked. Speed is our defense. With moderate loss of altitude and certainly without going all the way to the water and running for home, the enemy can be outdistanced, and then altitude and position recovered for further attacks.

16. Close attention must be given to the efficiency of our firepower. Our guns' loading, their boresighting, their cleanliness, and their general performance at altitude as well as at the lower levels, must be perfect. As a result of tests of the comparative destructive power of tracer, armor piercing and incendiary ammunition, our squadron changed its belting from 1-1-1 to 2 incendiary - 1 armor piercing - 2 incendiary - 1 tracer. In actual combat, we found this load much more satisfactory. We also found it desirable to use the ring sight entirely in determining range and establishing lead, using the tracer merely to check the bore sighting.

17. It must be remembered that with our armor plate, our self-sealing orpurged fuel tanks, and with proper evasive action, our rear vulnerability is not great.

18. On the other hand it is apparent that our most successful runs against fighter opposition are from eleven to one o'clock ahead and from five to seven o'clock astern, from a level just above to a level just below.

19. The most common maneuver of the Jap fighter at present is a split-S, which happens usually when he is approached from ahead or from astern. In normal combat, if he can not be hit before he has started down, he is usually gone.

20. In normal combat in enemy territory it is not desirable, particularly for a single plane, to go below a base altitude, which might well be 10,000 feet. To go lower with a section of two planes may be desirable if both planes carry ample speed and are prepared to cover each other when necessary.

21. In normal combat, clouds may provide cover either for us or for the enemy and must be considered constantly in both connections.

22. All squadrons must keep the white star on their insignia freshly painted. Cleaning of the fuselage causes them to become indistinct in a matter of days.

23. In all missions involving layers of aircraft stacked up through considerable air space, all must remember the difficulty of maintaining visual contact through all the layers.

24. All pilots must check their oxygen equipment (as well as everything else) thoroughlt before takeoff. To return to base early for oxygen reasons can hardly indicate anything less than negligence in preparation for the flight.

25. When a pilot decides that for some reason he must return to base, he should make a visual signal to the other member of his section that he must do so, and should also indicate by a visual signal whether he is able to go back alone.

26. When a plane drops out, the other member of the section should join up on some other single plane, if

any is available. A one-plane section is about as useless as a three-plane section.

27. Jap fighters approaching from angles ahead will usually turn away at the suggestion of a run on them, or at any other suggestion that we mean business.

28. Fighters must hold their fire until within range, as indicated by the size of the target in the ringsight. Otherwise, the Jap will be warned by that first over-anxious burst, will split-S and will be gone. On the other hand fire should be opened sooner in a head-on run because then we are closing faster and because the plane opening fore last usually turns away first and is a good target during that turn.

FIGHTER SWEEPS

29. The larger a striking force, the greater its power, provided that it is not so large as to be unmanageable. At the present time it would seem desirable to restrict sweeps to thirty-six to forty-eight planes, upon the assumption of course that all or very nearly all of them will continue to the target and will participate in the action. Later on the tactics of such sweeps may reach such development that larger forces can be handled efficiently

30. On each particular sweep the number of squadrons represented should be as small as possible, i.e. each squadron which does participate should have a large number of planes.

31. On each particular sweep the number of different types of fighters participating should be as small as possible.

32. The leader must fly in a position where he can be seen and followed easily. At the present time enemy patrols are not ordinarily airborne, or at least are not at altitude, before our arrival. Such being the case the sweep leader can fly satisfactorily in the bottom layer with the upper layers stepped back from his layer. However if enemy patrols should be at altitude, it would be better for the sweep leader to be in the uppermost layer. On some sweeps the leader has led the middle layer. By and large, therefore, the sweep leader should be at that level where it is expected that the first contact will be made.

33. The fighting should be kept in the same part of
the air. It should not degenerate into a number of
small fights, some going in our favor and some going
otherwise, with some planes out of the action
altogether.

34. After the initial contact it is hardly possible
to keep a division together, although it would be
desirable if it could be done without throwing the
division into a tail chase with only the leader doing
any good. A section is a thoroughly satisfactory
combat unit, and can be kept together much more easily
than a division. Every effort should be made to keep
the section together, but the wingman should not be
simply chasing his leader. If the efforts to
keep together fail, the separated planes should join up
as soon as possible on other friendly planes.

35. A rally point should be designated before hand
for all planes on the sweep. If for any reason this is
not done, those planes from any one squadron should
have their own rally point. The rally point should be
at a certain altitude, not too far removed from the
probably center of action and preferably into the sun.

36. Our fighters must keep in the fight for the time
specified unless lack of fuel, lack of oxygen, or some
other good reason requires otherwise.

BOMBER ESCORTS

37. The responsibility for the success of a bombing
mission rests partly upon the bombers and partly upon
their escort. When the bombers do a good job they
(aside from hitting their target) do the following:
     (a) They keep good formation, with all units
massed as closely as possible.
     (b) They select courses which will allow
sufficient, clear air space above the bombers for the
fighters to maintain visual contact.
     (c) They select courses avoiding anti-aircraft
fire as much as possible.
     (d) They use imagination in varying their times of
     attack, their altitudes of attack, their courses
of approach and retirement, etc.
     (e) They carry sufficient air speed for the
fighters to stay together comfortably during the non-

dangerous part of the approach and retirement as well as during the dangerous part.

38.   The layers of fighter cover are ordinarily roving high, high, medium, low and close. On the approach all layers will tend to lean ahead of the bombers; on the retirement they will be over the bombers. The higher the particular layer, the farther sideways its coverage should extend.

39.   The roving high cover should fly as high as possible consistent with good visual contact with the bombers (not more than a 10,000 foot spread), but not at more than 30,000 feet. It should fly well ahead of the bombers on the approach and ordinarily behind them on the retirement. Its mission is the engagement and annihilation of enemy interceptors operating anywhere but particularly at the upper levels. It may leave the air space over the bombers if that is necessary for the performance of its mission. It is a free unit.

40.   The high and medium covers are ordinarily the second and third highest covers. Their positions are respectively about 6000 and 4000 feet above the bombers. Unlike the roving high cover, the high cover is not authorized to leave the air space above the bombers.

41.   The fighters' air speed should be considerably greater than that of the bombers, for the safety of the fighters as well as for their greater maneuverability. As a result they must weave, in order to keep their assigned positions. The low and close covers will weave back and forth over the bombers' line of flight. The other covers ordinarily will put half of their strength on each side of the line of flight, each half then keeping to its side of the line of flight.

42.   The low and close covers are respectively 2000 to 1500 feet and 1000 to 500 feet above the bombers. They must hold those positions at all costs.

43.   When the bombers are SBD's and TBF's (which usually approach in that order and a mile or a mile and a half apart), the low and close covers must go down with the bombers, levelling off at about 5000 and 2000 feet respectively. The upper layers must settle down proportionately.

44. Ordinarily the low cover must see that the straggling bombers are covered.

45. It is desirable for the bombers to open up on the radio if the fighter cover is inadequate at any particular point. i.e. Someone in the bomber force should act as a fighter director or fire control officer. The fighters are often innocently unaware of enemy pressure at some particular point.

46. Fighter divisions should be able to keep together and fighter sections must keep together. The lower the layer in which a particular fighter happens to fly, the more vulnerable his position and the more prepared he must be to operate defensively with his section.

47. No fighter straggling can be permitted, on the part of single planes, sections or even divisions. Fighters in real trouble should dive under the bombers.

48. A bomber strike should be preceded by a fighter sweep, timed to arrive at the target at least half an hour before the bombers.

STRAFING

49. The importance of thorough planning and briefing is particularly great in strafing. Every scrap of knowledge with regard to terrain, vulnerability of targets, location of anti-aircraft defenses, etc., must be utilized. Each pilot must know exactly what his approach will be and where his targets will be found.

50. Probably no target is completely invulnerable to successful strafing. But strafing missions can not be run off under just any circumstances. Surprise is absolutely essential. All cover of weather, darkness, etc., must be utilized. A mission which has succeeded largely because the attack was not expected certainly can not be repeated immediately.

51. Strafing restrictions issued by the intelligence and operations authorities must be strictly observed. But in the unrestricted areas there should be no hesitation or delay in destroying enemy targets which

present themselves. Something which is wide open one moment may be gone the next.

52. We in the air sometimes fail to appreciate the effect of strafing upon enemy morale. We know the actual physical destruction which .50 caliber guns can cause, but we sometimes forget the amount of less tangible damage which those guns can inflict. Often such a target as a bivouac area in a coconut plantation can not be seen but strafing of such targets has inestimable value.

53. High speed runs are essential. Speed will reduce the number of rounds which can be delivered and will diminish the opportunity for observation, but it must be maintained. Ordinarily each plane should make but one run - if more firepower is desired the number of planes should be increased.

54. Particularly if the approach is made in line or in a flat echelon, the last mile or two of the approach should be made at a constant power setting so that all pilots will be able to devote full attention to the target. Any pilots who unconsciously jam on the throttle just before reaching the target, will run the risk of entering the fire of other planes and colliding with those planes later in their attempts to get back into position.

55. Strafing must not be done in a column. The greatest safety factor is achieved with a line or flat echelon. IF the target is so small that all planes can not get their guns to bear from a line or flat echelon, they should approach from different angles attacking as simultaneously as possible.

56. The approach must be as low as possible, with a momentary pull-up just before reaching the target, for the purpose of identifying the particular targets and getting the guns to bear.

57. Any impulse to fire too early must be restrained. For effectiveness and for saving gun barrels, fire should be held until one is definitely within range.

58. The retirement must be low and very fast, with an eye for possible water spouts from heavy fire.

59. Upon the word to scramble, it is important first to get the fighters off the ground, and only second to get them joined up in their usual order. Any four planes can make a division if the take off has been mixed up. And if the take offs are unduly delayed, any two planes should proceed together as soon as possible. Planes should never proceed singly.

60. Since fighter direction by radio is never perfect, due to the failures of radar, the adversities of the weather, etc., it may be possible to locate the enemy only if our planes operate as a scouting force. i.e. It may be necessary to break the interception force into smaller units such as divisions, which should keep each other in sight but should make their coverage as wide as possible. Of course upon establishment of contact the force should be reunited. It should be exactly like locating the enemy in operations upon land or sea.

61. When an enemy force is approaching and the fighter go out, some of them should be required to remain over the area or object in danger of attack, in case the interception is not a complete success.

62. When it is expected that bombers are included among the approaching bogies, our interceptors should have as little as possible to do with enemy fighters. In such a case our mission is to prevent those bombers from doing any damage with their bombs. This means that the bombers must be located, and shot down, or at least their formation must be broken up and the individual bombers forced to jettison their bombs.

PATROLS, INCLUDING DUMBO AND TASK FORCE COVERS

63. Too often, fighters consider patrols and dumbo and task force covers a waste of time. However, along with performing the mission properly, the time involved can be utilized to good effect.
    (a) Wingmen can develop their formation flying, making it perfect but effortless.
    (b) Leaders cab exchange the lead with their wingmen, to see how well the wingmen can lead and to see how well they themselves can fly wing.
    (c) Divisions can perfect their teamwork and section manoeuveres by practising tight turns, violent scissors, etc.

(d) Leaders can select patterns for flight the basis of which will be readily apparent to those following them, so that a minimum of concentration will be necessary in keeping the planes together.

(e) All pilots can practice their own systems of observation, particularly in focussing upon very distant objects.

(f) In the case of a dumbo cover, the fighters can fly as if escorting bombers.

(g) Quite frequently, upon completion of the mission, the divisions can go into tail chases which will release energy and improve technique. The average tour of combat involves much too much straight and level flying.

64. As much altitude should be held as is consistent with good visual contact with the objects or area being covered. The position should be into the sun and generally between the object or area being covered and the enemy's territory.

Appendix 4
Wartime radio program "Let Yourself Go"

After I completed my third combat tour and returned to the states, some of my military assignments were public-relations oriented. One of my more memorable "missions" was an appearance in New York, on a radio show called "Let Yourself Go". The radio show was hosted by Milton Berle, a famous comedian of the era. Also appearing on that radio show was Errol Flynn–a famous movie actor of the era. My radio spot came at the end of the program. Following is the script:

LET YOURSELF GO - February 21, 1945

```
[Music plays - the Marine hymn]

BERLE:
Now ladies and gentlemen, it is my pleasure to present
Eversharp honor guest… a young man whose guns have many
times blasted treacherous Jap Zeros from the skies.
Here he is, Captain Robert W. McClurg of the United
States Marines.

[APPLAUSE]

BERLE:
Captain McClurg, I want to welcome you to Let Yourself
Go, and tell you how very proud we are to have you with
us tonight.

MC.C:
Thank you, Mr. Berle.
```

BERLE:
Captain, were you pretty excited the day you got your
first Zero?

MC.C:
I was more like a kid who's broken his first window. I
was so scared, I turned right around and beat it home.

BERLE:
I'll never forget the day I got my first zero. I left
school and didn't go home for a week!... What outfit
did you fly with, Captain?

MC.C:
Marine Air Group 11, and I was lucky enough to fly as
wingman for one of the finest men I ever knew, and one
of our greatest fliers, Major Gregory Boyington.

BERLE:
Boyington's record was 26 enemy planes shot down,
wasn't it?

MC.C:
Yes, but I saw him get a lot more he never counted. He
was a real hero.

BERLE:
Well, Captain, tell us about that day when your plane
was crippled and yet you shot down two zeros?

MC.C:
I just got a break that day, Mr. Berle. Something went
wrong with the carburetor, and my engine stopped. So I
called to Boyington that I was going down. I was
hoping to crash somewhere I could be picked up. Down
at about five thousand feet the motor started again -
but it only had enough power to keep me sitting in the
air like a clay pigeon. And just then I saw two Zeros
coming up below me. If I'd had good sense I'd have
stayed out of their way.

BERLE:
I see.

MC.C:
But instead, I dived down on them. I guess they didn't
see me coming. Because I only gave them each one burst
and they rolled over and burned to the water and I
limped on home to our base.

BERLE:
Ladies and gentlemen, for the gallant action against
the enemy, and for many similar heroic achievements in
the South Pacific, the President of the United States
presented to Captain McClurg the Distinguished Flying
Cross.

[APPLAUSE]

BERLE:
Now Captain, comes time for you to tell us your secret
ambition? What is your secret ambition?

[Musical fanfare]

MC.C:
Well, Mr. Berle, my father died when I was very young,
my mother started teaching school to take care of me.
She worked for most of her life, and she sacrificed a
lot for me.

BERLE:
Well, that's how mothers are.

MC.C:
So it's always been my secret ambition to be able to
take care of her, and to give her everything she's
missed, and a lot more. And that's what I'm going to
try to do as soon as this war is over.

BERLE:
Well, Captain, that is a wonderful ambition, and as a
start toward fulfilling that, my sponsor, the Eversharp
Company, would like you to accept this check so that
you can do anything you've ever wanted to do for your
mother.

[APPLAUSE]

MC.C:
Thank you very much, Mr. Berle.

BERLE:
Well, Captain, you're very very welcome. But while
you're here, do you have any other secret ambition?

MCC:
Yes Mr. Berle, I think I have. It's not only mine, but
the ambition of a lot of other people I know, too… an
ambition for the future.

BERLE:
Tell us about it, Captain.

MC.C:
When I was in the South Pacific the Marines I knew were
fellows with names like Magee... Hill... Heier...
Moore... Czarnecki... and all the other names you've
ever heard. And those are the fellows who right now
are storming the pill-boxes and roaring through the sky
to take Iwo Jima Island.
All I can say is - they'll take it!
But they'll take it only because we've all learned
something fighting in this war. And that is - when a
Jap fires his rifle... his machine-gun... his mortar...
or his bomb, he doesn't put a tag on it marked
"catholic," "protestant," "Jew," "rich or poor," "black
or white." He makes no distinction. So, in battle
we've learned that all have to live, and work, and
fight together - and for each other - against our
common enemy. So, out of the thunder and smoke of
Salerno, the Coral Sea, Tarawa, and all the other
battles, came this truth - for us to have a future of
peace and freedom and happiness, the people of all
races and creeds must live and work and fight together
- and for each other - for the common good. That's the
ambition that gives those boys the courage to fight and
die to take Iwo Jima.

[APPLAUSE]

I used the check to pay for travel tickets so my mother could take
some long overdue vacation to visit friends and family. Personally,
I would have the memory of having met a comedic icon whose
name was a household word.